"The Maker Movement promises a revolution in education that the *Makeology* volumes beautifully describe. Adults and children work together to develop designs and products they can be proud of, involving science, technology, engineering, and the arts. This is the kind of collaborative education that helps people develop identities as lifelong learners and producers."

—Allan Collins, Professor Emeritus of Learning Sciences, Northwestern University, USA

"*Makeology* is the first broad and comprehensive examination of the Maker Movement as a catalytic force for young people's learning. Practitioners and scholars interested in implementing and studying making as a force for creative expression and student-centered learning will find in this two volume collection a wealth of thoughtful and significant information."

—Margaret Honey, President & CEO, New York Hall of Science, USA

Kylie Peppler is Associate Professor of Learning Sciences at Indiana University. An artist by training, she engages in research that focuses on the intersection of arts, media, new technologies, and informal learning. Her current work focuses on maker culture.

Erica Rosenfeld Halverson is Associate Professor of Digital Media and Literacy in the Department of Curriculum & Instruction at the University of Wisconsin–Madison. Her work focuses on what it means to learn in and through the arts across a range of contexts, including out-of-school arts organizations, museums, libraries, and arts-based classrooms.

Yasmin B. Kafai is Professor of Learning Sciences at the University of Pennsylvania. She is a researcher and developer of online tools and materials to promote computational participation, crafting, and creativity across K–16.

MAKEOLOGY

MAKERS AS LEARNERS

VOLUME 2

EDITED BY
KYLIE PEPPLER, ERICA ROSENFELD HALVERSON,
AND YASMIN B. KAFAI

Routledge
Taylor & Francis Group
NEW YORK AND LONDON

First published 2016
by Routledge
711 Third Avenue, New York, NY 10017

and by Routledge
2 Park Square, Milton Park, Abingdon, Oxon OX14 4RN

Routledge is an imprint of the Taylor & Francis Group, an informa business

Library of Congress Cataloging-in-Publication Data
Names: Peppler, Kylie A., editor. | Halverson, Erica, editor. | Kafai, Yasmin B., editor.
Title: Makeology / edited by Kylie Peppler, Erica Halverson, and Yasmin Kafai.
Description: New York : Routledge, 2016. | Includes bibliographical references and index.
Identifiers: LCCN 2015047214 | ISBN 9781138847767 (v. 1 : hardback) | ISBN 9781138847774 (v. 1 : pbk.) | ISBN 9781315726519 (v. 1 : ebook) | ISBN 9781138847804 (v. 2 hardback) | ISBN 9781138847811 (v. 2 : pbk.) | ISBN 9781315726496 (v. 2 : ebook)
Subjects: LCSH: Maker movement in education | Makerspaces.
Classification: LCC T65.5.M35 M35 2016 | DDC 607.1—dc23
LC record available at http://lccn.loc.gov/2015047214

ISBN: 978-1-138-84780-4 (hbk)
ISBN: 978-1-138-84781-1 (pbk)
ISBN: 978-1-315-72649-6 (ebk)

Typeset in Minion
by Apex CoVantage, LLC

Contents

Foreword

On my way to Pittsburgh, I was again delayed in Chicago, and while regretting my decision to make the flight connection from San Francisco, a stranger struck up a conversation about our respective travels. Asked what I would be doing in Pittsburgh, I mentioned I was excited about going to the Maker Faire. He stared at me with a puzzled look. I continued, "You know. The big festival that happens every year in San Mateo? New York? . . . (pause) . . . Detroit? *Everyday people who make things and celebrate in the making*?" As he further knit his eyebrows together in silence, I realized that the Maker Movement is not only still in its infancy, but is already forming boundaries of insiders and outsiders found in more mature communities. While many of us are immersed in maker culture—making, designing, fabricating, engineering, and crafting with combinations of physical materials with digital tools, this movement hasn't reached everyone, even though President Obama has declared that every child is a maker. A huge and wonderful opportunity exists to lead, shape, and design making to appeal and bring joyful learning to all children and families, the young and old, schoolteachers and students alike.

A yet even smaller group of us are immersed and studying the phenomenon of making in the way that scientists study a new field with purposeful intent and a search for evidence to support emerging theories and practices. Like any new phenomenon, the scientists are trying to document human activity, create shared observations, and study the people, programs, and organizations that form maker communities. Others are acting as engineering scientists, concurrently inventing novel methods, curricular lenses, and tools needed to focus its signal and capture evidence from distributed data sources and instruments. From fine-grained studies, surveys, and interviews to examining maker artifacts, scribbles, and conversations, each scientist is collecting and contributing data that is helping to build a shared understanding of the unknown. When cosmologists coordinate big telescopes to understand a piece of the night sky together or marine scientists cast multiple nets with different sizes of mesh to see what organisms and ecosystems exist in our living oceans, researchers and practitioners are collectively gathering information, making observations and insights from data, working together to better understand this local and global phenomenon of making as reflected in the title of this book—*Makeology*—an emerging science of making.

With this second volume, Kylie Peppler, Erica Rosenfeld Halverson, and Yasmin Kafai together have coalesced a scientifically minded maker community that each brings their own sets of tools, lenses, and perspectives to the education enterprise. Together, they bring artistic sensibility, fluency in media literacy, their scholarship in the Learning Sciences, and deep understanding and appreciation of how to use computation for broadening participation in science, technology, engineering, and math (STEM) and non-STEM fields. Kylie Peppler and Erica Halverson are education researchers that both come from arts traditions and have been instrumental in knitting together people across sectors, disciplinary boundaries, neighborhoods, and communities of teachers, urban youth activists, technology developers, librarians, artists, museum educators, and school-aged children. These overlapping communities involved in the making and doing provide the necessary test beds for studying activity in and across varied settings and problem spaces. As long as I have known Yasmin B. Kafai, she has been a designer, a scholar, and champion for gender equitable child-centered learning through expressive design and making, whether they are children programming new digital avatars, teen constructors of games and media software, or adults who stitch fabric, make circuits, and chat about electricity. Beyond being a scholar, she is an informal educator who not only taught my eldest son game-based strategies when he was five, but also showed us how to implement use-inspired research to help us better study and understand issues of learning, equity, and participation.

The Maker Movement from the view of innovation is creating novel technologies from low-cost programmable hardware, responsive materials, digital cutting machines, and smart sensors to DIY (do-it-yourself) kits to create self-made health monitors, agile robots, and 3D-printed toys. Communities of interest and local economies are thriving from the exchange of goods, services, and goodwill over the Internet and at mini-festivals happening in many cities and local communities. However, the Maker Movement from an education standpoint is in its early stages. Learning by making is at risk of becoming another fad in education or a boutique field that raises higher walls for outsiders because of their specialized language, exclusionary practices, and reinforced gender norms for participation. Our hope is that if we take this business of equitable participation seriously in an emerging field that is still expanding and morphing, we have a real chance at enacting inclusive practices and pedagogies from the start and embracing all forms of making and participation across disciplinary boundaries and practices.

These chapters together offer a window into the biggest promise of the Maker Movement—to give children agency and meaning in their own learning. This doesn't happen by accident. The contributors of *Makeology* focus their attention and concern with the knowledge of *how*—how to effectively orchestrate people, tools, and settings; how to scaffold new digital literacies; and how to position knowledge resources, assign roles, mix media, and arrange learning environments to promote learner agency. We learn that making can foster intrinsic motivation, build new kinds of expertise and literacies, and support collaborative resource sharing. As a potentially transformative practice and field of scholarship, *Makeology* has the opportunity to catalyze the attention of researchers, teachers, school administrators, parents, curriculum developers, and policy makers, because these authors offer insights into the ways one can begin to study, model, and understand these phenomena of learning.

I applaud the editors and contributors of *Makeology* who are situated in local maker communities, work side-by-side with makers, and are creative artistic makers themselves. Together, they bring the needed coherence to this emerging trend in education and growing interdisciplinary area of research and give hope to the possibility of keeping participation open, culturally relevant, accessible, and equitable. Let's read, drink in the ideas, and celebrate in the making of this collective endeavor.

Sherry Hsi
Research Director, Lawrence Hall of Science
University of California, Berkeley, USA

Acknowledgments

Chapter 1 Introduction to This Volume

The editors would like to thank Beau Johnson and Janis Watson for their editorial assistance throughout the process!

Chapter 3 Making, Thinking, and Understanding: A Dispositional Approach to Maker-Centered Learning

The research presented in this chapter was made possible thanks to the generous support of the Abundance Foundation.

Chapter 4 Making Matters: A Framework for Assessing Digital Media Citizenship

This research is funded by National Science Foundation REC-238524 A, John D. and Catherine T. MacArthur Foundation grant from the Digital Media and Learning initiative, and through the LIFE (Learning in Informal and Formal Environments) Science of Learning Center, an NSF-funded (REC-354453) effort seeking to understand and advance human learning through a simultaneous focus on implicit, informal, and formal learning, thus cultivating generalizable interdisciplinary theories that can guide the design of effective new technologies and learning environments.

Chapter 5 Is Sewing a "Girl's Sport"? Addressing Gender Issues in Making With Electronic Textiles

This work was supported by a collaborative grant from the National Science Foundation (#0855868) awarded to Yasmin B. Kafai. Any opinions, findings, and conclusions or recommendations expressed in this article are those of the authors and do not necessarily reflect the views of the National Science Foundation, the University of Pennsylvania, or Utah State University.

Chapter 6 Motivation for Making

Funders for this project include the National Science Foundation (1027848, 1348876), LEGO Foundation, and the Scratch Foundation.

Chapter 9 Bridging Crafting and Computing in Making: Designing Interactive Touchpads and Board Games With MaKey MaKey

This work was supported by a collaborative grant from the National Science Foundation (#0855868) awarded to Yasmin B. Kafai. The views expressed are those of the author and do not necessarily represent the views of the National Science Foundation or the University of Pennsylvania.

Chapter 11 Making as a Pathway to Engineering and Design

This material is based upon work supported by the Spencer Foundation under Grant No. 201300079 and from the National Science Foundation under Grant No. EEC-1351605.

Chapter 12 Making, Tinkering, and Computational Literacy

This work was supported by National Science Foundation Grants EEC-1025243 and EEC-0748186. The opinions expressed in this article are the author's and do not necessarily represent those of the National Science Foundation.

Chapter 13 ReMaking Arts Education Through Physical Computing

This work is supported by the ReCrafting Math NSF grant (#1420303), Dr. Kylie Peppler, PI.

CHAPTER 1

Introduction to This Volume

KYLIE PEPPLER, ERICA ROSENFELD HALVERSON, AND YASMIN B. KAFAI

White House Maker Faire

In February 2012, the US White House hosted its first-ever science fair showcasing the talent and ingenuity of the next generation of scientists, engineers, and innovators. Students—many winners from local and national science fairs, competitions, and state fairs—had brought their posters and exhibits, among them the extreme marshmallow cannon designed by Joey Hudy, of Anthem, AZ. The picture of President Obama testing the contraption shooting marshmallows across the State Dining Room—surely a first in its history—went around the world. More importantly, Hudy's business card that read "Don't be bored, make something," inspired the President to encourage all students to become "makers of things, not just consumers of things." In July 2014, the White House announced that it would also be hosting its very own Maker Faire, joining hundreds of mini and large Maker Faires around the world.

Introducing the Maker Movement

To date, much of the interest in the Maker Movement concerns how excitement can be leveraged to fuel the next generation of STEM (science, technology, engineering, and mathematics) innovators (Honey & Kanter, 2013). Such interest has ranged from White House Maker Faires (Kalil, 2010) to President Obama's Educate to Innovate campaign (Obama, 2009). Though this potential holds promise, these volumes take a concerted effort to better understand making as a new domain unto itself, rather than in service of other learning outcomes. While connected to traditional disciplinary ways of understanding, we think making deserves to be understood and studied in its own right.

Open exploration, intrinsic interest, and creative ideas are but a few of the commitments at the core of today's Maker Movement—a grassroots culture dedicated to hands-on making and technological innovation. Popularized by *MAKE* magazine, Maker Faires, and online communities like Etsy, Ravelry, and Instructables, the Maker Movement embodies Do-It-Yourself (DIY) production across a host of domains, ranging from textile crafts to electronics, advanced robotics to traditional woodworking (Peppler & Bender, 2013). Across these applications, the Maker Movement is propelled by (a) the introduction of new technologies, like 3D printers, laser cutters, and Arduino robotics, that allow for faster prototyping and new forms of digital fabrication; and (b) the rise of the Internet, which allows for the sourcing of parts as well as the widespread sharing of ideas (Dougherty, 2013).

At the same time, there is a growing grassroots movement behind the technology that reclaims the deeply held cultural values arcing back to the DIY culture of mid-20th-century America. While these practices still have a distinct place among 21st-century makers, the influx of new technologies reinvigorates these ideas through a capacity for "long tail" production that allows makers to produce at the appropriate scale (Anderson, 2008) and pushes the limits of what's possible in traditional domains. This burgeoning and distributed community identifies making as an alternative to the consumer culture and seeks to hack, mod, tinker with, create, and reuse tools and materials.

Who, then, are makers? In practice, anyone who builds or adapts objects by hand, often with the simple pleasure of figuring out how things work, creating an aesthetic object, or seeking to solve an everyday problem, falls under this distinction. Makers frequently take pride in and desire to share projects and/or their creative processes with others, which is what fuels the larger communities of physical and online makerspaces, as well as pop-up events like world and regional Maker Faires. At the same time, the Maker Movement has begun to infiltrate the education enterprise. Schools are building makerspaces and FabLabs in their facilities and incorporating making into curricula. As with any instructional innovation, questions about the pedagogical value of making as a discipline are front and center, and researchers are beginning to wrap their heads around how people learn to make as well as how they make to learn.

Current research on the Maker Movement in education can be classified into three categories: understanding *making* as a set of designed learning activities, studying *makerspaces* as communities of practice, and exploring *makers* as identities of participation (Halverson & Sheridan, 2014). While there is clearly overlap among these three categories, it is useful to explore activities, communities, and identities independently, especially if we want to avoid reductive policy questions like, "Is making good for kids?" or "Should we put a makerspace in our school?" Rather, we should be asking questions like, "In which ways can making connect to learning?" "Who gets into making and who does not?" and "What affordances do different materials have for learning through making?"

We have organized this growing movement of makerspaces, activities, and materials for learning in two volumes. In the first volume, *Makerspaces as Learning Environments*, we covered the wide range of makerspaces that provide multiple pathways to learning, with participants creating projects that vastly differ in terms of scope, function, production time, and support received. This introduction to making and makerspaces described making in a variety of educational ecosystems, spanning nursery schools, K–12 environments, higher education, hip-hop communities, museums, afterschool spaces, and online learning environments and offering practical takeaways for parents, educators, and researchers along the way.

In this volume, *Makers as Learners*, we highlight leading researchers and practitioners in the field as they discuss and share current perspectives on the Maker Movement and research on educational outcomes in makerspaces. We discuss a range of perspectives on learning through making, including the role of tinkering in the process of teaching and learning; how adaptive expertise and identity development are supported through making; and how new and playful tools can be used to assess informal learning. Throughout, we consider linkages among learning outcomes, equity issues, and the social and historical uses of materials within makerspaces. This volume also highlights a key set of transformative tools and materials that heightens possibilities for learning and create consequential invitations for a broader and more diverse group of learners to participate. While not comprehensive of the range of making found in maker communities, this volume provides the reader with an innovative range of maker tools, materials, and processes that expand what it means to merge high and low technologies and to learn in and through making.

The Maker Movement and the Future of Learning

When it comes to promoting specific learning outcomes, the Maker Movement is a bit of a paradox. It simultaneously embodies a new and innovative grassroots approach to learning, yet it is well rooted in established theories and the time-honored truisms of high-quality education. Certainly, a central facet of the learning promoted by the Maker Movement is that it is *interest driven*; today's Maker Movement encourages the making and sharing of artifacts with high personal and social significance, ranging from robotics, 3D-printed objects, high-tech fashion, hydroponic gardens, videogames, culinary oddities, textile crafts, and woodcrafts—in short, making and sharing nearly anything. As such, the Maker Movement presents unique and timely opportunities toward reimagining the future of learning in ways that will resonate with the time-honored traditions of a democratic education, yet pushes us forward to embrace the necessary changes inherent to the 21st century.

Core Issues and Challenges

With the advent of the Maker Movement, the focus on learning and learners has shifted to new contexts, activities, and artifacts. For instance, Piaget was one of the first who moved discussions about learning from the armchair of philosophy to observations of actual learners. He started by closely observing his own three children and then devising sets of experimental activities and clinical interviews (Elkind, 1968). With Skinner and colleagues, learning research moved into the laboratory, trying to establish laws of learning and schedules of reinforcements that would provide teachers with control over materials and feedback (Skinner, 1968). Then educational psychologists moved learning into classrooms, realizing that they needed to understand the contexts in which students and teachers operated (Bruer, 1993). A first turn away from schools came with Lave and Wenger's (1991) understanding that much of learning doesn't just happen in classrooms, but also in homes and workplaces. With Gee's (2003) discussion of games as successful models of learning environments, digital media finally became an acceptable context in which to situate learning activities that are complex and collaborative. With each of these shifts, researchers and educators developed new perspectives on what learners do and how and where they engage in learning with others.

What the Maker Movement has to offer here in terms of learning opportunities is an emphasis on engaging the world through design and sharing with others by making learning visible and tangible. This connects to the efforts of many early predecessors, such as Friedrich Froebel's building blocks (Brosterman, 1997), John Dewey's real-life experiences (Dewey, 1938), Maria Montessori's letter planes (1912), and Seymour Papert's turtle (1980). The focus of hands-on learning is a welcome shift away from the focus on minds-on efforts that has been dominating so much of academic learning, particularly in the upper grades. While kindergarten and elementary school years still make extensive use of manipulatives and model building, this aspect of learning is largely absent when the focus is on printed materials, on or off the screen. Here the work of education writer Mike Rose on the learning in vocational trades (2004) illuminates how far our focus has shifted toward the mind, especially in our college-bound education tracks. Rose places equal value on the "intelligence" required in trades like carpentry, plumbing, and waitressing and provides compelling illustrations of how learning in everyday work is complex, collaborative, and challenging. Maker activities legitimize hands-on activities, often in conjunction with computational coding, illustrating that complexity and collaboration are not limited to talk but can also be situated in the building of models and artifacts that are shared with others. This connects to Seymour Papert's notion of *constructionism* (1991), where the building of artifacts, be it a program, robot, or sand castle, that can be shared with others is seen as a particularly promising context for learning.

In some ways it can be argued that maker activities are the "shop class for the 21st century," as computer science educators Mike and Ann Eisenberg (1998) proposed when they argued for an integration of coding and crafting, predating the actual Maker Movement by more than a decade. What is key here is not just a different notion of learning that connects minds-on and hands-on, but one that also brings back a different pedagogy where learners are engaged in projects that are more long-term, challenging, and personally meaningful. This interest in project-based learning, of course, is not new, drawing on Dewey's legacy of situating learning in meaningful contexts. It had a quick but short-lived surge in the early 1990s when educators like David Perkins (1986) became interested in bringing design into education and many saw the emergence of web-based tools as an opportunity to engage students in making, albeit mostly on the screen. They saw classrooms as contexts where students would become designers (Harel, 1990; Kafai, 1995; Roth, 1998) of their own learning. These studies offer promising models and insights for educators interested in bringing making into schools.

Fast-forward to the 2010s and maker activities also offer a connection to interest-driven learning as promoted in the connected learning framework that describes learning as production-centered, openly networked, and conducted with peers (Ito et al., 2012). The key idea here is to leverage youths' interests in *using* media toward *making* media, as a key form of 21st-century participation (Gauntlett, 2011; Knobel & Lankshear, 2010). Specifically, making can be seen as a form of computational participation (Kafai & Burke, 2014) that allows youth to engage in the digital public. The online world abounds with examples where youth "hang out" to share and connect, dig deeper by "messing around" with different media, and ultimately also "geek out" in more extreme forms to outline different trajectories of participation (Ito et al., 2009). There is an abundance of DIY sites where kids make media designs, often using mainstream media experiences as a jumping-off point for their ideas and collaborative explorations (Grimes & Fields, 2015).

This focus on interest-driven projects raises questions of whose interests are promoted and valued in the Maker Movement. While popular media are a promising starting point, they are not always the most open to value everyone's and all forms of participation and content. Many youth DIY sites have millions of contributions, but most of the productions are connected to mainstream commercial content with only few examples of content related to the interests of underrepresented communities (Margolis, Estrella, Goode, Holme, & Nao, 2008; Warschauer, 2003). Why does this matter? If we want making to be a global activity, we need to make sure that who is making and what is being made is open and accessible to everyone. The artifacts and images of makers signal to others what is valued in this culture and what not, and ultimately they also signal who belongs to the maker culture and who does not. It is here where we see the greatest challenges in broadening participation in making.

Overview of Volume 2

Current research on understanding learning in making is far behind the growing enthusiasm for making in the educational world. The second volume of *Makeology* closes this gap by addressing three overarching themes: Section 1 approaches the Maker Movement from a cultural perspective, examining closely the complex relationship between gender, background, and accessibility with regard to the design and use of maker environments; Section 2 investigates how makers' tools and materials differentially shape their creative output and, consequently, their learning in the process; Section 3 then unpacks the promise of the Maker Movement as a vehicle for advancing disciplinary learning and closes with a comparative discussion between making, writing, and coding. Across the 14 chapters that constitute this volume, we seek to illustrate the impact of making on learning and development.

The first section, on the culture and identities of makers, presents a thorough investigation into the ways that learners' cultural and personal histories inform the way they engage in making. Here, Lisa Brahms and Kevin Crowley (Chapter 2) identify the core learning practices of making as revealed through analysis of the field's most seminal maker publication, *MAKE* magazine. Their findings suggest that educators seeking to harness the appeal of the Maker Movement should take a critical look at who is most visible in the community and what forms of participation emerge as most valued as a result. Next, Jennifer Oxman Ryan, Edward Clapp, Jessica Ross, and Shari Tishman (Chapter 3) examine how the learning that comes from maker experiences is affecting the way that learners see themselves as agents of change in the world. Such a view stands in contrast to the oft-presumed outcome of the Maker Movement as an avenue for advanced STEM or innovation mindsets. Such a dispositional view of the benefits of making is extended by Brigid Barron and Caitlin Martin's (Chapter 4) systematic comparison of several 21st-century out-of-school pursuits, including video gaming, social media participation, and making. The evidence presented here provides yet another reason to consider making as more than just a potential improver of students' academic outcomes but an activity that can help develop the creative and mindful dispositions important to being an active participant in the 21st century. Kristin Searle, Deborah Fields, and Yasmin Kafai (Chapter 5) then address how a more considered view of the role of gender and tool choice can help educators design more inclusive making activities for youth from a variety of backgrounds. The authors use workshop data from students engaging in e-textile production to identify how youths' awareness of the gendered cultural histories of crafting, computer science, and engineering shape their participation and learning. Finally, Natalie Rusk (Chapter 6) investigates what motivates young people to take initiative, persist, and learn new skills in the process of making. By better understanding the motivation for making, Rusk seeks to help the field design and support maker experiences that help young people create, connect, share, and learn in physical as well as online communities.

In section two, we dive into how makers leverage the tools and materials on hand in the learning process. This section begins with Mike McGalliard's (Chapter 7) presentation of how cardboard used in the documentary *Caine's Arcade* transformed into one organization's global quest to support and extend youth creativity wherever it is found. In this discussion, key themes emerge about how creativity can be supported through activities using materials as basic as cardboard. On the other side of the technology spectrum, Sophia Bender (Chapter 8) presents a view of e-textile production as a fundamentally different way of relating to technology from what we are accustomed. Examining a range of tools and materials for e-textile creation, Bender illustrates a way of fostering powerful ideas using a softer, more intimate and transparent approach to technology that marries high and low tech, masculine and feminine, and technology with craft. Veena Vasudevan and Yasmin Kafai (Chapter 9) then illustrate how contemporary making can utilize tools and materials that further intertwine the concepts of arts & crafts and technology. The authors examine the bridge between everyday and craft materials and electronics in context of making games for learning, expanding ways into more technical topics for youth who are more comfortable with arts and crafts but also allowing those who might not have seen themselves as makers to engage in creative design. Finally, Karen Wilkinson, Luigi Anzivino, and Mike Petrich (Chapter 10) engage constructionist pedagogy to frame the learning experiences in the Tinkering Studio at the Exploratorium in San Francisco. Drawing on over two years of visitor observations, the authors present four dimensions and indicators of learning based on observable behaviors they recognized in the tinkering activities in their studio. The findings suggest that learning in makerspaces is tightly tied not only to the spaces created for it, but also to the material context.

We close out the volume with an examination of the connections between making and disciplinary learning. Lee Martin and Colin Dixon (Chapter 11) investigate how aligning making endeavors with Next Generation Science Standards can help inform efforts to integrate making into K–12 engineering education. Matthew Berland (Chapter 12) turns our focus to the impact that a holistic view of play and tinkering can have on advancing computational literacy. Finally, Kylie Peppler (Chapter 13) presents how the "art of making" presents new opportunities for creativity and innovation in education. The volume concludes with Mitchel Resnick, Elyse Eidman-Aadahl and Dale Dougherty's (Chapter 14) conversation around the commonalities and compelling differences between writing, coding, and making. The authors provide us with thoughtful vignettes to consider as we move forward to envision the future of learning through making.

References

Anderson, C. (2008). *The long tail: Why the future of business is selling less of more.* New York, NY: Hachette Books.

Brosterman, N. (1997). *Inventing kindergarten.* New York, NY: Abrams.

Bruer, J. (1993). *Schools for thought: A science of learning for the classroom.* Cambridge, MA: MIT Press.

Dewey, J. (1938). *Experience and education.* New York, NY: Simon & Schuster.

Dougherty, D. (2013). The maker mindset. In M. Honey & D. E. Kanter (Eds.), *Design, make, play: Growing the next generation of stem innovators* (pp. 7–11). New York, NY: Routledge.

Eisenberg, M. & Eisenberg, A. (1998). Shop class for the next millennium: Education through computer-enriched handicrafts. *Journal of Interactive Media in Education, 98*(8), 1–30.

Elkind, D. (1968). Introduction. In J. Piaget (Ed.), *Six psychological studies* (pp. v–xxiii). New York, NY: Random House.

Gauntlett, D. (2011). *Making is connecting.* Malden, MA: Polity Press.

Gee, J. P. (2003). *What videogames have to teach us about learning and literacy.* New York, NY: Palgrave Macmillan.

Grimes, S. & Fields, D. (2015). Children's media making but not sharing. The potential and limitations of child-specific DIY media websites for a more inclusive media landscape. *Media International Australia, 154,* 112–122.

Halverson, E. R. & Sheridan, K. M. (2014). The Maker Movement in education. *Harvard Educational Review, 84*(4), 495–504.

Harel, I. (1990). *Children designers.* Norwood, NJ: Ablex.

Honey, M. & Kanter, D. E. (Eds.). (2013). *Design, make, play: Growing the next generation of STEM innovators.* New York, NY: Routledge.

Ito, M., Baumer, S., Bittanti, M., boyd, d., Cody, R., Herr, B., . . . Tripp, L. (2009). *Hanging out, messing around, geeking out: Living and learning with new media.* Cambridge, MA: MIT Press.

Ito, M., Gutierrez, K., Livingstone, S., Penuel, B., Rhodes, J., Salen, K., . . . Watkins, S. C. (2012). *Connected learning: An agenda for research and design.* Irvine, CA: Digital Media and Learning Research Hub.

Kafai, Y. B. (1995). *Minds in play: Computer game design as a context for children's learning.* Mahwah, NJ: Lawrence Erlbaum.

Kafai, Y. B. & Burke, Q. (2014). *Connected code: Why children need to learn programming.* Cambridge, MA: MIT Press.

Kalil, T. (2010). *Remarks on innovation, education, and the Maker Movement.* Retrieved November 4, 2015 from radar.oreilly.com/2010/10/innovationeducation-and-the-m.html

Knobel, M. & Lankshear, C. (Eds.). (2010). *DIY media: Creating, sharing, and learning with new technologies.* New York, NY: Peter Lang.

Lave, J. & Wenger, E. (1991). *Situated learning.* New York, NY: Cambridge University Press.

Margolis, J., Estrella, R., Goode, J., Holme, J. J., & Nao, K. (2008). *Stuck in the shallow end: Education, race, and computing.* Cambridge, MA: The MIT Press.

Montessori, M. (1912). *The Montessori method.* New York, NY: Frederick A. Stokes Company.

Obama, B. (2009). *Remarks by the President on the "Education to Innovate" campaign.* [Press release]. Washington, DC: White House Office of the Press Secretary. Retrieved November 1, 2015 from www.whitehouse.gov/the-press-office/remarks-presidenteducation-innovate-campaign

Papert, S. (1980). *Mindstorms.* New York, NY: Basic Books.

Papert, S. (1991). Situating constructionsim. In I. Harel & S. Papert (Eds.), *Constructionism* (pp. 1–11). Norwood, NJ: Ablex Publishing.

Peppler, K. & Bender, S. (2013). Maker Movement spreads innovation one project at a time. *Phi Delta Kappan, 95*(3), 22–27.

Perkins, D. N. (1986). *Knowledge as design.* Hillsdale, NJ: Lawrence Erlbaum Associates.

Ratto, M. & Boler, M. (Eds.). (2014). *DIY citizenship.* Cambridge, MA: The MIT Press.

Rose, M. (2004). *The mind at work.* London: Viking Penguin.

Roth, W.-M. (1998). *Designing communities.* Dordrecht: Kluwer Academic Press.

Skinner, B. F. (1968). *The technology of teaching.* New York, NY: Prentice Hall.

Warschauer, M. (2003). *Technology and social inclusion: Rethinking the digital divide.* Cambridge, MA: The MIT Press.

Section 1

The Cultures and Identities of Makers

CHAPTER 2

Making Sense of Making
Defining Learning Practices in *MAKE* Magazine

LISA BRAHMS AND KEVIN CROWLEY

Introduction

Born from individual basement tinkerers and garage-mechanic hobbyists, the Maker Movement has evolved to support a strong community among makers. Makers increasingly gather together in makerspaces, hackerspaces, tech shops, and FabLabs, where groups composed of diverse ages, genders, and backgrounds are motivated to learn with and from one another on how to use and combine materials, tools, processes, and disciplinary practices in novel ways. The growth of the international Maker Faires' annual showcases of makers' inventions and investigations have become celebrated meccas of maker culture, attracting hundreds of thousands of makers of all ages and interests. And, finally, makers widely disseminate projects, culture, and ideals through *MAKE* magazine and online communities such as etsy.com, ravelry.com, DIY.org, and others.

The field of education has embraced the Maker Movement as a potential context for innovative and more inclusive STEM education experiences. Making has been hailed by the White House for its potential to encourage youth to become interested and engaged in STEM education, as a potential pathway to providing specific jobs skills to youth to engage in the STEM workforce (e.g., Kalil, 2010), and a wellspring of potential political and economic rebirth (The Economist, 2011). It has been positioned widely in the nonprofit sector as key to engaging new and traditional users of informal learning spaces, such as museums and science centers, as well as to the retooling of libraries (Honey & Kanter, 2013). Educational platforms in high school tech labs, community makerspaces, and afterschool youth programs have been created to strengthen and associate the many individuals and organizations that seek to integrate and study making as a means of learning (Sheridan et al., 2014).

So what is making, exactly? Is it poised to serve as the on-ramp to STEM careers that the educational policy world hopes it to be? In this chapter, we turn to the pages of *MAKE* magazine for data on which to base our first approximation of some core principles of the maker community. We draw upon the communities of practice framework (Lave & Wenger, 1991; Wenger, 1998), which asserts an understanding of learning as fundamentally tied to the social and cultural contexts in which it occurs and focuses on the "practices" that define communities (Brown, Collins, & Duguid, 1989; Greeno, 1997; Gutierrez & Rogoff, 2003; Hutchins, 2002; Lave & Wenger, 1991; Wenger, 1998). This framework implies a process of social learning whereby learners participate legitimately in the practices of the community, local or distributed, moving, over time, from peripheral participation as a "newcomer" towards mastery as an "old-timer." This results in learners' development of knowledgeable skill and identity as a member of the community.

Thus, assuming that makers are part of a community of practice, we set out to define making in terms of the distinct making practices that are at the center of the community. To find these practices, we analyzed the most popular and nationally recognized textual source of maker community participation: *MAKE* magazine. In quarterly publication since February 2005 and with a readership of more than 300,000 (makermedia.com/press/fact-sheet/), this magazine is perhaps the oldest and most visible textual marker of the Maker Movement. As an introduction to the inaugural volume, the editors welcomed readers through a declaration of community identification and an invitation to join a burgeoning movement: "More than mere consumers of technology, we are *makers*, adapting technology to our needs and integrating it into our lives . . . MAKE is a new magazine dedicated to showing how to make technology work for you" (Dougherty, 2005, p. 7, emphasis original). Each 200-page volume contains approximately 40 articles, written and edited by makers, including profiles of makers and projects, how-to guides, product reviews, and thematic features. *MAKE* magazine, through its longevity and visibility, could be considered the archival journal of the maker community—establishing, shaping, and reinforcing practices, beliefs, and values of the community by way of its contributors, editors, and readership.

As a data source, *MAKE* magazine is not a direct observational record of the making process, nor is it the only publication associated with the Maker Movement. Therefore, our findings should be interpreted as representing the sample from which they were derived—a primarily adult, male, well-educated, and affluent population of makers who, through wide distribution and esteem, have come to represent a broad movement of individuals whose ages, genders, educational aspirations, and financial situations vary far more than those selected for representation in the pages of this publication. Despite these limitations to generalizability, we consider *MAKE* magazine a useful benchmark for identifying and characterizing the qualities and behaviors of this emerging community.

Our analyses of one year of the magazine's articles focus on two questions: What are the learning practices of the making community, as represented in *MAKE* magazine? And, who are the makers who contribute to *MAKE* magazine and, for analytic purposes, represent central participation in making community practice? To answer these questions, we will begin with an introduction to the learning practices of the community that we identified across the articles. To illustrate these practices, we will take a close look at how they are exemplified through an analysis of a single feature article. This is followed by a description of the attributes of the makers who authored each article, and therefore comprise the community of makers.

Content Analysis of *MAKE* Magazine

To identify the core learning practices of the contemporary making community, we coded volumes 30 to 33 (the most recent volumes of *MAKE* magazine when we started analysis) to gain a comprehensive sense of the data (Tesch, 1990), collecting lists and memos of key characteristics, qualities, and emergent patterns of maker practice that surfaced through this initial reading. We then engaged in several cycles of inductive coding of two volumes of *MAKE* magazine (Vols. 30 & 31) until defining patterns of the maker community's practices emerged. From these, we iteratively developed a set of codes reflective of these identified patterns of practice. This included extensive discussion, examination, re-examination, and definition of categories.

A coding scheme and manual was created to identify the qualities and quantities of these specific practices, as well as other attributes of the makers featured throughout the volumes, such as gender and disciplinary affiliation. We then recoded all textual data (n = 162 articles). Texts were segmented by the main idea being conveyed. Since our goal was to identify and characterize maker community practices, codes were not exclusively assigned to specific text segments, as some segments described multiple practices. Inter-rater agreement, performed on roughly 60% of the data, was 92%. To reduce the data, conceptually ordered matrices (Miles & Huberman, 1994) were created using the coded text and to more clearly see, compare, and contrast examples and dominant factors.

Our analysis revealed a set of seven core learning practices associated with recognizable participation in the maker community: *explore and question; tinker, test, and iterate; seek out resources; hack and repurpose; combine and complexify; customize;* and *share* (Table 2.1). We will explore each of these learning practices in more depth in the article analysis.

Each of the seven practices are relatively common across articles, with percentages of identified practices ranging from 51% of articles containing the practice *Seek Out Resources* to 28% of articles containing

Table 2.1 Maker community learning practices

Maker Community Practice	*Definition*	*% of articles coded as exemplifying a practice*
Explore & Question	Interrogation of the material properties of the context in order to find inspiration or to determine intention for a process or project.	49%
Tinker, Test, & Iterate	Purposeful play, experimentation, evaluation, and refinement of the context.	29%
Seek Out Resources	Identifying and pursuing the distributed expertise of others, includes recognition of one's own not-knowing and desire to learn.	51%
Hack & Repurpose	Harnessing and salvaging component parts of the made world to modify, enhance, or create a product or process.	38%
Combine & Complexify	Developing skilled fluency with diverse tools and materials in order to reconfigure existing pieces and processes and make new meaning.	28%
Customize	Tailoring the features and functions of a technology to better suit personal interests and express identity.	43%
Share	Making information, methods, and modes of participation accessible and usable by members of the community.	42%

the practice *Combine & Complexify*. Making practices tend to co-occur within an article. Seventy five percent of articles contained two or more practices and more than a third of the articles contained four or more practices. This finding suggests that the practices may be commonly part of a repertoire that characterizes making, or participation in the community of makers, as opposed to specialized practices that some makers use and others do not.

Beyond identifying the practices of making, we were also interested in the identities and affiliations of the makers who publish in *MAKE* magazine. Each article was coded as being framed, or not, by one or more of the disciplines of science, technology, engineering, math (STEM), and art. STEM disciplinary affiliation was determined based on the core learning practices of each discipline as they have been described in the most recent consensus reports published by the National Research Council (e.g., NRC, 2001, 2007, 2010). In the case of art, where authoritative consensus documents are unavailable or inconclusive, foundational learning research studies supplement these identified practices (e.g., Eisner, 2002; Hetland, Winner, Veenema, & Sheridan, 2007). If the authors' description of their process or featured product clearly encompassed discernable aspects of disciplinary practice, the entire article was coded as being framed by that discipline. Each article could be framed by one, two, or three representative disciplines. In cases where more than three disciplines may have been present, researchers discussed the representation and agreed on which disciplines were dominant.

Who Publishes in *MAKE* Magazine?

Figure 2.1 shows the disciplinary-based professional affiliations of each article's author(s) and featured makers. These professional affiliations were determined based on authors' own explicit identification with a disciplinary profession either within the body of the text or within the byline of the article. The majority of authors did not identify as working in the disciplines. Rather, within the context of *MAKE* magazine, many makers' self-identification was with their diverse and often playful interests outside of their professional affiliations. For example, one author who shows readers how to grow and use bhut jolokia chili peppers in Volume 33 (O'Reilly Media, Inc., 2013) describes himself as "a web geek living in Portland, OR, who loves building tall bikes, brewing beer, and growing unusual edibles" (pp. 88–91), while another author, the maker of The Electronic Nag from Volume 30 (O'Reilly Media, Inc., 2012a), describes himself as "a forgetful, loving husband and the proud father of three beautiful little girls. He has always had to learn how everything works"

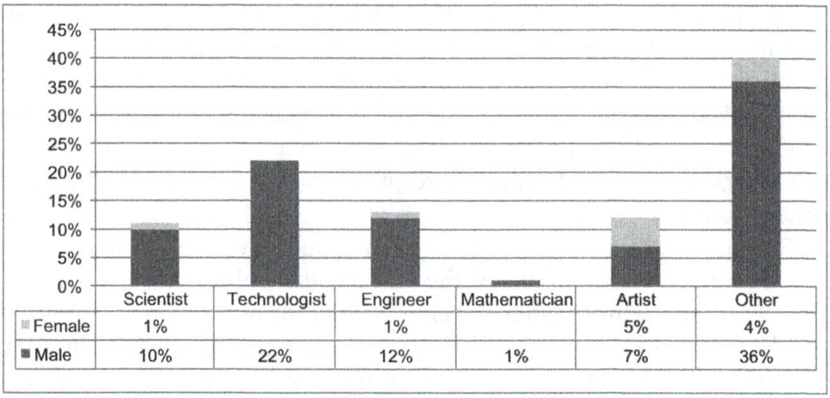

Figure 2.1 Authors' professional disciplinary affiliation.

(pp. 50–53). Those authors who were identified as "other" describe themselves as a polyglot of professions and interests, ranging from students (as young as 8 years old) to teachers (Vol. 30), lawyers (Vol. 30), community organizers (Vol. 31), and even a naval officer (Vol. 32), physical therapist (Vol. 31), and "fireworks master" (Vol. 33) (see O'Reilly Media, Inc., 2012a, 2012b, 2012c, and 2013).

Even when authors identify as working in a discipline, it did not necessarily mean that their making activity was aligned to their professional affiliation. When we compared the disciplinary framing of the articles with the disciplinary self-identification of the authors, 61% of makers wrote or were featured in an article that was framed by a discipline other than their stated professional discipline.

Makers, as featured in *MAKE* magazine, are overwhelmingly men: 89% of the authors or featured makers across the sampled articles of *MAKE* magazine were men and only 11% were women. Most (64%) of the time when women appear as authors or featured makers, they were part of a team that included at least one man.

The majority of articles were multidisciplinary. Figure 2.2 shows that these disciplines are present in the activities of makers, yet rarely does each discipline occur independently of others. Science, technology, and engineering were the most common disciplinary framings for the articles, although art was also common. This analysis begs the question of what disciplinary communities makers are most connected to or aligned with. This analysis supports the idea that the activity of making may well lead to participation in the STEM disciplines, or at least the disciplines of science, technology, and engineering, but disciplinary affiliations were not comprehensive, either within or among disciplines.

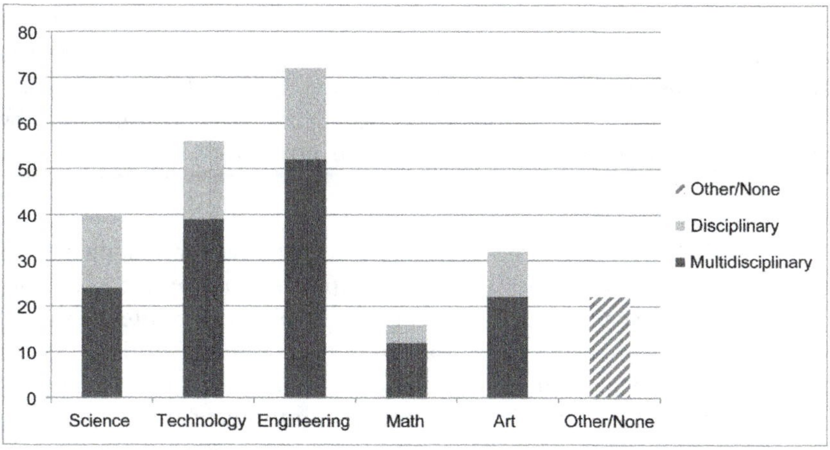

Figure 2.2 Disciplinary framing of articles and co-occurrence.

How Is Making Defined in *MAKE* Magazine?

We turn now to a deeper exploration of each of the core practices we identified in *MAKE* magazine. To do so, we will describe one example of making, the Rocket-Ship Treehouse, featured in *MAKE*, Volume 31 (O'Reilly Media, Inc., 2012b, pp. 144–151). Rocket-Ship Treehouse is the story of a dad, Jon, his friend and colleague Jeremy, and their process of building a backyard play structure for Jon's 6-year-old son Eliot. What began with the simple idea of beautifying a small backyard space developed into an elaborate project that spanned two years, evolved to include a host of neighborhood friends, exponentially expanded Jon, Jeremy, and Eliot's knowledge base and skill set, harnessed their imagination and creative spirit, and above all, solidified their identities as makers. Through the authors' description of their process and project, we may come to qualitatively understand the identified practices of the maker community.

The rocket ship idea emerged when Jon's wife suggested that Jon install a treehouse for their son Eliot under the trees in the backyard. Jon, a researcher at Microsoft, took the request as a challenge, and through an elaborate and imaginative process, decided to instead build a stationary rocket ship as a play structure for his son. As the vision for the project became more elaborate, Jon recruited his colleague Jeremy to collaborate on the electrical aspects of the rocket ship.

The rocket ship, or RULAV (Ravenna Ultra-Low Altitude Vehicle, named after the makers' Seattle, Washington, neighborhood) is a hexagonal prism-shaped capsule, rising 15 feet off the ground, atop a tripod structure. The capsule is 6.5 feet wide and is framed in welded steel with a riveted aluminum skin. Inside, the rocket contains nearly 800 LEDs forming flashing lights and numeric display panels. The "pilot" controls the rocket using a joystick, switches, knobs, and buttons. The rocket "takes off," "rumbles" and "docks," by way of "thrusters" that shoot compressed air and water, accompanied by vibration and sound effects (rocket.jonh.net/intro.html).

Explore and Question

Makers in *MAKE* magazine generally approach a project or making process through the practice of questioning and exploring the context of activity and/or problem space. Makers are curious people, whose interest in and wonder about a particular topic leads to inquiry and exploration. Makers interrogate the past, researching and referencing former projects and ideas related to their future intentions. Contributing authors of articles to *MAKE* magazine often introduce the reader to their motivation for engagement in the particular project, medium, or process of making to be considered, through an explanation of their process of investigating personal and/or collaborative inquiries.

For Jon and Jeremy, the question came as a suggestion posed by Jon's wife to build a simple treehouse for their son, yet taken up as an exploratory challenge by Jon, Eliot, and eventually Jeremy. Their exploratory process began with a trip to Boeing Surplus to scrounge for inspiration amidst the piles of used parts. Jon and Eliot brought home a few big sheets of aluminum and some aluminum tube to test their initial idea: a geodesic structure formed entirely by bending and riveting. Yet, the authors attest, "early prototypes wouldn't stand up, proving that we really didn't know much about mechanical engineering" (p. 144). Through their questioning and testing of materials, the makers realized "weight wasn't a design constraint for a rocket that never leaves the ground; it would be just fine to use steel" (pp. 144–146). Thus, they defined the design of the rocket's exterior, or chassis and skin, through an exploration and questioning of the material constraints.

Tinker, Test, and Iterate

Makers explore materials and processes through purposeful play, experimentation, and ongoing evaluation. Makers are doers, rather than planners. Yet, the doing is iterative and sequential. Makers model designs with software, they build and test paper prototypes, and they evaluate their process to discover what is possible or to improve upon what has come before. Makers try, make mistakes, and fail—a lot. Makers value the iterative process of engagement in making and testing out ideas as much as the finished product. For makers, each successive iteration of a project presents an opportunity to develop applicable skills and grow relative knowledge for oneself and for the community of makers.

The authors' portrayal of the design and development of the treehouse's internal electronics showcases their deep investment in their iterative learning process. Jon and Jeremy's original goal was to fill the rocket's interior with an array of flashing LED lights, numeric displays, and dials. Jeremy went about designing a circuit board that would light up an 80-segment numeric display that the makers intended to build themselves. The authors describe the intricacies of the electrical system and attest, "An early prototype worked, but even with only 2 LED digits, it took a week of evenings to construct. We had to carefully modify a prototyping board with a rotary tool, and solder in each component and wire connection" (p. 148). Although they describe the process as "time-consuming, error-prone, and not very fun," the challenge provoked them to persist with their iterative design:

> Sane treehouse builders might decide to scale back their ambitions. We went the opposite direction: why not design our own printed circuit board (PCB) and have it fabricated in bulk? The only problem was, we hadn't done anything of the sort before—in fact, we'd only recently learned how to light up an LED.
>
> (p. 148)

Jon and Jeremy describe an intense readiness to try in the face of the unknown, to test ideas and push beyond their existing boundaries of ability, to persist when challenged, to pursue creative solutions, and to turn to the resources of the maker community for support in order to make progress on their personal project.

Seek Out Resources

Makers are resourceful. They seek out and rely on the expertise of others. Makers know where and to whom to turn for guidance and collaboration. They willingly seek and give advice and feedback. They interact flexibly with the distributed tools, materials, and expertise of the community. This practice of seeking out resources is often enacted through Internet searches and online forums. It is also frequently played out through the recruitment of friends and colleagues with diverse skill sets and knowledge, as well as through the active use of local community-developed resources for discussion, design, and fabrication.

Jon and Jeremy overcame the challenge of generating enough customized circuit boards to ignite the inside of their rocket ship with flashing lights and numbers through a little resourcefulness. The authors declare, "The thriving DIY community came to the rescue" (p. 148). Jon and Jeremy turned to their online community for instruction and feedback when creating their own printed circuit board (PCB). They learned PCB design through online tutorials and discussion boards, used readily available software to hone their previously rudimentary skills, created a working schematic and layout drawing, and virtually sent their design to be professionally fabricated. Although there was a learning curve, Jon and Jeremy researched, discovered, and activated community resources to suit their creative and functional needs. In so doing, they developed their own knowledge of electronic processes and related design skills, and they also gained a deeper sense of the wealth of expertise among makers that can be harnessed and channeled.

Hack and Repurpose

Makers see the world as made of component parts: pieces and platforms that can be opened, deconstructed, modified, and repurposed to create something new, improved, altered, or recombined to better suit the needs and desires of an individual or community. Makers would rather repurpose a found object or salvaged component than buy something new. The community of makers is one that values affordability, accessibility, and ingenuity over sleekness and precision. Hacking and repurposing is a practice of problem solving and improving functionality, but it is also an act of improvisation and creativity, and an opportunity to put the stamp of individuality on a project or process.

To simulate the experience of a pilot's launch, positioning, and landing, Jon and Jeremy sought to create just the right rumble, vibration, and sound effects of the rocket's engine using pressurized gas to produce mechanical motion. To do this, they hacked and repurposed a few commonly found products from a hardware supply store. The "booster" was made from an old paint shaker that creates the perfect vibratory feeling during "takeoff," and the thrusters were made of repurposed automotive engine-cleaning wands, "that aerate water using a supply of compressed air, producing a convincing jet blast of mist" (p. 150). Having mastered electronic programming, the makers nostalgically decided to connect the "boosters" and "thrusters" to the main control panel through electronically actuated valves controlled by a repurposed vintage PC joystick from the computer games of their own youth. Jon and Jeremy intentionally chose to use repurposed materials that were readily available and inexpensive, familiar simulations of more complex system.

Combine and Complexify

Makers look towards a future of endless innovative possibility. Yet, they do so with the recognition that they are standing on the shoulders of past craftspeople and makers who created tools, products, and platforms, both analog and digital, which can be harnessed, combined, and adapted to enable future ingenuity. The practice of developing skilled fluency with a diverse set of physical and digital tools, materials, and processes of construction, in order to put these existing pieces and processes together differently, is central to making and enables makers to extend what is possible. Inherent in this practice is an impulse to learn and an acknowledgment that there is always more to learn—that what is not yet known is of deep personal interest, is learnable, usable, and useful to oneself and to the community of makers. The practice of combining and complexifying is a practice of lifelong learning.

Jon and Jeremy liken their ongoing and increasingly complex project to the "opening of floodgates." The authors write, "we realized the rocket's electronics could do far more interesting things than just display a random number" (p. 150). The makers took it a step further by combining individual elements to create an overall effect of a takeoff sequence: "A countdown is displayed on a control panel while audio from the real Apollo 11 sequence is played. At zero, the lights start to flicker, and the rocket starts to rumble from the movement of the paint shaker and the bass from our subwoofer" (p. 150). The authors recount with pride:

> Rarely does building a treehouse require welding, grinding, painting, riveting, bending, crimping, plumbing, brazing, laser cutting, sound design, printed circuit board fabrication, distributed network protocols, an embedded operating system, sewing, and even embroidery.
>
> (p. 144)

Each newly envisioned feature of the rocket revealed a novel skill or tool for the pair to learn, use, and hone. As the project expanded in scope, so did the makers' roster of familiar tools, materials, and processes that they could combine to extend what was possible for this and future making endeavors.

Customize

Making is a personal pursuit. The subtitle of *MAKE* magazine originally read, "technology on your time." Since its inception, the community of makers has sought to alter technology to suit individual and community needs and to express personal and collective beliefs. In 2005, founding editor Dale Dougherty identified the communal drive of makers: "adapting technology to our needs and integrating it into our lives" (2005, p. 7). Through the practice of customization, makers tailor the features and functions of a technology to make it their own.

As the project evolved, Jon and Jeremy learned about and integrated many maker processes to create a highly customized technological system that combines mechanics, electronics, pneumatics, and software to create a singular experience. Moreover, it is evident that Jon and Jeremy's ambitious rocket ship project was not only motivated by personal aspiration—a treehouse for Jon's young son—it became a highly collaborative and joyful pursuit of learning and making that stretched across generations. The authors explain, "It became transparent that the treehouse was just as much an engineering playground for the adults, a place for us to share our joy of making and teach it to the kids" (p. 144). For example, the authors explain, "we even created a rocket version of the classic video game *Pong*, to keep crew morale high during long trips to the Moon" (p. 151). Such associations both personalized the experience and introduced Eliot to an element of the adults' own childhood adventures. The practice of customization can be seen in the incorporation of other personal touches, from the joystick from the makers' youth to the way in which Jon and Jeremy strongly identify with the process and products of their pursuit, to the intentionality of communicating a shared family and community value through the making process. The authors conclude, "since Eliot was with us every step of the way, he also learned that toys aren't just something you buy, they're something we can build—together" (p. 151).

Share

Makers openly share and access the stuff of making with the entire community of makers through diverse platforms for presentation, reception, and communication. Often characterized as open source, the maker community works to develop repositories of information, kits, and systems of communication, which make tools, materials, methods of design and fabrication, and products accessible, customizable, and usable by the entire community. This practice of sharing is at the core of *MAKE* magazine itself.

Within the pages of *MAKE* magazine, Jon and Jeremy's story is accompanied by photos and drawings of their process, as well as sidebars in which the authors share tips and resources related to the many processes they engaged and eventually mastered through their project: welding, riveting, brazing, etching, and programming. The authors provide advice, compare sources and prices of products, review software, link to related articles previously published in the magazine, and add personal tips to encourage the reader to engage in similar endeavors.

The makers also created their own website to share their project (rocket.jonh.net/), which describes the entire process, from conception to blast-off, in detail. The extensive site walks the reader through each step in the process, complete with photographs and videos, as well as open-source links to download the makers' plumbing and operating system designs and electronic and PCB schematic files. Here, Jon and Jeremy invite the visitors to provide feedback, and even encourage visitors to "schedule a flight" if ever in the Seattle area.

Conclusions

As the educational community rushes to understand and promote the spread of making, a first goal must be to define what we mean by making. In this paper, we provide evidence that identifies seven core learning practices of making as it is recounted in the pages of *MAKE* magazine. Our analysis suggests that the practices that characterize participation in making cannot be simply described as practices that come from or point to any one educational disciplinary pathway such as engineering, science, or math. It can be argued that aspects of maker practice are drawn from or resemble certain disciplinary practices, but no one discipline or singular set of established disciplinary practices captures the essence of participation in the making community. Makers have developed a set of sophisticated community practices and modes of participation that, as a whole, are organic and, possibly, unique to making.

So if learners participate in making activities, are they more likely to be interested and successful in STEM? The answer to this question is beyond the scope of the current chapter. Yet, our findings concerning the practices of making do encourage us to ask whether participation in the community of makers would necessarily guarantee a member's orientation towards participation in STEM disciplines. We identified practices that in some ways seem consistent with STEM practices, but also that may have important differences. At the least, we do not see evidence in our work that becoming expert in making would necessarily involve developing practices that foster expertise in STEM disciplines.

On the other hand, as disciplinary practices are applied through the community's making activities, becoming a more practiced maker does encourage community members to tinker at the edges and intersections of other disciplines. Making may promote an understanding, and the purposeful use, of specific facets of disciplinary knowledge and skill that inform and extend making community participation. Consequently, as a multidisciplinary endeavor, making may have the potential to render STEM experiences more accessible, interactive, and motivating for the community of makers, as well as for individuals and communities seeking to integrate making into their own community practice, such as teachers and informal educators. Positioning themselves and their activity at these edges, intersections, and boundaries of participation in disciplinary (and other diverse) communities, makers work to transform the refined and inaccessible aspects of disciplinary participation to become accessible to community members. For example, one scientist described how she makes research-grade equipment out of repurposed common kitchen items (O'Reilly Media, Inc., 2012b, p. 42). Rather than emphasizing the exotic and refined aspects of disciplinary understanding and practice, makers work across disciplinary boundaries to piece together everyday objects and processes in innovative ways. This boundary work, drawing connections across disciplines, is central to maker participation.

Yet, in light of its potential, making and the ways in which it is publicly represented and positioned with regard to education must be further questioned as a movement of inclusivity and accessibility. For example, we found that makers featured in *MAKE* magazine are primarily men. We note that the readers of *MAKE* magazine reflect the same sex disparity, as reported by the magazine itself—81% are male. The readers are also less diverse than the broader population, with a median age of 44 and median household income of $106,000. Ninety-seven percent graduated from and/or attend college, 80% have a post-graduate degree, and 83% are employed (Maker Media, Inc., 2013). As the magazine launched, a *New York Times* Op-Ed hailed it as a haven for men and boys who tinker:

> Make . . . is a throwback to an earlier time, before personal computers, to the prehistory of geekiness—the age of how-to manuals for clever boys, from the 1920's to the 50's. . . . The technology has changed, but not the creative impulse . . . Make is not just a clubhouse for guys with Skittle breath and abbreviated social skills. Beneath all the home-brewed gadgets and cool software tricks lies a sly and subversive agenda.
>
> (Downes, 2005)

Our findings suggest that educators, and the making community itself, must take a critical look at who, exactly, is most visible in the community, and what forms of participation are being positioned as central, and therefore valued, by the community. If making is represented as being, for example, mostly male, mostly white, and mostly about hobbyist technology, how does it differ in substantive ways from other recent educational phenomena that were similarly thought to be new supports and motivations to participate in STEM, such as educational gaming or robotics, and that continue to foster a complex relationship to gender and access with regard to design and use (e.g., Kafai, Heeter, Denner, & Sun, 2008)? Will making experiences really become more accessible and motivating to young people and communities who do not see others like themselves and their creative interests reflected in the public face of the movement? The current framing of *MAKE* magazine—as one of the most popular and visible characterizations of the community—runs the risk of perpetuating current trends, making STEM experiences more motivating for only those to whom those experiences are already accessible (see Blikstein & Worsley, 2016, in Volume 1 of this series for more on this). As an educational endeavor, our goal should be to create and nurture spaces and opportunities that are accessible and encouraging for *all* youth to engage and to feel as though each of them is a legitimate member of the community.

Making is a multidisciplinary, interest-driven, distributed, and evolving form of informal learning. To help realize the educational potential of making, future work must focus on identifying and designing accessible and representative educational platforms, experiences, and assessments that draw clear connections between making and educational outcomes, such as STEM success. Currently, our research-based understanding of making is still far behind the growing enthusiasm for making in the educational world and, with it, the ongoing spread and scaling of making to formal and informal learning environments. The pathway from making to, for example, STEM education and STEM workforce participation, although assumed, is not clear, well defined, or inclusive. If such connections are a priority for education, then we must study and design with awareness of the intricacies of community participation, what forms they take and where such pathways point.

References

Blikstein, P., & Worsley, M. (2016). Children are not hackers: Building a culture of powerful ideas, deep learning, and equity in the maker movement. In K. Peppler, E. Halverson, & Y. Kafai (Eds.), *Makeology: Makerspaces as learning environments* (Volume 1) (pp. 64–79). New York, NY: Routledge.

Brown, J. S., Collins, A., & Duguid, P. (1989). Situated cognition and the culture of learning. *Educational Researcher, 18*(1), 32–42.

Dougherty, D. (2005, February). The making of make. *MAKE* magazine, p. 7. O'Reilly Media, Inc. Retrieved on April 12, 2013 from m-cdn.dashdigital.com/make/vol01/data/make200504-dl.pdf

Downes, L. (2005, June 12). A new magazine's rebellious credo: Void the warranty! *The New York Times*. Retrieved on October 15, 2015 from www.nytimes.com

The Economist Technology Quarterly. (2011, December 3). *More than just digital quilting*. New York, NY: The Economist Newspaper Limited, 3–4.

Eisner, E. (2002). *The arts and the creation of the mind*. New Haven, CT: Yale University Press.

Greeno, J. G. (1997). On claims that answer the wrong questions. *Educational Researcher, 26*(1), 5–17.

Gutierrez, K. D. & Rogoff, B. (2003). Cultural ways of learning: Individual traits or repertoires of practice. *Educational Researcher, 32*(5), 19–25.

Hetland, L., Winner, E., Veenema, S., & Sheridan, K. (2007). *Studio thinking: The real benefits of visual arts education*. New York, NY: Teachers College Press.

Honey, M. & Kanter, D. (Eds.). (2013). *Design, make, play: Growing the next generation of STEM innovators*. London: Routledge.

Hutchins, E. (2002). *Cognition in the wild* (5th ed.). Cambridge, MA: MIT Press.

Kafai, Y. B., Heeter, C., Denner, J., & Sun, J. (Eds.). (2008). *Beyond Barbie and Mortal Kombat: New perspectives on gender and gaming*. Cambridge, MA: The MIT Press.

Kalil, T. (2010, September 29). Remarks on innovation, education, and the Maker Movement. *New York Hall of Science*. [Transcript]. Retrieved on October 15, 2015 from radar.oreilly.com/2010/10/innovation-education-and-the-m.html

Lave, J. & Wenger, E. (1991). *Situated learning: Legitimate peripheral participation.* New York: Cambridge University Press.

Maker Media, Inc. (2013). *Fact sheet.* Retrieved November 3, 2013 from makermedia.com/press/fact-sheet/

Miles, M. B. & Huberman, A. M. (1994). *Qualitative data analysis: An expanded sourcebook.* Thousand Oaks, CA: Sage.

National Research Council. (2001). *Adding it up: Helping children learn mathematics.* Mathematics Learning Study Committee, J. Kilpatrick, J. Swafford, & B. Findell (Eds.). Center for Education, Division of Behavioral and Social Sciences and Education Washington, DC: National Academies Press.

National Research Council. (2007). *Taking science to school: Learning and teaching science in grades K–8.* Committee on Science Learning, Kindergarten through Eighth Grade, R. A. Duschl, H. A. Schweingruber, & A. W. Shouse (Eds.). Board on Science Education, Center for Education. Division of Behavioral and Social Sciences and Education. Washington, DC: National Academies Press.

National Research Council. (2010). *Report of a workshop on the scope and nature of computational thinking.* Committee for the Workshops on Computational Thinking. Washington, DC: National Academies Press.

O'Reilly Media, Inc. (2012a). *MAKE* magazine, Volume 30 (April). Sebastopol, CA.

O'Reilly Media, Inc. (2012b). *MAKE* magazine, Volume 31 (July). Sebastopol, CA.

O'Reilly Media, Inc. (2012c). *MAKE* magazine, Volume 32 (October). Sebastopol, CA.

O'Reilly Media, Inc. (2013). *MAKE* magazine, Volume 33 (January). Sebastopol, CA.

Sheridan, K., Halverson, E., Litts, B., Brahms, L., Jacobs-Priebe, L., & Owens, T. (2014). Learning in the making: A comparative case study of three makerspaces. *Harvard Educational Review, 84*(4), 505–531.

Tesch, R. (1990). *Qualitative research: Analysis types and software tools.* Bristol, PA: Falmer.

Wenger, E. (1998). *Communities of practice: Learning, meaning, and identity.* Cambridge, England: Cambridge University Press.

CHAPTER 3

Making, Thinking, and Understanding

A Dispositional Approach to Maker-Centered Learning

JENNIFER OXMAN RYAN, EDWARD P. CLAPP, JESSICA ROSS, AND SHARI TISHMAN

In the past five years, hundreds of articles have appeared in magazines, journals, and blogs extolling the virtues of the Maker Movement. Advocates praise the possibilities and potentials of making to ignite a new system of democratized manufacturing, to inspire a shift from a consumer to a producer mentality, and to instill within the next generation of young people a renewed interest in the science, technology, engineering, and mathematics (STEM) professions. Communities are taking note: downtowns are developing makerspaces and FabLabs; municipal libraries and church spaces are presenting opportunities to make, hack, tweak, iterate, and invent; and employers are wooing prospective employees by celebrating their company's practices of innovation, invention, and collaboration—the hallmarks of maker culture.

As this volume makes clear, the educational sector is taking note as well. Schools are building out or repurposing spaces for making-centered activities (see, for instance, Wardrip & Brahms, 2016, in volume 1 of this series). Shop classes that were once decommissioned and cut from curricula are being rebranded as makerspaces and tinkering labs. Tech Ed positions are replacing Ed Techs, as schools move to embed technology teachers into their programs. Across the country educators, policy makers, and researchers alike are beginning to investigate the tools, tricks, and trends of the maker trade.

In 2012, the Agency *by* Design (A*b*D) initiative at Project Zero, a research organization at the Harvard Graduate School of Education, began to investigate the practices and pedagogies of maker-centered learning. Our team was particularly interested in the educational responses to the Maker Movement and the various promises being made about maker education—by the popular press, community advocates, and even the White House. Amidst a sea of advocacy statements based on the purported outcomes of maker experiences, we sought to understand what educators who actively engaged young people in making perceived to be the foundational benefits of maker-centered learning. In this chapter, we present these emergent ideas, explore what it means to look at maker-centered activities through both a learning and a dispositional lens, and conclude by discussing opportunities that may help shape the field of maker education by focusing on thinking, learning, and understanding.

Throughout this chapter, we are intentional about our choice of the words *making* and *maker*, and give each its own connotation. We use *making* to refer to the general human activities of creating, building, designing, and tinkering. When we use the term *maker*, such as in maker education and maker-centered learning, we refer to a unique constellation of characteristics we've identified within the design and making realms. These particular characteristics exemplify the culture (e.g., collaborative, distributed, creative);

Figure 3.1 The flexible student-built and -designed interior space of the Brightworks school in San Francisco, CA.

approaches to making (e.g., iterative, interdisciplinary, flexible); and features of physical spaces (e.g., easy access to materials, shared workspaces, and technological and traditional tools) typical of maker experiences. Each individual and organization that participated in our study embodies many, though not necessarily all, of these characteristics.

Looking at Maker Through a Learning Lens

By human nature, we are all makers. Though some of us may be more accustomed to making than others are, each one of us can recall a time in our lives when we've made *something*. And so, to enter into our discussion of looking at making through the lens of learning, we draw from our own experiences and begin with a simple thought experiment. We invite you to pause from your reading for a moment to consider the following:

> *Reflect for a moment and try to recall a standout experience you've had making something.*

At workshops and conference presentations facilitated throughout the United States, the Agency *by* Design team has used the above prompt to introduce educators, parents, and policy makers to the nature of our research and the maker education landscape. After providing our participants with the time and space to reflect on a memorable making experience, we then ask: *What about your memorable making experience makes it so memorable?*

If you are like many of our participants, your response to this question may be that your most memorable making experiences were those that involved working closely with others. You may have recalled a time when you worked side by side with a grandparent, an older sibling, a role model—or within a collective of diverse individuals. Alternatively, your most memorable making experience may have been a time when you experienced the thrill of learning how to do something new, a time when you had a shift in perspective, a time when you felt empowered to effect change in the world, or a time when the process or product of your making had a positive impact on your character or community.

We can't know for sure, but we can speculate that, like our many workshop participants, your conception of what makes a memorable making experience was not just (if at all) about acquiring STEM skills, pitching the next five-digit Kickstarter campaign, developing manufacturing jobs for future generations, or boosting the American economy. We offer this simple thought prompt as an entryway into a discussion of differences between the rhetoric surrounding the benefits of maker-centered education and the real outcomes of maker learning—as expressed to us by maker educators and thought leaders throughout the United States.

Maker-Centered Learning: A Survey of Early Promises

When we began our study, the Agency *by* Design research team was naturally curious to know more about the purported benefits and outcomes associated with maker-centered activities. We started with a review of the contemporary literature, looking first to the popular press—magazines and journals such as *Smithsonian*, the *Atlantic*, the *New York Times*, the *Huffington Post*, *Wired*, and the *Economist*, to name just a few—where hundreds of short articles had been printed over the past five years heralding the benefits of the Maker Movement. We eventually focused our inquiry on 44 articles that more specifically addressed the effects of the Maker Movement. The majority of the articles we reviewed placed maker-related activities at the center of discussions around a future with a more democratized economy, industry, and manufacturing (e.g., More Than Just Digital Quilting, 2011; Royte, 2013; Walker, 2012), with the most widely celebrated benefits of the Maker Movement underscoring the economic potentials (Ryan, 2015).

Turning from the popular press to an exploration of more academic or formal literatures provided a slightly different perspective on the potential benefits of the Maker Movement. Some authors looking through an educational lens considered the more cognitive, character-building, and intellectual potentials of maker-centered and related learning (e.g., Ackermann, 2013; Dougherty, 2012, 2013; Honey & Kanter, 2013; Martinez & Stager, 2013; Quinn & Bell, 2013). Others highlight promises of the movement such as innovation and agency (e.g., Peppler & Bender, 2013). And Petrich, Wilkinson, & Bevan (2013) consider notions of making and tinkering that focus on "the socially situated developing self (being and becoming) as central to activities and processes of learning."

And yet, while there is an emergent body of scholarly work and empirical research addressing the cognitive benefits of maker-centered learning—we share the staging area with colleagues from MIT, Stanford, Tufts, and Indiana University, to name just a few—the championing from the field continues to take cues from popular rhetoric centering on STEM and skill acquisition. Positioning maker-centered opportunities as part of an economic future has subsequently fueled conversations about the importance of training an emergent workforce that can best take advantage of the tools associated with the future of manufacturing. As Kalil (2013) asserts:

> The spirit and practices of the maker community . . . present an enormous opportunity for educators of the young, particularly those who teach science, technology, engineering, and math (STEM) education whether in formal or informal educational settings.
>
> (p. 13)

Indeed, the idea that STEM education would be essential to the future success of the American economy is now a keystone of the Obama administration's Educate to Innovate initiative and a stated priority for the future of American education (White House, 2009, n.d.). Perhaps adding urgency to this message were reports that US students lag behind other countries on standardized tests of STEM subjects (Kalil, 2013; OECD, 2010) and that there is a lack of young people pursuing higher education degrees in STEM content areas (Committee on Conceptual Framework for the New K–12 Science Standards/National Research Council, 2012).

Yet despite the advocacy statements suggesting that maker-centered learning experiences foster proficiency in the STEM subjects and an interest in the STEM professions, the relationship between the two is still unsettled. As University of Pittsburgh researchers Lisa Brahms and Kevin Crowley have found through their content analysis of articles in *MAKE* magazine (see chapter 2 of this volume), "we do not see evidence in our work that becoming expert in making would necessarily involve developing practices that foster expertise in STEM disciplines" (p. 25).

Maker-Centered Learning: Practitioner Perspectives

Curious as to whether maker educators themselves would echo the emphasis on STEM disciplines/professions, next-wave economy, and entrepreneurship extolled by the popular press, the Agency *by* Design team interviewed maker education practitioners across the United States working in a variety of contexts. Among the individuals we interviewed was Mariano Ulibarri from The Parachute Factory, a makerspace in Las Vegas, New Mexico, that brings making experiences to rural communities in partnership with the New Mexico library system. We spent time with Melissa Butler and Jeremy Boyle from the Pittsburgh Public Schools and the Children's Innovation Project, as they worked on building habits of mind through hands-on work with electronics, circuitry, and innovation with technology. We interviewed Gus Goodwin at King Middle School in Portland, Maine, where engineering, 3D printing, and robotics combine with traditional woodworking and fabrication processes. We also visited The Athenian School in Danville, California, and spoke about prototyping and student agency with Bruce Hamren in the Makers Studio.

In addition to these educators, our list of interviewees included administrators and practitioners from public and private K–12 schools, makerspaces, library programs, and museums. Though we are still in the midst of fully analyzing these data, a clear picture has already begun to emerge. Overwhelmingly, the learning outcomes these educators described have less to do with the development of skills and more to do with the development of self and community (for a similar sentiment, see Blikstein & Worsley,

Figure 3.2 Young patrons of the Corrales Community Library work with LED lights and conductive thread during a traveling Parachute Factory workshop in Corrales, New Mexico.

2016, in volume 1 of this series). Our interviewees occasionally mentioned STEM skills, but they did so in the context of much larger outcomes. For instance, in our interview with Steve Teeri, founder of the HYPE teen center at the Detroit Public Library, we learned that, along with teaching creative thinking, problem solving, and tech skills, HYPE is focused on developing "interesting people that go out into the world and have good ideas and are able to accomplish things." As Teeri explained,

> I am not actively rooting for any of the teens to become an engineer or computer programmer. If they do that's wonderful. My goal here is to just aid them in becoming better people and better able to interact with the world around them.

Many of our interviewees discussed how maker experiences help students learn to pursue their own passions and become self-directed learners, proactively seeking out knowledge and resources on their own. They described how students learn to problem solve, to iterate, to take risks, to see failure as opportunity, and to make the most out of unexpected outcomes. They shared examples of how students learn to collaborate, to build on each other's strengths and interests, to persist in difficult tasks, and to be confident in their capacity to learn new things. Perhaps most strikingly, they each mentioned examples of how students come to see themselves as capable of effecting positive change in their own lives and in their communities.

Now it is true that young people in these programs certainly have been acquiring technical and STEM skills; in fact, learning how to use tools, the potentiality of materials, and the processes of fabrication are all components of these educational opportunities. However, for the educators we spoke with, skills and expertise were merely one of many by-products in the service of the larger outcome of self-development. David Clifford from the East Bay School for Boys in Berkeley, CA, for example, cited learning goals such as "inquiry, observation, idea generation, practicing the muscle of creativity, developing character, [and] cultural competency." Though there has been great emphasis on making and learning maker-centered skills at his school, he insisted: "We're not building woodworkers. We're not building metalworkers. We're just *utilizing* metalworking, 3D printing, a laser cutter . . . they're just catalysts for developing these [goals]."

To focus on STEM skills and the like as the primary outcome of maker-centered learning would be to sadly miss the point—it is like saying that learning to cut your food with a knife and fork is the most important outcome of eating a nutritious meal. In contrast, what we have been hearing from maker practitioners on the ground is the power of maker-centered learning to help students develop a sense of personal agency and self-efficacy. These two concepts are often cited as key aspirations of human development. Albert Bandura, a psychologist who has written extensively about agency and its companion concept, self-efficacy, notes that "to be an agent is to intentionally make things happen by one's actions" (Bandura, 2001, p. 2). Bandura views agentic capabilities as fundamental to a well-lived life: "The core features of agency enable people to play a part in their self-development, adaptation, and self-renewal with changing times" (Bandura, 2001, p. 2). Our interviewees also see agency and self-efficacy to be key aspirations of maker-centered learning.

Taking a Dispositional Approach Towards Maker-Centered Learning

In an attempt to articulate our interviewees' best hopes about what young people might gain through maker-centered educational experiences, we developed a concept we call *maker empowerment.* The concept looks at agency through the lens of maker and aims to give a name to the self-making our interviewees described so eloquently: students' discovery of their own passions, their capacity to pursue them, and the confidence and resourcefulness developed as they learn with and from others. Maker empowerment is meant to encompass more than mere cognitive development; it includes character development. Accordingly, the concept aims to describe a kind of *disposition* that students develop—a way of being in the world—that is characterized by understanding oneself as a person of resourcefulness who can muster the wherewithal to change things through making (for more on resourcefulness in making, see Sheridan & Konopasky, 2016, in volume 1 of this series).

An example of this kind of dispositional shift in behavior can be found in a recently published comparative case study of three makerspaces (Sheridan et al., 2014). In this study, Sheridan and colleagues demonstrated a change in how young people saw their world after beginning to make things. Students reported that before their maker experiences, they never thought about how the everyday objects in their world were made—things like bikes, electric appliances, and T-shirts. But, even after just a few experiences in a makerspace, they began to see the world differently. For instance, in reference to everyday objects, one student explained: "Now I kind of think about everything—like, what makes it tick." Another student reported: "Now I get out, I do things, I help people, I have ideas" (as quoted in Sheridan et al., 2014).

From the standpoint of education, the goal of empowering students is nothing new: it is the deep rationale behind much of what we teach. We teach art, or history, or mathematics, not solely to the group of students who will go on to make their livings in these areas, but to *all* students, because we believe it is empowering for everyone to learn how to engage with the world through the lenses of these disciplines. The concept of maker empowerment aims for this same breadth. Not all students who are exposed to maker education will go on to become scientists, technology specialists, engineers, or carpenters. But perhaps, through high-quality maker-centered learning experiences, they might all acquire a sense of maker empowerment.

Maker empowerment, as we have come to understand it, can be defined as a *sensitivity to the designed dimension of objects and systems, along with the inclination and capacity to shape one's world through building, tinkering, re/designing, or hacking*. Three distinct ideas come together to form this definition. The first phrase, *a sensitivity to the designed dimension of objects and systems,* points to the importance of simply noticing that many of the objects, ideas, and systems we encounter in the world—from desktops to democracy to driver education classes—are human-made designs. They are comprised of specific parts that fit together to serve one or more purposes, and they can be understood and analyzed from the standpoint of design. The second part of the sentence mentions both the inclination and the capacity to make (or remake) things. These two terms are separated intentionally: inclination has to do with motivation to do something; capacity has to do with skill or wherewithal to actually do it.

This three-part definition, with its emphasis on the triad of sensitivity, inclination, and capacity, extends a concept of dispositional behavior developed at Project Zero (Perkins, Jay, & Tishman, 1993; Perkins & Tishman, 2006; Perkins, Tishman, Ritchhart, Donis, & Andrade, 2000; Tishman, 2001; Tishman, Jay, & Perkins, 1993) proposing that ability alone is not enough to ensure action. For example, to be called a cyclist you not only need to have the ability to ride a bicycle, but you have to be motivated to ride your bike on a regular basis, and you have to be alert to occasions to do so. Dispositional behavior occurs when these three things coalesce—the ability to do something, the motivation to do it, and the sensitivity to appropriate occasions to do it.

From an educational standpoint, it's easy to imagine that the biggest bottleneck to developing dispositions is motivation. We teach skills in school; it is up to students to be motivated to use them. However, in their investigation of thinking dispositions, researchers found that in fact the biggest obstacle to cultivating dispositions is alertness to opportunity (Perkins et al., 2000). Specifically, students often fail to develop the habits of mind we as educators aim to inculcate, not because they cannot do something, and not because they don't want to, but mainly because they do not notice opportunities to do so—in other words, they have a lack of sensitivity. This doesn't mean that young people's inner detection mechanisms are woefully flawed. Rather, sensitivity has everything to do with the saliency of cues in the environment.

A Sensitivity to Design

The Project Zero research mentioned above was originally conducted to investigate *thinking dispositions*—habits of mind like open-mindedness, reason-seeking, and perspective-taking—in fairly traditional school settings. So perhaps findings about a lack of sensitivity are not surprising, considering that schools typically cue students to think in certain ways at certain times, rather than encourage them to be alert to occasions on their own. For example, at 10:00 a.m. students might be asked to start thinking about math, and then at 10:45 a.m. to redirect their attention to thinking about art. We cannot know for sure if the findings about sensitivity transfer to the notion of developing a disposition towards maker empowerment, but it's easy to see that there are lots of cues in our everyday environments that prompt us *not* to notice design and *not* to make things on our own: The endless stream of cheap, ready-made objects; a culture of disposable goods; little time for or valuing of prolonged making or tinkering.

Maker culture is different, of course. What goes on inside makerspaces and in maker classrooms is usually just the opposite, and that is part of the point. Here—where looking closely, making, and thinking critically about design are celebrated—is the opportunity to explore how we might cultivate the sensitivity dimension of dispositional behavior. How might this sensitivity be developed? One way is to offer students regular opportunities to notice and become alert to design, encouraging them to notice not only that much of our world is designed by humans, but that our human-made designs are malleable.

Opportunities for Intervention

Our interest in the sensitivity dimension of maker empowerment led to an action research strand of the Agency *by* Design work in which we partnered with classroom teachers in Oakland, California. Over the course of two years, we worked with educators from six public, private, and charter schools, who teach pre-K through 12th grades, and are based in disciplines ranging from general education and literacy to art and technology. None was primarily a "maker educator," but all were willing to explore the possibilities of maker-centered learning within their curriculum.

Pathways to Sensitivity

Working with these educators, we developed a conceptual framework that offers three practices aimed at cultivating a sensitivity to the designed dimension of our world. The three practices are *looking closely* (noticing nuances and intricacies of object and system design), *exploring complexity* (considering the people, interactions, and motivations associated with objects and systems), and *finding opportunity* (noticing if and where there are opportunities for imagining how an object or system might be otherwise).

For an illustration of how we hope these practices might benefit a young learner, let's return to our cyclist. Initially motivated by the joy of riding, through ongoing observation and experience, we begin to see how the cyclist might slowly build an appreciation for the design of the object (her bike) as well as the associated systems connected to bike riding: as she interacts with the numerous components of her bike, she would begin to consider it as a whole as well as a myriad of subsystems. She would become familiar with the design and function of its gears, brakes, tires and wheels, and a variety of safety features. She would investigate the complexities of the many external systems she interacts with each time she rides: bike lanes, traffic patterns, pedestrian crossings. As her circle of acquaintances comes to include other bike enthusiasts, she would likely gain a peer-to-peer learning network with whom she could both learn and share her knowledge. She would make informed assessments about how her bike and biking systems are functioning and finally begin to recognize opportunities for redesign—of the bike itself or the many internal or external systems within which her bike is situated. Through looking closely and exploring complexity, our cyclist would have exercised *sensitivity*: she would recognize the design cues in her environment and notice opportunity for change.

Developing Maker-Centered Thinking Routines

How can educators help students develop a sensitivity to design? The practices of looking closely, exploring complexity, and finding opportunity provide a useful framework; however, simply naming these capacities isn't enough. They need to be accompanied by structures that weave attention to design into the daily fabric of learning. How can sensitivity to design become a routine mode of thinking in the classroom? To answer this question, we again look to a concept developed at Project Zero—the concept of *thinking routines.*

Thinking routines are short, widely applicable, easy-to-use strategies that can be used by students across contexts and subjects. Their purpose is to habituate and make visible certain kinds of thinking (Ritchhart, Palmer, Church, & Tishman, 2006). To navigate through the practices of looking closely, exploring complexity and finding opportunity, the Agency *by* Design team—with help from its action research partners—developed maker/design-focused thinking routines to provide teachers and learners with specific thinking moves they might make along the way.[1] As just one example, a routine called Parts-Purposes-Complexities helps students step into the practices of looking closely and exploring complexity. The simple structure begins with observations and ideas about an object or system, as the learner responds to the prompt, "What are the parts?" Next, the learner is prompted to construct evidenced-based interpretations and explanations in order to respond to, "What are its purposes? or What are the purposes of the parts?" With the open-ended final question, "What are its complexities?" learners are invited to ask questions, seek out problems, notice relationships, and challenge previously held assumptions.

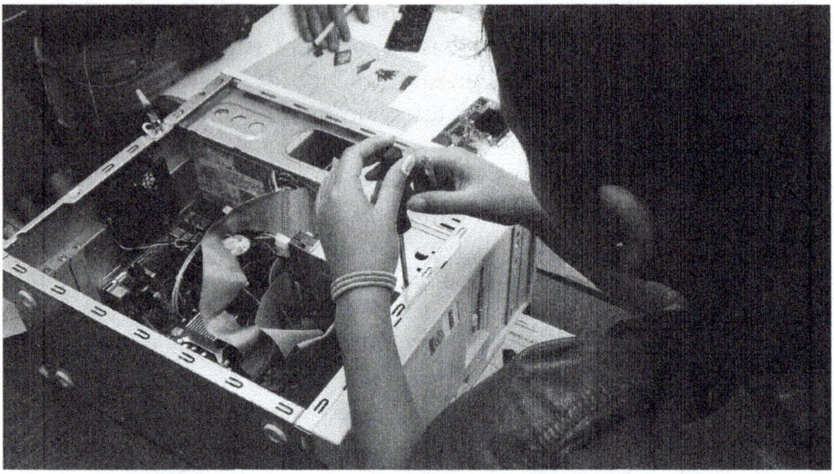

Figure 3.3 Students in Thi Bui's computer class take apart a computer CPU to get a better understanding of how it works at Oakland International High School in Oakland, CA.

As we saw in the work of our teacher partners, the use of this particular routine can play out in myriad ways in the classroom, from Alex Kane's 4th graders exploring the complexities of the civil rights movement to Thi Bui's high school students using the exercise to understand the design and functionality of computers. Third grade teacher Renee Miller incorporated the Parts-Purposes-Complexities routine into a unit on electricity and circuits. She noted a shift in her planning at the start of the unit when students looked closely at light bulbs:

> The light bulb lesson always required a great deal of "telling as teaching" and many students never really understood as I tried to explain what was happening on the inside of a light bulb. Drawings and diagrams only got us so far.

Once the students began using the thinking routine, Renee explained that students became interested in seeing *all* of the parts. "They *finally* asked to break it open. I hadn't offered this as an option but I knew it was where we were headed." Renee's students continued to follow the steps of the thinking routine as they donned safety glasses and gloves and engaged in taking apart light bulbs. The language of these routines is accessible and their structure is spare in order to help learners notice, ask questions, and arrive at new understandings about the designed world.

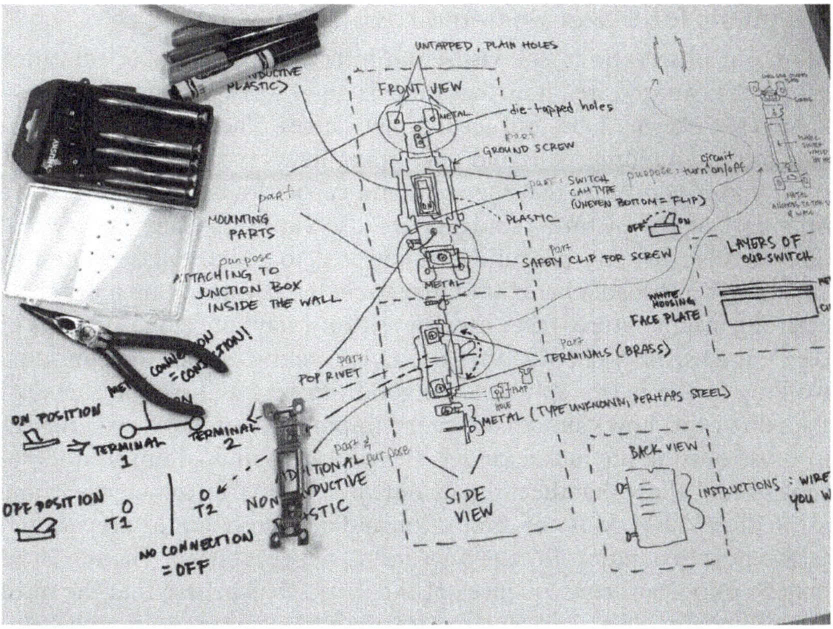

Figure 3.4 After engaging in a mechanical dissection activity, Agency *by* Design workshop participants map out the parts, purposes, and complexities of a light switch.

Figure 3.5 Third grade students looking closely at the internal parts of a light bulb during a unit on electricity in Renee Miller's class at Park Day School in Oakland, CA.

Jeanine Harmon.

Potentials for Maker-Centered Learning

From our observations, site visits, and interviews with maker educators across the country, we know that there is good work happening in makerspaces, tinkering labs, and technology classes. There is no doubt that students are building skills and developing new capacities. But we know from maker educators that the skills and capacities being developed are only part of the picture—students are also exploring their agency and self-efficacy; they are becoming empowered to build, tinker, re/design, and hack. The broader benefits of maker-centered learning are more characterological in nature—they are dispositions, ways of being, and ways of seeing the world. So how can we encourage young people and educators working in the maker sphere to be good thinkers *and* good makers? At the same time, how can we convey the importance of maker experiences to those outside the maker circle? The educators and administrators we spoke with believe that the ultimate outcomes of maker-centered learning are neither STEM skills nor innovation and invention nor the preparation of the next generation for the next industrial revolution. Though these may be important consequences of the work, they believe that the most salient benefits of maker-centered learning have more to do with helping young people realize their capacity to shape the designed dimension of their worlds—that they have the inclination, motivation, and wherewithal to effect change.

Return, for a moment, to the standout making experience you recalled at the beginning of this chapter. In the same way that you connected with a memorable making experience that helped build your character, we hope likewise to lay the foundation for young people to engage in making experiences that not only equip them with valuable skills, but also shape the way they engage and interact with the world. Through our research, we hope to help educators and young people recognize and realize the *dispositional* benefits of maker education—to help them think well with the maker capacities they have and are learning, to encourage them to be good thinkers *and* empowered makers. To do this, to develop a dispositional approach to maker-centered learning, it is necessary for students to learn to notice the intricacies and nuances of their worlds . . . to develop, in other words, a sensitivity to design.

Note

1 Visit the Educator Resources of the Agency *by* Design website to access our full set of thinking routines: www.agencybydesign.org.

References

Ackermann, E. K. (2013). Cultures of creativity and modes of appropriation: From DIY (Do it Yourself) to BIIT (Be in it Together). *Essay Prepared for the LEGO Foundation Report on Cultures of Creativity*. Retrieved on November 10, 2014 from www.legofoundation.com/en-us/research-and-learning/foundation-research/cultures-of-creativity/

Bandura, A. (2001). Social cognitive theory: An agentic perspective. *Annual Review of Psychology, 52*, 1–26.

Blikstein, P., & Worsley, M. (2016). Children are not hackers: Building a culture of powerful ideas, deep learning, and equity in the maker movement. In K. Peppler, E. Halverson, & Y. Kafai (Eds.), *Makeology: Makerspaces as learning environments* (Volume 1) (pp. 64–79). New York, NY: Routledge.

Committee on Conceptual Framework for the New K–12 Science Standards/National Research Council. (2012). *Framework for K–12 science education: Practices, cross-cutting concepts, and core ideas.* Washington, DC: National Academies Press. Retrieved on November 10, 2014 from www.nap.edu/catalog.php?record_id=13165

Dougherty, D. (2012). The Maker Movement. *Innovation: Technology, Governance, Globalization, 7*(3), 11–14.

Dougherty, D. (2013). The maker mindset. In M. Honey & D. E. Kanter (Eds.), *Design, make, play: Growing the next generation of STEM innovators* (pp. 7–11). New York: Routledge.

Honey, M. & Kanter, D. E. (2013). *Design, make, play: Growing the next generation of STEM innovators.* New York: Routledge.

Kalil, T. (2013). Have fun—Learn something, do something, make something. In M. Honey & D. E. Kanter (Eds.), *Design, make, play: Growing the next generation of STEM innovators* (pp. 12–16). New York: Routledge.

Martinez, S. L. & Stager, G. (2013). *Invent to learn: Making, tinkering, and engineering in the classroom.* Torrance, CA: Constructing Modern Knowledge Press.

More than just digital quilting. (2011). Retrieved on November 10, 2014 from www.economist.com/node/21540392/

OECD. (2010). *PISA 2009 results: What students know and can do—Student performance in reading, mathematics and science (Volume I).* Retrieved on November 10, 2014 from dx.doi.org/10.1787/9789264091450-en

Peppler, K. & Bender, S. (2013). Maker Movement spreads innovation one project at a time. *Phi Delta Kappan, 95*(3), 22–27.

Perkins, D. N., Jay, E., & Tishman, S. (1993). Beyond abilities: A dispositional theory of thinking. *Merrill-Palmer Quarterly, 39*(1), 1–21.

Perkins, D. N. & Tishman, S. (2006). Learning that matters: Towards a dispositional perspective on education and its research needs. *A Report Prepared for the Spencer Foundation.*

Perkins, D. N., Tishman, S., Ritchhart, R., Donis, K., & Andrade, A. (2000). Intelligence in the wild: A dispositional view of intellectual traits. *Educational Psychology Review, 12*(3), 269–293.

Petrich, M., Wilkinson, K., & Bevan, B. (2013). It looks like fun, but are they learning? In M. Honey & D. E. Kanter (Eds.), *Design, make, play: Growing the next generation of STEM innovators* (pp. 50–70). New York: Routledge.

Quinn, H. & Bell, P. (2013). How designing, making, and playing relate to the learning goals of K–12 science education. In M. Honey & D. E. Kanter (Eds.), *Design, make, play: Growing the next generation of STEM innovators* (pp. 17–33). New York: Routledge.

Ritchhart, R., Palmer, P., Church, M., & Tishman, S. (2006). *Thinking routines: Establishing patterns of thinking in the classroom.* Paper Presented at the 2006 Annual Meeting of the American Educational Research Association (AERA), San Francisco, CA.

Royte, E. (2013). *What lies ahead for 3-D printing?.* Retrieved on November 10, 2014 from www.smithsonianmag.com/science-nature/What-Lies-Ahead-for-3-D-Printing-204136931.html

Ryan, J. (2015). Moving beyond the hype of the 3-D printer. *Education Week, 35*(11), 18–19.

Sheridan, K., Halverson, E., Litts, B., Brahms, L., Jacobs-Priebe, L., & Owens, T. (2014). Learning in the making: A comparative case study of three makerspaces. *Harvard Educational Review, 84*(4), 505–531.

Sheridan, K. M., & Konopasky, A. (2016). Designing for resourcefulness in a community-based makerspace. In K. Peppler, E. Halverson, & Y. Kafai (Eds.), *Makeology: Makerspaces as learning environments* (Volume 1) (pp. 30–46). New York, NY: Routledge.

Tishman, S. (2001). Added value: A dispositional perspective on thinking. In A. Costa (Ed.), *Developing minds: A resource book for teaching thinking* (3rd ed.) (pp. 72–75). Alexandria, VA: Association for Supervision and Curriculum Development.

Tishman, S., Jay, E., & Perkins, D. N. (1993). Teaching thinking dispositions: From transmission to enculturation. *Theory into Practice, 32*(3), 147–153.

Walker, R. (2012). Meet your maker. *Fast Company* (162), 90.

Wardrip, P. S., & Brahms, L. (2016). Taking making to school: A model for integrating making into classrooms. In K. Peppler, E. Halverson, & Y. Kafai (Eds.), *Makeology: Makerspaces as learning environments* (Volume 1) (pp. 97–106). New York, NY: Routledge.

White House. (2009, April 27). *Remarks by the President at the National Academy of Sciences annual meeting.* Retrieved on November 10, 2014 from www.whitehouse.gov/the-press-office/remarks-president-national-academy-sciences-annual-meeting

White House. (n.d.) *Educate to innovate.* Retrieved on November 10, 2014 from www.whitehouse.gov/issues/education/k-12/educate-innovate

CHAPTER 4

Making Matters

A Framework for Assessing Digital Media Citizenship

BRIGID BARRON AND CAITLIN K. MARTIN

> If you think it can be done, then it can probably be done.
> (Shurbham Banerjee, 8th grade)

The 13-year-old middle school student quoted above is the latest example of a teen tinkerer turned entrepreneur. Shurbham Banerjee's story was reported on the front page of the San Jose *Mercury* in early November of 2014 with the headline "Teen now V[enture] C[apital] wunderkind—13-year-old inventor youngest ever to gain venture capital funding" (Sommerville, 2014). Banerjee's invention is a low-cost braille printer, a project launched after he learned about the high cost of current printers designed for home use by the blind. Armed with a programmable LEGO robotics kit, Banerjee launched a rigorous prototyping process—cycling through seven models before hitting on a solution just in time for his middle school's science fair. Banerjee's story exemplifies the Silicon Valley version of the classic maker—confident, persistent, entrepreneurial, and impassioned to create a specific product that is personally and socially relevant.

In this chapter, we focus specifically on digital makers who, like Banerjee, are creating with technology and computing devices, though often with fewer resources. While the beneficial outcomes of Banerjee's efforts are obvious, what else is going on when young people create with technology? We are particularly interested in this mode of creation for two reasons related to trends in media opportunity and access. First, current free and widely distributed technologies allow children access to creation activities that were previously reserved for professionals trained within complex systems. Examples include youth creating full-length movies with various transitions using tools bundled with Apple products, and assembling and coding multiplayer games with freely distributed mobile apps. To develop making and creating projects, devices are important, but learning opportunities that can provide inspiration and skills are essential. We expect that these learning opportunities are less equally distributed and we believe it is important to know how widely these making and creating hobbies are being adopted. A second reason for interest in digital creation lies in its potential as a unique catalyst for the development of an innovative mindset and the social and technical skills that will be important for the future. The notion that all young people should be creators, as opposed to simply consumers, in the world (Freire, 1970) is especially relevant and critical, as mobile devices and expanded connectivity allow young people to spend hours of their day engaging in media-enabled consumption, be it watching YouTube, shopping online, or scanning Facebook. It is likely that not all digital hobbies yield the same benefits and we want to be able to start measuring different kinds of outcomes. This kind of evidence can help make the case for giving all young people opportunities to develop the capacity for digital production, not just consumption, in order to have agency in this increasingly digital world.

The hypothesis that sustained engagement in making and creating activities can help nurture an innovative mindset, a robust sense of creative self-efficacy, and an identity as someone who can come up with interesting ideas is a core premise of the Maker Movement (Blikstein, 2013; Vossoughi & Bevan, 2014). These ideas have roots in earlier theories of constructivist learning (e.g., Papert, 1980; Piaget, 1964) and the progressive education movement that emphasized the importance of inquiry-oriented, interest-driven, and project-based learning (Barron et al., 1998; Dewey, 1897; Kilpatrick, 1918) that can help connect knowledge with contexts of authentic application. Their current instantiation in the Maker Movement frequently includes a modern focus on technologies for fabrication and the blending of the material and digital in products that range from robots to video games. This conjecture is also consistent with qualitative and ethnographic research that shows that sustained engagement with interest-driven digital hobbies can be consequential for learning and development. Across several studies, we have used a learning biography approach to document the development of students' interests, identities, and the diversification of their learning ecologies as they become more involved in digital hobbies (Barron, 2006; Barron, Wise, & Martin, 2013). Learning biographies tap into the life histories of learners, using retrospective interviews and prospective observations to identify key events, activities, and learning partners over time and across different settings in which youth spend their time. These longitudinal portraits begin to reveal the resources related to expertise and the ways that interest-driven hobbies can spark independent decisions to learn more, as projects evolve and learners seek out new opportunities. These choices to keep learning can take many forms—defining new projects, deciding to take an elective at school, pursuing information online, recruiting mentors, and making choices to teach others. These interest-based pursuits tend to cross boundaries—that is, they show up in settings across life spaces including homes, schools, community centers, and online. And, each learning opportunity can be consequential, leading young people to develop new ideas about their capacities as creators, their possible futures, practice-linked identities, confidence with digital tools, and new sustained relationships with adults and peers (Barron, 2006; Barron, Gomez, Pinkard, & Martin, 2014; Ito et al., 2009).

Despite ample grounding in ethnographic research and the expansion of opportunities for making of all kinds, there is a scarcity of large-scale research that reveals nuances in different types of production and making and what outcomes they might be linked to. Few quantitative studies have identified the types of digital making young people are involved in, nor have they established relationships between experience in building, designing, and creating and other metrics that we might care about. In this chapter, we provide evidence for the relationship between experience with a set of digital hobbies—such as website creation, digital art, and robotics—and a set of dispositions that are posited to be important for young people to capitalize on new technologies to enhance their own lives and contribute to the well-being of their local communities.

Defining Dispositions Important to 21st-Century Citizenship

Frameworks defining 21st-century competencies organize the skills, abilities, and attitudes slightly differently, but they share a similar focus on both cognitive and noncognitive outcomes and pay attention to individual skills and attitudes, as well as social orientations (e.g., Binkley et al., 2012; Pellegrino & Hilton, 2012; Partnership for 21st Century Skills, 2009). Attending to cultural, social, and ethical dimensions of participatory cultures has led to the articulation of additional considerations of what might be developing as young people learn to contribute, circulate, and curate content online, including abstract concepts such as collective intelligence, or shared knowledge that emerges from collaboration, and multimodality, or the ability to communicate in various ways such as written, verbal, special, and visual (Jenkins, 2009). The capacity to find and evaluate sources of information online to determine their credibility are increasingly garnering attention, and empirical work shows how education levels and histories of experience with networked resources are linked to these skills (Hargittai, 2005, 2011). Although measurement of conceptual knowledge and technology skills is important, in this work we address more noncognitive outcomes. Attention to these types of social and individual dispositions have been identified as critical to the design and implementation of equitable learning environments (Barron, 2014; Margolis, Goode, & Chapman, 2015). Dispositions associated with related skills and abilities have been called out in a number of ways by different researchers; for example, encapsulated by terms such as "creative confidence" (Kelley & Kelley, 2012) and "intrepid explorer" (Turkle, 1984). "Creative confidence" is defined as belief in your ability to create change in the world around you (Kelley & Kelley, 2012). To be an "intrepid explorer" is to delight in taking risks and tinkering without a fear of getting lost in the complex or breaking something in the process of exploration (Turkle, 1984; also see Denner & Bean, 2006 for an elaboration of this construct).

In this chapter, we present an assessment approach based on the Digital Youth Network (DYN) Digital Media Citizenship design framework. This framework guided the development and iteration of a program to cultivate "digital media citizenship," specifying three dispositions as youth became *constructive producers* of digital media, *social advocates* for better futures, and *critical consumers* of digital media (Pinkard & Austin, 2011). The *constructive* disposition incorporates creative identity, experience, and expertise with digital production and a propensity to seek out resources and opportunities for learning more. The *social* disposition includes participation in a learning network around digital making, including collaborators, more knowledgeable instructors, and learners, across different environments such as family, school, community, and online. The *critical* disposition is an understanding that all media is authored and reflects the values, biases, and possible inaccuracies of those who created it, thus positioning learners to analyze information found online as well as contribute their own perspectives on social or political issues. DYN designed and implemented a cross-setting school and afterschool program in Chicago intended to ensure that digital production activities and the fluencies that developed from technological creation and collaboration activities were not limited to youth from areas of higher socioeconomic status or from areas that typically had more technology-based resources in schools and homes.

We had the opportunity to study a cohort of students involved in the DYN program over three years, and as part of this work we created an assessment framework that included quantitative measures mapped onto the DYN Digital Media Citizenship framework to operationalize a set of dispositions that emphasizes the multidimensional nature of participation, as well as the importance of interests and identities (Martin, Barron, Matthews, & Stringer, 2014). In this chapter, we use these measures to look at a sample of youth from Silicon Valley and focus our analysis on the relationship between the 21st-century dispositions outlined in the DYN framework and digital making experience.

Research Aims and Our Approach

Our three primary questions we set out to address were: (1) What types of digital hobbies do these students spend time on? (2) Are digital makers at an advantage in terms of dispositions related to constructive, social, and critical dispositions? (3) Who has access to digital making and creating activities in terms of youth gender and home access to technology?

To help answer these questions, we recruited students from a public middle school in the Silicon Valley region of California. The school, with 1,300 6th- through 8th-grade students, was high performing (over 90% of students met or exceeded standards in math and English language arts on California state tests) and affluent (only 3% were eligible for subsidized lunch programs). We had the opportunity to survey the entire 8th-grade cohort (n = 367 students) at the end of the 2009 school year. Approximately half of surveyed students were male (51.1%). The sample had a high Asian-American population: 34.2% self-selected Chinese as their ethnicity, 25.6% Asian Indian, 23.3% White, 19.4% other Asian (Japanese, Vietnamese, Korean), and 4.7% Hispanic-Latino. Almost a quarter of these students (23.2%) were born outside the United States, and many lived in multilanguage households: Although only 1% of the school population was classified as English Language Learners, 33.5% reported speaking a Chinese dialect at home, 11% an Asian Indian dialect, and 5.2% Spanish.

Students were administered a survey of *Access, Experience, and Interest* (Barron, 2004; Barron, Walters, Martin, & Shatz, 2010), including the DYN Digital Media Citizenship framework measures. The paper-based survey was given during students' 40-minute mathematics period. In this chapter, we report on a subset of measures from the survey, including home access, prior experiences, current digital activities, and those related to constructive, social, and critical dispositions as defined in Table 4.1. The survey also included items about general academic and social self-efficacy, prior classes and other learning opportunities, parent expertise and support, and ideas for future careers and learning.

Table 4.1 DYN Digital Media Citizenship Framework and corresponding measures (see Appendix A for measures)

Disposition	*Description*	*Measures*
Constructive	Confident and able users of technology who see themselves as creators and who seek out new opportunities and resources to advance learning. Skilled in finding information online and familiar with technical vocabulary.	• Creative identity • Technological confidence • Internet proficiency proxy • Independent learning sources
Social	Shares expertise with peers, family, and community. Participates in online communities related to their interests. Imagines using media skills for promoting social change.	• Teaching network • Making media to promote social change • Online affinity groups
Critical	Uses networked resources to learn about and contribute to political conversations. Aware that all media is authored and uses strategies to evaluate information online and find converging evidence.	• Critical approach to online information • Exchange of political information online • Addressing political issues through media creation

Framework of Digital Media Citizenship

In this chapter, we provide an analysis of how making and creating experiences relate to the three dispositions articulated by DYN. We recognize that the definitions of these dispositions are broad and could be operationalized in many ways. Table 4.1 provides a brief description of each disposition and the survey measures we used to assess them.

What We Found

What Types of Digital Hobbies Do Students Spend Time On?

To get a sense of what digital activities these Silicon Valley youth pursued on their own time, we looked at the proportion of students who reported regular engagement with different computer and online activities and media and technology projects that involve elements of designing, building, and troubleshooting.

Regular digital hobbies. Students were asked how often they used a computer anywhere to do a range of technology activities on an 8-point scale ranging from Never (1) to Several times a day (8). Activities included hobbies such as gaming, social networking, and digital creation. When we looked at the percentage of students who reported at least weekly participation, gaming was by far the most common regular digital hobby (see Table 4.2), while digital making occurred less frequently.

Digital making experience. To find out more about what the Silicon Valley students were creating and had ever created using computers and technology, we looked at their history of experience with a set of nine digital maker activities, each of which involve some aspect of designing, inventing, or building. Students indicated their participation from a choice of: never, once or twice, three to six times, and more than six times. Table 4.3 shows the percentage of participants who reported having ever participated in each, revealing a range of variability between activities. Making a piece of digital art and creating a digital video stand out as activities that were highly accessible to these youth. Meanwhile, while we know that the majority of these youth were playing digital games, only 23% reported any experience creating a computer game of their own.

Table 4.2 Percentage of students who reported activity at least once a week

Play games	*62.7%*
Edit/design your blog/social networking page	46.5%
Work on digital media projects outside of school assignments	20.2%

Table 4.3 Percentage of students who reported having participated in each activity at least once

Created a digital video	82.5%
Created a piece of digital art	80.5%
Created an animation	47.9%
Built a robot or created an invention of any kind using technology	47.1%
Created a piece of digital music	46.0%
Created a website	42.3%
Written computer program (code) using a computer language	38.0%
Designed a 2D or 3D model or drawing	37.0%
Created a computer game	23.1%

To put our sample in the context of broader teen digital media trends, we looked at international reports collected around the time of our survey research. In general, our sample was similar to other young people in terms of their computer-enabled gaming and social networking. A 2010 Pew Research Internet Project publication reported that 78% of US teens 12–17 played online games and 73% used social networking sites when they used the Internet (Zickuhr, 2010). Another national study from the Kaiser Family Foundation reported that on average, youth 11–14 years old were spending 29 minutes a day on social network sites and 1 hour and 45 minutes gaming on computers and other devices (Rideout, Foehr, & Roberts, 2010). A 2010 report from a sample of over 25,000 9- to 16-year olds across 25 European countries found similar frequency of digital activities: 83% had played computer games in the past month and 62% had visited a social networking profile.

As indicated earlier, there is little empirical data about youth technological production experiences, but similar to our sample, indications are that it occurs less than other computer-based activities. In the PEW study, only 14% of teens reported that they worked on their own blog. Although the Kaiser survey did not ask specifically about creation and production activities, the 11–14 age group reported an average of only two minutes a day on any computer activities other than those asked about. In the EU study, 39% of youth reported having posted photos, videos, or music to share with others in the past month and 11% had contributed to a blog or an online diary (Livingstone, Haddon, Görzig, & Ólafsson, 2011). An updated report from Europe found kids doing more online that they were in the original 2010 study, but that media creation and contributions remained less frequent than other activities such as social networking and watching video clips (Mascheroni & Ólafsson, 2014).

Are Digital Makers at an Advantage in Terms of Literacies Related to Constructive, Social, and Critical Dispositions?

Given the variability of the students involved in digital making in this sample, we were interested to look at different profiles of digital producers. We created three groups of students who differed in their breadth and depth of experience as digital makers and then contrasted these groups with respect to our measures of constructive, social, and critical dispositions (see Table 4.1). Because this data is correlational and collected at a single time point we cannot make causal claims, but instead report on relationships between experience and these valued dispositions.

Defining maker experience profiles. A digital making experience score was created for each student based on the total number of production activities they had done at least three times. We created three maker profiles based on these

Table 4.4 Percentage of students who reported activity at least once a week, by maker group. Significance should be read across rows ($p < .05$). Items that share a common superscript or that do not have superscripts do not differ significantly.

	Beginner Makers	*Intermediate Makers*	*Experienced Makers*
Weekly gamer	65.5%	55.0%	68.1%
Weekly social networker	36.8% ^{a}	48.3% ^{a,b}	58.9% ^{b}
Weekly project work	8.4% ^{a}	14.3% ^{a}	45.3% ^{b}

scores. Beginner Makers (40% of the sample) had scores of zero or one, indicating that they had repeated experience with no more than one of the nine digital making activities; Intermediate Makers (33% of the sample) had scores of two or three; and Experienced Makers (27% of the sample) had scores from four to nine.

To connect this to the first analyses, we looked at the digital hobbies of these three profile groups (see Table 4.4). Although they did not differ in the likelihood of regularly playing games, Experienced Makers were significantly more likely to work on their own digital projects outside of class time than the other two groups and were more likely than the Beginner Makers to regularly edit or update their social networking sites. This data shows that beginners were not idle in terms of technology use, but Experienced Makers had greater breadth of regular digital activities. Three-quarters of Beginner Makers pursued one or less of these activities on their own time ($M = 1.10$, $SE = 0.06$), whereas 60% of Experienced Makers reported regularly doing at least two ($M = 1.73$, $SE = 0.82$).[1]

Constructive Dispositions

To explore constructive dispositions of the three different digital production profiles, we looked at student ratings of creativity, confidence with computers and technology, Internet proficiency, and number of learning resources.

Creative identity. A creative identity score was constructed by taking the average rating of agreement with two statements, "I can be creative" and "I can come up with new and interesting ideas," on a 5-point Likert scale from 1 (strongly disagree) to 5 (strongly agree).[2] The Experienced Makers considered themselves significantly more creative than the other two groups, and Intermediate Makers reported significantly higher creativity than Beginner Makers.[3]

Technological confidence. A confidence measure developed in earlier studies[4] was constructed by taking the average rating of agreement (using the same 5-point scale) of three statements: "I feel confident about my abilities to use computers," "I am good with computers," and the reverse of "I am NOT the kind of person who works well with computers." Again, Experienced Makers had significantly higher confidence ratings than the other groups, and the Intermediate Makers were significantly higher than the Beginner Makers.[5]

To find out more about the specific types of confidences students had with computers and technology, we asked them to indicate their level of expertise with a range of technology tools from options of: I don't know what this is; I have no experience but have heard of it; I've played around with it; I have used it to make something; and I am an expert and can teach others how to use it. Experienced and Intermediate Makers were more likely than Beginner Makers to report expertise with word processing, presentation, and video production tools. Experienced Makers were more likely than the other two groups to consider themselves expert for each tool listed with the exception of word processing and LEGO Mindstorms, on which the Experienced and Intermediate Makers did not differ. Overall, expertise with expressive (art, video graphics, music) and productivity (word processing and presentation) tools was more frequently cited, with more direct computational tools (such as programing and game design) being less frequently nominated (see Table 4.5).

Internet proficiency proxy. Eszter Hargittai validated a measure of Internet proficiency by correlating actual search success with a survey-based measure

Table 4.5 Percentage of students who reported expertise with tools, by maker group. Significance should be read across rows ($p < .05$). Items that share a common superscript or that do not have superscripts do not differ significantly.

	Beginner Makers	*Intermediate Makers*	*Experienced Makers*
Word processing programs (MS Word, Pages)	46.9% [a]	64.2% [b]	75.8% [b]
Presentations (PowerPoint)	36.4% [a]	52.5% [b]	77.7% [c]
Video production (iMovie)	2.8% [a]	10.0% [b]	26.3% [c]
Digital graphics programs (Photoshop, Illustrator, Fireworks)	2.8% [a]	6.7% [a]	28.4% [b]
Music creation programs (Garageband, Fruity Loops, ProTools)	1.5% [a]	3.4% [a]	21.7% [b]
LEGO Mindstorms Robotics	1.4% [a]	5.9% [a,b]	12.6% [b]
Web creation tools (iWeb, Dreamweaver)	0.7% [a]	0.0% [a]	18.9% [b]
Games and animation tools (Flash, Scratch, Game Star Mechanic)	0.7% [a]	0.0% [a]	12.8% [b]

of familiarity with technical vocabulary (Hargittai, 2005; Hargittai & Hsieh, 2012). The proxy was determined to measure both effectiveness (percentage of tasks completed successfully) and efficiency (amount of time spent on tasks). This proxy uses the average ratings of understanding of 15 Internet-related terms on a 5-point Likert scale from 1 (none) to 5 (full). Experienced Makers had significantly higher scores than the other two groups and the Intermediate Makers had significantly higher scores than the Beginner Makers.[6]

Independent learning sources. Students were asked to rate the importance of a variety of ways they learned to use computers on a 5-point Likert scale from 1 (not at all) to 5 (extremely much). We created a learning sources score by summing the different resources students rated as "important" or "very important" contributors to their learning. This five-item index included books, magazines, online articles or discussion boards, step-by-step tutorials or instructions, and software help menus. Experienced Makers had significantly more sources of learning than the Intermediate Makers and the Beginner Makers, who did not differ from one another.[7]

In summary, more digital making experience was associated with more evidence of a constructive disposition, and this was true for each level of experience profile. The Intermediate Makers had a higher sense of their own creativity, more confidence with technology, and greater Internet proficiency than the Beginner Makers, and the Experienced Makers were higher on these measures than both Beginner and Intermediate Makers. The Experienced Makers also reported more sources of learning on their own than the other two groups, perhaps indicating that those trying new genres of production (breadth of experience) or going deep into production activities (depth of production) were more likely to reach a point where they needed to seek out and incorporate novel resources for learning as they moved beyond what they were introduced to in a class, in an afterschool program, or by a person.

Social Dispositions

To look at the social disposition of the three different digital production profiles, we examined whom they taught about computers and technology, their perceptions about the likelihood of creating media for social change, and their use of online affinity groups.

Teaching network. Students were asked whom, if anyone, they taught about computers and technology from a list including mother, father, brother, sister, cousin, friend(s) grandparents, and other. Experienced and Intermediate Makers reported teaching significantly more types of people in their lives than the Beginner Makers, but did not significantly differ from one another.[8]

Table 4.6 Percentage of students who reported participation in social technology activities, by maker group. Statistical significance at the level of $p < .05$ is denoted in this table through a series of superscripts. Significance should be read across rows. Items that share a common superscript or that do not have superscripts do not differ significantly.

	Beginner Makers	*Intermediate Makers*	*Experienced Makers*
See themselves creating media for social change	13.8%[a]	26.1%[b]	31.9%[b]
Report regular participation in online affinity groups	29.6%[a]	42.0%[a,b]	53.7%[b]

Creating media to promote social change. Students were asked to rate the likelihood of a number of possible future activities on a 5-point Likert scale from 1 (definitely no) to 5 (definitely yes). Significantly more Experienced Makers and Intermediate Makers agreed that they might create and share media to promote social change in their community or more globally (marked a 4 or a 5, indicating probably or definitely yes) compared to the Beginner Makers (see Table 4.6).

Online affinity groups. Students indicated how often they used the Internet (blogs, social networking sites, wikis, or other websites) to talk to others about their hobbies on an 8-point scale from 1 (never) to 8 (several times a day). Experienced Makers were significantly more likely than Beginner Makers to report regularly discussing hobbies online (at least once a week) (see Table 4.6).

While Experienced Makers and Intermediate Makers did not differ in their evidence of social dispositions, the two groups were significantly more likely to exhibit these indicators than the Beginner Makers. Those with more experience reported teaching more people about what they know about computers and technology, were more likely to discuss their own hobbies with others in online networks, and were more likely to create media to promote social change. These results suggest that sustained digital making experiences connect learners to a social network around digital technologies, both online or in person, and foster ideas about how they can use their knowledge and abilities to impact others.

Critical Dispositions

To explore the critical disposition of the maker profiles, we looked at how students analyzed information they found online and their likelihood of addressing political issues through online discussion and/or media creation and sharing.

Critical approach to online information. Students indicated the frequency with which they enacted practices of critical review of online sources from a selection of never, rarely, sometimes, often, or very often. An online content validation score was constructed by taking the average of three practices: "Check to see if webpage is current," "Consider whether the site is factual or opinion," and "Validate information through other sources (e.g., books, teachers, encyclopedias, magazines)."[9] Experienced Makers were significantly more likely than the other groups to report often engaging in critical practices to validate online information. We also looked at how often they evaluated sources by investigating authorship, creating an author validation score by taking the average of four practices: "Check to see who the author is," "Check if contact information is provided on the website," "Check the qualifications or credentials of the author," and "Go to the About Us pages."[10] Experienced Makers and Intermediate Makers did not differ from each other but were more likely than the Beginner Makers to report doing these types of activities often, although few students reported this to be true across all groups (see Table 4.7).

Exchange of political information online. Students indicated how often they used the Internet (blogs, social networking sites, wikis, or other websites) to get or share information (news or opinions) about political issues on an 8-point scale from 1 (never) to 8 (several times a day). Experienced Makers were significantly more likely than Intermediate Makers and Beginner Makers to report having regular (at least once a week) exchanges of information of this nature online (see Table 4.8).

Addressing political issues through media creation. Using the same scale, students indicated how often they used the Internet to create and share media about a political message. Experienced Makers were significantly more likely to report regular creation of political media than Intermediate Makers and Beginner Makers (see Table 4.8).

To summarize these findings, Experienced Makers exhibited more evidence of a critical disposition than the other groups, including greater regularity of validating information found online and of addressing

Table 4.7 Percentage of students who report frequent use of critical online practices, by maker group. Statistical significance at the level of $p < .05$ is denoted in this table through a series of superscripts. Significance should be read across rows. Items that share a common superscript or that do not have superscripts do not differ significantly.

	Beginner Makers	*Intermediate Makers*	*Experienced Makers*
Content validation activities	15.4%^{a}	20.0%^{a}	41.1%^{b}
Author validation activities	0.0%^{a}	4.2%^{b}	6.5%^{b}

Table 4.8 Percentage of students who reported using media to explore political information, by maker group. Statistical significance at the level of $p < .05$ is denoted in this table through a series of superscripts. Significance should be read across rows. Items that share a common superscript or that do not have superscripts do not differ significantly.

	Beginner	*Intermediate*	*Experienced*
Regular exchange of political info online	22.4%[a]	16.7%[a]	37.9%[b]
Regular address of political issues in media	5.7%[a]	4.2%[a]	23.2%[b]

political ideas through making and sharing online. On these measures, the Intermediate and the Beginner Makers did not differ from each other. In this case, those students who were the most experienced with different genres of production had a more critical viewpoint, perhaps taking on authorship responsibility, analyzing deeply both what they consumed and created.

Who Has Access to These Making and Creating Activities in Terms of Youth Gender and Home Access to Technology?

Given the benefits of making suggested in our findings, we wanted to find out more about the particular students in the different maker groups to see how boys and girls, and youth from different home environments, were using productive technologies.

Gender

There was a significant relationship between gender and maker group. Boys and girls were equally represented in the Beginner Makers. This group consisted of 47.9% girls and 52.1% boys (40.6% of all the boys and 39.0% of all the girls in the sample were identified as Beginner Makers). However, of those youth who evidenced some making experiences, significantly more boys were categorized as Experienced Makers (31.7% compared to 21.5% of the girls in the sample), while girls were more likely to be classified as Intermediate Makers (39.5% compared to 27.8% of boys in the sample).[11] Intermediate Makers consisted of 57.6% girls and 42.4% boys, and the Experienced Makers consisted of 39.4% girls and 60.6% boys.

Home Access and Opportunity

Technology tools at home. Experienced and Intermediate Makers were heavy home users of technology with a lot of equipment at their disposal. Experienced and Intermediate Makers were more likely to report at least daily use of a computer at home (66.3% and 63.3%, respectively) than Beginner Makers (46.9%).[12] These groups were also more likely than Beginner Makers to have their own computer.[13] Whereas almost three-fourths (74.7%) of Experienced Makers and 67.5% of Intermediate Makers had their own computer, only just over half (54.5%) of Beginner Makers reported this to be true. A self-reported count of technology tools at home from a possible total of 10 (computer(s), printer, scanner, digital camera, movie camera, tablet, game console, digital music player, high-speed Internet [DSL or Cable], and wireless Internet) revealed that Experienced and Intermediate Makers reported significantly more devices at home than Beginner Makers.[14]

Discussion

In this chapter, we provide a set of analyses that showed significant relationships between experience in digital maker hobbies and a number of measures that reflect the *constructive*, *social*, and *critical* dispositions that all learners need to develop in order to make full use of technologies to advance their own learning and development. Although this study took place at one point in time and is correlational data, there is good theoretical grounding to suspect that causal relationships exist—that making matters. For example, the relationship between self-efficacy or confidence in being able to accomplish what one sets out to do and actual persistence in the activity is one of the most replicated findings in the motivation literature and has been documented across domains of health, weight loss, academic tasks, and interpersonal relationships (Bandura, 1988). Self-efficacy in turn is developed through experience. To prepare young people for the future, they need to have experiences that empower them to develop a sense of themselves as creators and contributors, confidence utilizing technical tools and learning on their own time, and an orientation to engage in civic and social issues. This study suggests that we can nurture these types of important dispositions through making and creating, helping to provide evidence for some of the claims made in, for instance, Regalla (2016) in volume 1 of this series and chapter 3 in this volume. In our sample of middle school students, there was a lot of variability of experience with digital making, despite the fact that these youth were growing up in one of the technology capitals of the world. And those with more digital making experience displayed evidence of more constructive, social, and critical dispositions. More making was associated with, among other things, higher reports of personal creativity, confidence with technology tools, independent learning sources, the use of technology to address social and political ideas, and teaching others what they knew about computers and technology. These important findings will hopefully energize educators and researchers and others who are interested in designing makerspaces and communities to start documenting these types of outcomes. We imagine that these findings would apply to makers who engage in nondigital making as well, but more extensive research is needed to clarify the nature of this relationship and how it may be nuanced by different types and tools of creation.

In this chapter, we also present an analysis of this data with respect to gender and access to tools at home to point to the importance of continuing to attend to issues of equity. Females and those without home access in the form of personal computers were less likely to inhabit the Experienced Maker group. The role that digital tools play in making creative work possible raises important questions about who is getting access to both the tools of production and the learning opportunities that support design and creation activities. Long-standing patterns of gender-, SES-, and ethnicity-related differences in participation in computing have led to an articulation of the implications of "experience gaps" (Barron, 2004; Margolis & Fisher, 2003) or "participation gaps" (Jenkins, 2009) for equity (Castells, 1996; New London Group, 1996; Reich, 2002). These older concerns are being revoiced within the Maker Movement, including by Brahms and Crowley in chapter 2 of this volume, bolstered by content analyses of *Make* Magazine that reveal portrayals of makers that are consistent with the stereotype of makers as male and either White or Asian (Quattrocchi, 2013).

Our work to analyze longitudinal qualitative data—the learning biographies discussed in the introduction—highlight the importance of configurations of resources, particularly in the early phases of interest development. Interests typically grow out of a confluence of opportunities that provide inspiring ideas along with the time to explore and the tools to do so (Azevedo, 2011; Barron, 2014). Peers and adults can serve as learning partners and guides who demonstrate or explain technology-related concepts, but also who engage in various forms of brokering, consulting, and collaboration (Barron, Martin, Takeuchi, & Fithian, 2009). Beyond providing instrumental help, our case portraits show that adults help socialize positive attitudes towards innovation and position young people in authentic roles as contributors.

We see similar dynamics in the inspirational maker story we started with. Although the young Shurbham Banerjee's talents and engagement are obvious in his creation of the braille printer, an equally important part of his story lies in the multiple supports that contributed to his success. As he says, "It is not that surprising for someone even as young as me to be able to do big things in Silicon Valley. It's filled with smart people who have helped me and there are so many opportunities here for anyone who wants to create something" (Chakraborty, 2014). His private school offered a child-centered environment that focused on individual learning interests, as well as specific school-day offerings in computer science (Terrapin Logo and Java languages) and robotics. The school also fostered STEM project creation, capitalizing on Silicon Valley competitions and opportunities, such as the county science fair in which six of Banerjee's peers also won top awards. At home, Banerjee has been deeply supported in his creative technology work by his parents, from general encouragement and shared values about helping others to business advice and large-scale funding of the initial design prototype. His father bought him his LEGO robotics set and worked at Intel, suggesting some expertise in the technology area. His mother monitored his tenacious pursuit, making sure he got enough sleep when he was trying to work late into the night, and is currently serving as CEO of Banerjee's company until he is old enough to take on this position. The outcomes of this support and work are clear; Banerjee has venture capital funding and a patented innovation, as well as plans for doing more in the future.

His story and those of others that have been published in research journals and in the popular press should convince us of the value of positioning learners to design, create, invent, and use technologies to enhance their personal lives and social worlds (Castells, 1996; New London Group, 1996; Reich, 2002). In the event that policy makers will want more than stories, we've laid the groundwork for the development of more representative quantitative studies or experiments that can marshal stronger evidence for the claim that "Making Matters," not just for young learners but for the communities that they might contribute to, now and in the future.

NOTES

1 Intermediate Makers $M = 1.18$, $SE = 0.066$.

2 Chronbach's alpha = 0.84.

3 ANOVA ($F(2,353) = 15.97$, $p < .001$) with post hoc Tukey; Beginner Makers $M = 3.69$, $SE = 0.07$; Intermediate Makers $M = 4.02$, $SE = 0.08$; Experienced Makers $M = 4.32$, $SE = 0.09$.

4 Chronbach's alpha = 0.83.

5 ANOVA ($F(2, 352) = 38.64$, $p < .001$) with post hoc Tukey; Beginner Makers $M = 3.54$, $SE = 060$; Intermediate Makers $M = 3.80$, $SE = 0.07$; Experienced Makers $M = 4.37$, $SE = 0.07$.

6 ANOVA ($F(2,337) = 76.90$, $p < .001$) with post hoc Tukey; Beginner Makers $M = 2.39$, $SE = 0.08$; Intermediate Makers $M = 3.07$, $SE = 0.08$; Experienced Makers $M = 3.85$, $SE = 0.09$.

7 ANOVA ($F(2,347) = 12.31$, $p < .001$) with post hoc Tukey; Beginner Makers $M = 1.62$, $SE = 0.13$; Intermediate Makers $M = 1.76$, $SE = 0.14$; Experienced Makers $M = 2.61$, $SE = 0.16$.

8 ANOVA ($F(2,348) = 11.85$, $p < .001$) with post hoc Tukey; Beginner Makers $M = 0.98$, $SE = 0.13$; Intermediate Makers $M = 1.58$, $SE = 0.14$; Experienced Makers $M = 1.92$, $SE = 0.15$.

9 Chronbach's alpha = .73.

10 Chronbach's alpha = .79.

11 Chi square analysis, $p < .05$.

12 Chi square analysis, $p < .05$.

13 Chi square analysis, $p < .05$.

14 ANOVA ($F(1,357) = 8.86$, $p < .001$) with post hoc Tukey; Beginner Makers $M = 6.45$, $SE = 0.11$; Intermediate Makers $M = 10.90$, $SE = 0.12$; Experienced Makers $M = 10.66$, $SE = 0.14$.

REFERENCES

Azevedo, F. (2011). Lines of practice: A practice-centered theory of interest relationships. *Cognition and Instruction, 29*(2), 147–184.

Bandura, A. (1988). Organizational application of social cognitive theory. *Australian Journal of Management, 13*(2), 275–302.

Barron, B. (2004). Learning ecologies for technological fluency: Gender and experience differences. *Journal of Educational Computing Research, 31*(1), 1–36.

Barron, B. (2006). Interest and self-sustained learning as catalysts of development: A learning ecology perspective. *Human Development, 49*(4), 193–224.

Barron, B. (2014). Formative assessment for STEM learning ecosystems: Biographical approaches as a resource for research and practice. *Report Commissioned by the Committee on Successful Out-of-school STEM Learning*, National Research Council.

Barron, B., Gomez, K., Pinkard, N., & Martin, C. (2014). *The digital youth network: Cultivating digital media citizenship in urban communities.* Cambridge, MA: MIT Press.

Barron, B., Martin, C. K., Takeuchi, L., & Fithian, R. (2009). Parents as learning partners in the development of technological fluency. *International Journal of Learning and Media, 1*(2), 55–77.

Barron, B., Schwartz, D. L., Vye, N. J., Moore, A., Petrosino, A., Zech, L., . . . Bransford, J. D. (1998). Doing with understanding: Lessons from research on problem- and project-based learning. *The Journal of the Learning Sciences, 7*, 271–311.

Barron, B., Walter, S., Martin, C. K., & Schatz, C. (2010). Predictors of creative computing participation and profiles of experience in two Silicon Valley middle schools. *Computers & Education, 54*(1), 178–189.

Barron, B., Wise, S., & Martin, C. K. (2013). Creating within and across life spaces: The role of a computer clubhouse in a child's learning ecology. In B. Bevan, P. Bell, R. Stevens, & A. Razfar (Eds.), *LOST opportunities: Learning in out-of-school time* (pp. 99–118). New York, NY: Springer-Verlag.

Binkley, M., Erstad, J., Herman, J., Raizen, S., Ripley, M., Miller-Ricci, M., & Rumble, M. (2012). Defining twenty-first century skills. In P. Griffin, B. McGaw, and E. Care (Eds.), *Assessment and teaching of twenty-first century skills* (pp. 17–66). New York, NY: Springer.

Blikstein, P. (2013). Digital fabrication and 'making' in education: The democratization of invention. In J. Walter-Herrmann & C. Büching (Eds.), *FabLabs: Of machines, makers and inventors* (pp. 1–21). Bielefeld, Germany: Transcript Publishers.

Castells, M. (1996). *The rise of the network society: The information age: Economy, society and culture, Vol. 1.* Massachusetts and Oxford: Blackwell.

Chakraborty, R. (2014). *Shubham Banerjee, the world's youngest entrepreneur to receive VC funding, on his life changing invention.* [Blog post]. Retrieved November 14, 2014 from yourstory.com/2014/11/shubham-banerjee-vc-funding/

Denner, J. & Bean, S. (2006). Girls, games, and intrepid exploration on the computer. *Encyclopedia of Gender and Information Technology, 1*, 727–732.

Dewey, J. (1897). My pedagogic creed. *School Journal, 54*(3), 77–80.

Freire, P. (1970). *Cultural action for freedom*. Cambridge, MA: Harvard Educational Review.

Hargittai, E. (2005). Survey measures of web-oriented digital literacy. *Social Science Computer Review, 23*(3), 371–379.

Hargittai, E. (2011). Minding the digital gap: Why understanding digital inequality matters. In S. Papathanassopoulos (Ed.), *Media Perspectives for the 21st Century* (pp. 231–240). New York, NY: Routledge.

Hargittai, E. & Hsieh, Y. P. (2012). Succinct survey measures of web-use skills. *Social Science Computer Review, 30*(1), 95–107.

Ito, M., Horst, H., Antin, J., Finn, M., Law, A., Manion, A., . . . Yardi, S. (2009). *Hanging out, messing around, and geeking out: Kids living and learning with new media.* Cambridge, MA: The MIT Press.

Jenkins, H. (2009). *Confronting the challenges of participatory culture: Media education for the 21st century.* Cambridge, MA: The MIT Press.

Kelley, T. & Kelley, D. (2012). Reclaim your creative confidence. *Harvard Business Review, 90*(12), 115–118.

Kilpatrick, W. H. (1918). The project method. *Teachers College Record, 19*(4), 319–335.

Livingstone, S., Haddon, L., Görzig, A., & Ólafsson, K. (2011). *Risks and safety on the Internet: The perspective of European children.* Full Findings. LSE, London: EU Kids Online.

Margolis, J. & Fisher, A. (2003). *Unlocking the clubhouse: Women in computing.* Cambridge, MA: MIT Press.

Margolis, J., Goode, J., & Chapman, G. (2015). An equity lens for scaling: A critical juncture for exploring computer science. *ACM Inroads, 6*(3), 58–66.

Martin, C., Barron, B., Matthews, J., & Stringer, D. (2014, June). Patterns of engagement: How depth of experience matters. In B. Barron, K. Gomez, N. Pinkard, & C. K. Martin, *The digital youth network: Cultivating digital media citizenship in urban communities* (pp. 203–235). Cambridge, MA: MIT Press.

Mascheroni, G. & Ólafsson, K. (2014). *Net children go mobile: Risks and opportunities* (2nd ed.). Milano: Educatt.

New London Group. (1996). A pedagogy of multiliteracies: Designing social futures. *Harvard Educational Review, 66,* 60–92.

Papert, S. (1980). *Mindstorms: Children, computers, and powerful ideas.* New York: Basic Books, Inc.

Partnership for 21st Century Skills. (2009). *P21 framework definitions.* Washington, DC: Partnership for 21st Century Skills. Retrieved on February 22, 2016 from www.p21.org/storage/documents/P21_Framework_Definitions.pdf

Pellegrino, J. W., & Hilton, M. L. (Eds.). (2012). *Education for life and work: Developing transferable knowledge and skills in the 21st century.* Washington, DC: National Academies Press.

Piaget, J. (1964). Part I: Cognitive development in children: Piaget development and learning. *Journal of Research in Science Teaching, 2*(3), 176–186.

Pinkard, N. & Austin, K. (2011). Digital youth network: Creating new media citizens through the affinity learning model. *International Journal of Learning and Media, 4*(2). doi:10.1162/ijlm_a_00055

Quattrocchi, C. (2013, October 29). *MAKE'ing more diverse makers.* [Blog post]. Retrieved September 9, 2015 from www.edsurge.com/news/2013-10-29-make-ing-more-diverse-makers

Regalla, L. (2016). Developing a maker mindset. In K. Peppler, E. Halverson, & Y. Kafai (Eds.), *Makeology: Makerspaces as learning environments* (Volume 1) (pp. 257–272). New York, NY: Routledge.

Reich, R. B. (2002). *The future of success: Working and living in the new economy.* New York, NY: Vintage.

Rideout, V. J., Foehr, U. G., & Roberts, D. F. (2010). *Generation M2: Media in the lives of, 8–18 year olds.* Report for the Henry J. Kaiser Family Foundation.

Sommerville, H. (2014). Intel funds Silicon Valley teen's Braille printer startup. *San Jose Mercury News,* November 4, 2014. Retrieved on February 22, 2016 from www.mercurynews.com/business/ci_26860580/13-year-old-venture-raises-vc-funding-braille-intel-capital

Turkle, S. (1984). *The second self.* New York: Simon and Schuster.

Vossoughi, S. & Bevan, B. (2014). Making and tinkering: A review of the literature. *Report Commissioned by the Committee on Successful Out-of-school STEM Learning.* National Research Council.

Zickuhr, K. (2010). Generations 2010. *Pew Internet & American Life Project, 16*(11). Retrieved on February 22, 2016 from www.pewinternet.org/files/old-media/Files/Reports/2010/PIP_Generations_and_Tech10.pdf

APPENDIX A

Full Survey Items

Table Appendix A Survey measures by construct*

Construct	*Survey measure*				
Digital maker production experience	How often have you **EVER** done the following computer-related activities?				
	Please mark only one box per item	**Never**	**Once or twice**	**3 to 6 times**	**More than 6 times**
	a. Written computer program (code) using a computer language *(e.g., C, Java, Visual Basic)*	□	□	□	□
	b. Created a website using HTML or an application *(e.g., Dreamweaver, iWeb)*	□	□	□	□
	c. Created a piece of art using an application *(e.g., Photoshop, Illustrator)*	□	□	□	□
	d. Designed a 2D or 3D model or drawing *(e.g., CAD or ModelShop)*	□	□	□	□
	e. Built a robot or created an invention of any kind using technology	□	□	□	□

* This survey was administered in 2009 and does not include many maker activities that are more common today, such as working with 3D printers and developing digital fabrications. We encourage researchers and practitioners to use our survey as a model, expanded to fit the experiences and activities young makers and producers are involved in.

f. Created a digital movie *(e.g., iMovie or MovieMaker)*	☐	☐	☐	☐
g. Created an animation *(e.g., Flash, Alice, Scratch)*	☐	☐	☐	☐
h. Created a computer game *(e.g., Stagecast, GameStar, Scratch)*	☐	☐	☐	☐
i. Created a piece of music *(e.g., GarageBand, FruityLoops)*	☐	☐	☐	☐

Digital hobbies

How often do you use a computer (anywhere) to do each of the following:

Please mark one box per item	**Never**	**Less than once a month**	**Once a month**	**A few times per month**	**Once a week**	**A few times a week**	**Daily**	**Several times a day**
Play games (on the computer, online, or on a game console)	☐	☐	☐	☐	☐	☐	☐	☐
Work on your own digital media projects outside of school/pod assignments	☐	☐	☐	☐	☐	☐	☐	☐
Edit/design your own blog/social networking page (e.g., MySpace or Facebook)	☐	☐	☐	☐	☐	☐	☐	☐

(*Continued*)

Table Appendix A (Continued)

Construct	*Survey measure*					
Creative Identity	Please rate how much you agree with the following statements					
	Please circle one number for each item.	**Disagree strongly**	**Disagree**	**Neutral**	**Agree**	**Agree strongly**
	a. I feel that I can come up with interesting new ideas.	1	2	3	4	5
	b. I feel that I can be creative.	1	2	3	4	5
Technological confidence	Please rate how much you agree with the following statements					
	Please circle one number for each item.	**Disagree strongly**	**Disagree**	**Neutral**	**Agree**	**Agree strongly**
	a. I feel confident about my ability to use computers.	1	2	3	4	5
	b. I am NOT the kind of person who works well with computers.	1	2	3	4	5
	c. I am good with computers.	1	2	3	4	5
	How would you describe your level of experience with the following computer applications/equipment?					
	Please circle one number for each item.	**I don't know what this is**	**I have no experience but I have heard of it**	**I've played around with it**	**I have used it to make something**	**I'm an expert and can teach someone how to use it**
	Flash	1	2	3	4	5
	Photoshop	1	2	3	4	5
	Illustrator	1	2	3	4	5
	Scratch	1	2	3	4	5

	GameStar Mechanic	1	2	3	4	5
	ComicLife	1	2	3	4	5
	FruityLoops	1	2	3	4	5
	ProTools	1	2	3	4	5
	iMovie	1	2	3	4	5
	iWeb	1	2	3	4	5
	GarageBand	1	2	3	4	5
	Word/Pages	1	2	3	4	5
	Powerpoint	1	2	3	4	5
	LEGO Mindstorms	1	2	3	4	5
	Dreamweaver	1	2	3	4	5
	Fireworks	1	2	3	4	5
Internet proficiency proxy	How familiar are you with the following computer and Internet-related terms? *1 represents "no understanding" and 5 represents "full understanding" of the item.*					
	Please circle one number for each item.	**None**	**Little**	**Some**	**Good**	**Full**
	a. JPEG	1	2	3	4	5
	b. Frames	1	2	3	4	5
	c. Preference settings	1	2	3	4	5
	d. Newsgroups	1	2	3	4	5
	e. PDF	1	2	3	4	5
	f. Refresh/reload	1	2	3	4	5
	g. Advanced search	1	2	3	4	5
	h. Weblog	1	2	3	4	5
	i. Bookmark	1	2	3	4	5
	j. Spyware	1	2	3	4	5
	k. Bcc (on email)	1	2	3	4	5
	l. Tagging	1	2	3	4	5
	m. Tabbed browsing	1	2	3	4	5

(*Continued*)

Table Appendix A (Continued)

Construct	*Survey measure*					
	n. RSS	1	2	3	4	5
	o. Wiki	1	2	3	4	5
	p. Malware	1	2	3	4	5
	q. Social bookmarking	1	2	3	4	5
	r. Podcasting	1	2	3	4	5
	s. Phishing	1	2	3	4	5
	t. Web feeds	1	2	3	4	5
	u. Firewall	1	2	3	4	5
	v. Cache	1	2	3	4	5
	w. Widget	1	2	3	4	5
	x. Favorites	1	2	3	4	5
	y. Torrent	1	2	3	4	5
	z. Blog	1	2	3	4	5
Independent learning sources	How important have the following items been in your learning how to use computers?					
	Please circle one number for each item.	**Not at all**	**A little**	**Some**	**Very much**	**Extremely much**
	a. Books or manuals	1	2	3	4	5
	b. Magazines	1	2	3	4	5
	c. Online articles, discussion threads, etc.	1	2	3	4	5
	d. Software help menus	1	2	3	4	5
	e. Step-by-step tutorials / instructions	1	2	3	4	5
	f. Playing around on my own	1	2	3	4	5

Critical approach to online information	When you use the Internet to look for information for school, how often do you do the following?					
	Please circle only one number for each item	**Never**	**Rarely**	**Some-times**	**Often**	**Very often**
	a. Check to see if the information is current	1	2	3	4	5
	b. Consider whether the views represented are facts or opinions	1	2	3	4	5
	c. Seek out other sources to validate the information (e.g., books, teachers, encyclopedias, magazines)	1	2	3	4	5
	d. Check to see who the author is	1	2	3	4	5
	e. Check if contact information is provided on the website	1	2	3	4	5
	f. Check the qualifications or credentials of the author	1	2	3	4	5
	g. Go to the "About us" pages (pages about who runs the site, who owns the site and so on)	1	2	3	4	5

(*Continued*)

Table Appendix A (Continued)

Construct	*Survey measure*
Exchange of political information online *AND* Addressing political issues through media creation	How often do you use the Internet (blogs, social networking sites, wikis, or other websites) to:

Please mark only one box per item	**Never**	**Less than once a month**	**Once a month**	**A few times per month**	**Once a week**	**A few times a week**	**Daily**	**Several times a day**
Get or share information (news or opinions) about political issues	☐	☐	☐	☐	☐	☐	☐	☐
Create and share media with a political message	☐	☐	☐	☐	☐	☐	☐	☐

Construct	*Survey measure*
Teaching network	Are you **teaching or helping** anyone to learn about technology / computers? ☐Yes ☐No *If yes,* please mark the boxes to indicate **ALL** the people you are teaching or helping: ☐ Mother or female guardian ☐ Father or male guardian ☐ A friend or friends ☐ Brother(s) ☐ Sister(s) ☐ Grandparents ☐ Other relatives (cousins, aunts, uncles, etc.)
Making media to promote social change	In the future, can you see yourself . . .

Please circle only one number for each item	**Definitely no**	**Probably no**	**Maybe**	**Probably yes**	**Definitely yes**
Creating and sharing media to promote social change in your community or more globally	1	2	3	4	5

Online affinity groups	How often do you use the Internet (blogs, social networking sites, wikis, or other websites) to:								
	Please mark only one box per item	**Never**	**Less than once a month**	**Once a month**	**A few times per month**	**Once a week**	**A few times a week**	**Daily**	**Several times a day**
	Talk to others about a hobby	☐	☐	☐	☐	☐	☐	☐	☐

CHAPTER 5

Is Sewing a "Girl's Sport"? Addressing Gender Issues in Making With Electronic Textiles

KRISTIN A. SEARLE, DEBORAH A. FIELDS, AND YASMIN B. KAFAI

Over the course of her first year in high school, Marcela, a 14-year-old Caucasian student, participated in a series of three workshops around learning how to sew, design circuits, and program lights and sensors on fabric with conductive thread, making electronic textiles (hereafter: e-textiles). What is unique about e-textiles as a making activity is that it integrates crafting with fabric, typically perceived as a more feminine activity, with coding and engineering, typically associated with the more masculine technology-driven activities of the Maker Movement (for more on this, see chapter 8 of this volume). Thus, making with e-textiles provides a unique opportunity to study how craft-based activities can support or challenge youths' gendered maker identities (Halverson & Sheridan, 2014).

For her third and final e-textile project of the workshop series, Marcela created a wearable belt of multicolored felt whose design was inspired by DNA's double-helix structure, something she was learning about in 9th-grade biology (see Figure 5.1). This design brought together her interests in crafts and arts with her love for science instilled by her father, a scientist at a local university. The code for Marcela's DNA belt was simple but purposeful: the lights blinked on and off in a carefully timed order. This programming addressed her desire for a particular aesthetic in which the lights complemented the project as a whole rather than drawing attention to themselves. In a final reflective interview, Marcela emphasized that while she was most proud of her "sewing pace and design," her greatest accomplishment came in the form of better understanding of what computer programming was.

Figure 5.1 Marcela's e-textile DNA belt.

While Marcela never went so far as to call herself a "maker" or a "techie," she recognized that she had gained valuable knowledge about coding and circuitry while crafting her e-textiles.

We view Marcela's newly gained technical knowledge—and her changed self-narrative about it—as an important first step in engaging students of all genders into engineering, computer science, and other domains historically gendered as masculine (Ensmenger, 2010; Oldenziel, 1999). But we also recognize the tensions students face between comfortable, familiar gendered positionings, such as Marcela's oft-articulated love of art and design, and newer, less comfortable positionings, such as professing an interest in programming, that break with traditional expectations. In this chapter, we explore the role of gender in youth's engagement with e-textile making activities and their willingness to take on particular making identities. Drawing on the experiences of Marcela and two other students, Lucas and Kyra, we argue that the hybrid, domain-crossing nature of e-textiles facilitated students' reshaping of their gendered cultural histories surrounding crafting, engineering, and computing. We begin by unpacking the ways in which our sociohistorical understandings of making are gendered and examine how e-textile projects challenge these taken-for-granted understandings.

Perspectives on Gender in Making and Tools

E-textile construction kits, like all tools and technologies, bring cultural histories that need to be taken into consideration if we want to understand the challenges as well as opportunities in broadening participation in making with e-textiles. The collision of craft, circuitry, and code in making activities involving e-textiles is not the brainchild of a mad scientist, but rather a very purposeful mash-up intended to complicate our cultural understandings of highly gendered domains (Buechley, 2006). Crafting is typically seen as "low tech" women's work, characterized by its "soft" and "feminine" properties, so much so that embroidery and other forms of stitchery were relegated to the domestic realm and siphoned off from consideration as fine art (Parker, 1986/2011). Meanwhile, despite women's early involvement in computing, engineering and computer science have come to be seen as "high tech" men's work, characterized by their "hard" and "masculine" properties (Ensmenger, 2010). As Oldenziel (1999) argues, these constructions are by no means new or arbitrary, but rather the products of historical struggles. E-textiles combine the high/low-tech dichotomy by integrating different traditions of gender-natured work and illuminate some of the challenges of creating appealing making activities for youth of all genders (Halverson & Sheridan, 2014).

Previous tangible computational construction kits such as LEGO Mindstorms have focused on robotic designs (Rusk, Resnick, Berg, & Pezella-Granlund, 2008), while the LilyPad Arduino focuses on textile crafts (Buechley & Eisenberg, 2008). The LilyPad Arduino e-textile construction kit (see Figure 5.2) and the community of users that has developed around

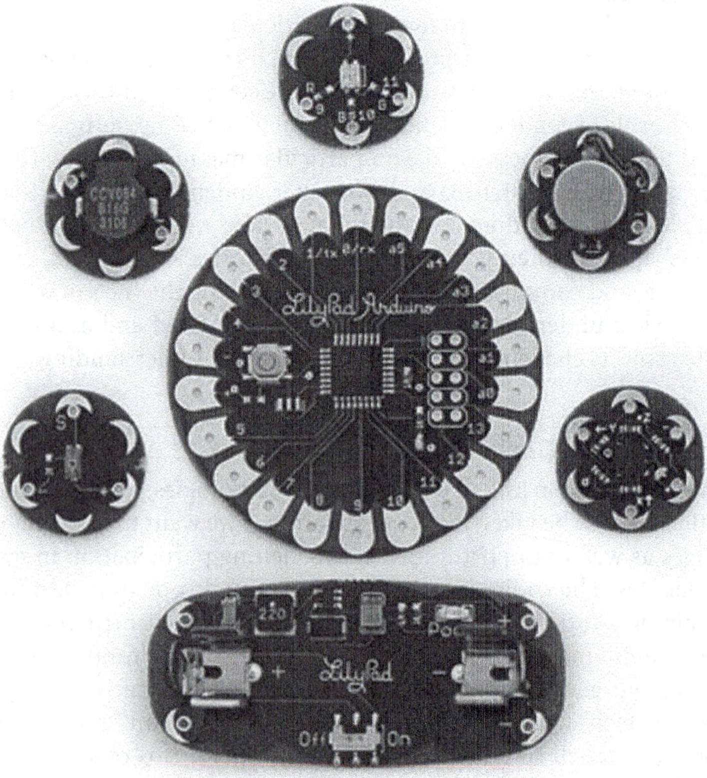

Figure 5.2 The LilyPad Arduino kit for making electronic textiles.

it are one example of a new kind of culturally and epistemologically distinct space for making. E-textiles combine traditional aspects of fabric crafts using needles, thread, and cloth with a microcontroller that is both sewable and programmable, various actuators such as LED lights or speakers, and novel materials such as conductive fabrics, paint, and even tinfoil (Buechley, 2006). In a study of LilyPad Arduino users (hobbyists), Buechley and Hill (2010) found that significantly more women use the LilyPad Arduino (57% male, 35% female) than the functionally identical Arduino (78% male, 9% female). This suggests that a culturally hybrid construction kit such as the LilyPad Arduino can combine high and low technologies and attract different groups of makers while still engaging them in the same technical complexities.

These contradictions between "high" and "low" technologies, old and new materials, and masculine and feminine domains are what make e-textiles a compelling context to examine how the gendered cultural histories surrounding engineering, programming, and crafting practices are playing out in the present Maker Movement (Buechley, Peppler, Eisenberg, & Kafai, 2013). How beginning makers respond to the seemingly contrasting histories of crafting and coding can illuminate (among many other possibilities) potentially gendered ways that youth approach contemporary technology. Our focus is to better understand how students initially align with these gendered cultural histories of crafting, coding, and engineering, and also how designing e-textiles might shift how students align with these cultural narratives, not only in terms of what they want to do with e-textiles but also how they think about them. These understandings will help us to design more inclusive making activities that support maker identities for youth from a variety of backgrounds.

E-Textiles Workshops With High School Youth

Our observations are drawn from a series of three e-textiles workshops conducted in partnership with a local science museum and a science-focused high school in a large, urban district. The school attracts students from diverse racial, ethnic, and class backgrounds who are already interested in STEM fields, providing a compelling space for studying making activities. All students at the high school are issued a laptop for use during the school year and all first-year students are required to take introductory engineering. To provide students with authentic learning experiences, all freshmen spend one afternoon each week engaged in a series of science-focused mini-workshops on topics ranging from forensics to human anatomy. These mini-workshops (ranging between 4 and 6 weeks) are often, though not always, linked to museum exhibits and students may request particular

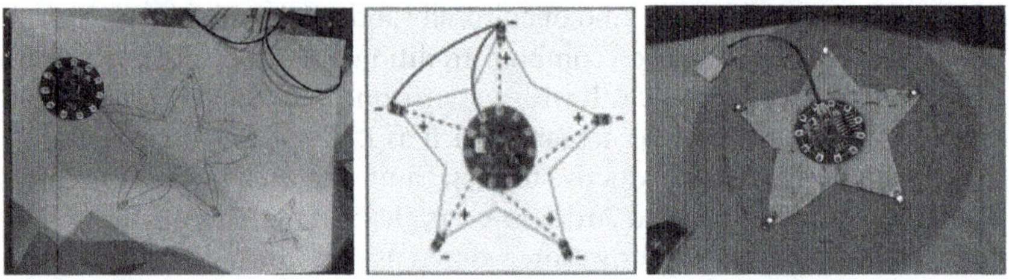

Figure 5.3 An initial sketch, a circuit diagram, and final e-textile design created by Amari, a 9th-grade girl.

workshops, though they are not guaranteed to get their first choice, meaning that there are varying levels of interest within any mini-workshop.

Over the course of the 2010–2011 school year, we conducted a series of three e-textiles mini-workshops with each successive workshop increasing in design complexity of the e-textiles. The final workshop required prior participation in one of the preceding workshops. In total, 35 high school freshmen (14–15 years old) participated in at least one of the workshops. Few of our participants had prior programming experience and none had ever worked with e-textiles before participating in our mini-workshops. Workshop sessions were held once a week and lasted for two hours. During this time, students learned how to design and create their own e-textile projects, beginning with drawings, followed by circuit schematics, sewing/crafting of designs, and programming (see Figure 5.3). In addition to the "techie" elements, such as sensors for light, touch, and sound and actuators for lights and sound buzzers associated with the LilyPad, we had various wearable items, such as hats and T-shirts, and crafting materials, such as felt, puffy paint, and colorful embroidery thread for students to use.

In addition to Marcela's case described earlier, we focus on two other students' experiences with e-textiles: Kyra, an African American girl, and Lucas, a Caucasian boy (pseudonyms are used for all students). What is compelling about these students' experiences is their differential engagement with all domains of e-textiles—designing and sewing circuits, writing computer code, and crafting a completed project that was personal, functional, and aesthetically pleasing. Kyra participated in one workshop and Lucas participated in two workshops several months apart. Addressing students' experiences across different time points allows us to explore the variation in their experiences.

Drawing upon logs of video data, field notes, transcripts of one-on-one reflective interviews conducted at the conclusion of each workshop (26 interviews, 10 girls and 16 boys), and artifact collection (design blueprints and photographs of projects in various stages of completion), we focused our analysis of what students found most challenging, where in the process of design and creation they learned the most, and what they were most proud of (see also Kafai, Fields, & Searle, 2014). This analysis revealed interesting patterns concerning how students thought about different domains within e-textiles. For instance, given that not all boys were asked about what they found most challenging (because the interview protocol evolved over time), it is striking that more than half of the boys we interviewed commented on their difficulties with sewing and only one commented on his difficulties with circuitry. In contrast, not a single girl commented on her difficulties with sewing, even though many had never sewn prior to our workshops. Across boys and girls, most students were proudest of their finished project, though they tended to emphasize one dimension of that project, such as sewing or programming the lights.

In a second stage of our analysis, we developed several case studies of students (Yin, 2008), two of which we describe here, documenting their design processes and the ways that their opinions about aspects of e-textiles and their own expertise changed over time. This approach allowed us to compare what they said about themselves (their narratives) with what they were actually doing (their practices) (Fields & Enyedy, 2013). We documented shifts in student opinion over time in conjunction with their design processes and interactions with others. These approaches enabled us to focus on the ways in which making with e-textiles engaged students' gendered identities and impacted the ways they positioned themselves through simultaneous engagement with multiple domains (crafting, coding, and circuitry).

Perspectives on Gender and Making With E-Textiles

Our goal was to understand how youth responded to the historically gendered domains that are present in e-textiles and to document changes in students' attitudes over time. While we might have expected more variation, in general, boys and girls initially positioned themselves and each other as most capable in the fields that had cultural histories of being gendered as masculine and feminine. We suggest that these positionings do not point to a lack of critical awareness on the part of the youth in our study but rather reveal the social power of the gender binary, especially in places like high school where performances of gender that do not adhere to the masculine/feminine binary are still heavily policed and reinforced (Pascoe, 2007). Thus, it shouldn't come as a surprise that in the earlier stages of e-textile workshops, boys typically positioned themselves and were positioned by others as good at the coding and circuitry aspects of e-textiles while struggling with crafting, even if they had no prior experience in these areas in practice. For instance, Jack told us that "sewing is evil" (Interview, 12/15/10) and John lamented his lack of sewing skills saying, "I wish I was, like, a better sewer because it—it does look bad" (Interview, 12/15/10). Like many of the boys, John was displeased with his sewing and desired to improve, but also did not express worry about the computer programming. Boys new to e-textiles tended to complain vociferously about the sewing component while simultaneously proclaiming their programming prowess and shouting out answers to exercises intended to test their knowledge of circuitry, even if these answers were incorrect.

In contrast, most girls initially positioned themselves and were positioned by others in classroom interactions as comfortable with crafting knowledge, even if they had no prior sewing experience. For instance, Amari reflected that she was terrified that she wouldn't understand e-textiles on the first day of her first workshop, but felt considerably more at ease when she saw that it involved sewing. She said:

> I was like "Oh, I can—Oh, this is probably easy," so I did that and then I just sewed it onto felt and then I was like it's time for lights and techie stuff and then slowly I started to understand it.
>
> (Interview, 5/27/11)

Importantly, Amari demonstrated a shift from being uncomfortable with circuitry and computer programming to seeing them as within her grasp. While many of students' initial positionings reinforced historical gender binaries between "feminine" sewing practices and "masculine" engineering and programming practices, we also saw how these sociohistorical narratives around the gendered nature of these practices shifted over time as students had exposure and gained experience with them.

When students completed their projects, their reflections complicated the initial, stereotypical gendered positionings that we saw enacted throughout the course of each workshop. At the end, we found that boys most frequently expressed pride about the physical, crafting elements of their projects such as sewing while the girls were most frequently proud of the "techie" elements of their projects such as creating working circuits and coding them properly. We also noted that girls seemed more open to learning about circuitry and coding than boys were open to learning about crafting. Repeatedly girls reflected that they were initially worried about the "techie" elements of e-textiles but then learned what they needed to learn. For a fuller exploration of these themes, we turn to two case studies, Kyra and Lucas, to examine the ways in which the domain-crossing activity of e-textiles made computing and crafting more personally relevant for a broader range of students and opened up possibilities for new, more inclusive types of makerspaces to emerge.

Kyra

Kyra, a 14-year-old African American girl, demonstrated a typical path of many of the girls who participated in the e-textile workshops discussed here. Regardless of actual ability, most girls in our workshops initially positioned themselves as less comfortable with electronics and computing. Later they positioned themselves as not only competent but also confident in those areas. Unlike many of her peers who didn't even know how to thread a needle, Kyra had prior sewing experience from home. She participated in one e-textile workshop, in December 2010, and made a pink heart with one blinking LED (see Figure 5.4), which she later posted on a website devoted to e-textile projects with the description "it blinks and I'm proud." We selected Kyra as a case study because her experience illustrates how even participating

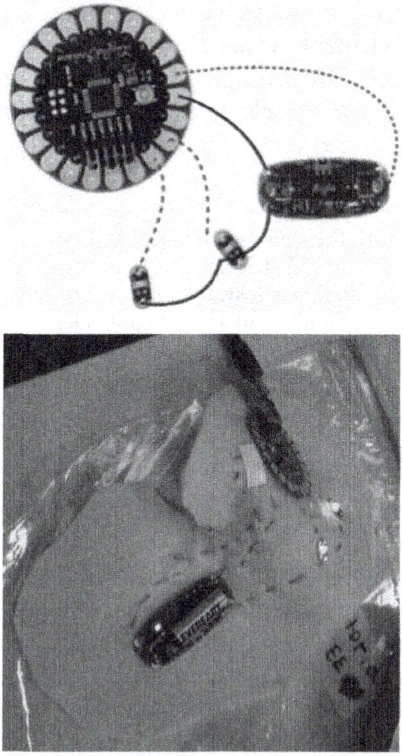

```
int first LED = 8;
int secondLED = 10;

void setup () {
pinMode (firstLED, OUTPUT);
pinMode (secondLED, OUTPUT):
}

void loop () {
digitalWrite (firstLED, HIGH);
digitalWrite (secondLED, HIGH);
delay (500);
digitalWrite (firstLED, LOW);
delay (500);
delay (500);
digitalWrite (secondLED; LOW);
delay (500);
```

Figure 5.4 A circuit schematic for Kyra's project, Kyra's completed blinking heart, and Kyra's Arduino code.

in a single e-textile workshop over several weeks and making a simple project has the potential to alter how students see themselves in relation to the gendered cultural histories of crafting, engineering, and programming.

Kyra initially presented herself as a typical girl who was less confident about her ability to write computer code for her project. After some time spent in the workshop learning about and doing coding and circuitry, however, she began to position herself as someone who was not only knowledgeable about these topics but confident in her own abilities. In fact, Kyra was able to pinpoint the exact moment when she went from being less comfortable to more comfortable with the technology aspects of e-textiles:

> Where I was, um, connecting the positives and the negatives . . . at that point, I just felt like, this feels good—because I know how to do this. And I felt kinda like an expert. . . . I'm proudest that it actually blinks.
>
> (Interview, 12/15/10)

For Kyra, having functional code for her e-textile was the most important achievement. While this was true for many students, we noticed that girls tended to be proudest of the "techie" elements while boys tended to be proudest of their crafting achievements. Not surprisingly, the elements that felt like the biggest accomplishments were also the elements where students perceived that they struggled the most. Asked about the most frustrating part of making her e-textile artifact, Kyra said:

> The most frustrating thing was probably the coding. Because, at first, I didn't know what to do. I was just like, coding? What do you mean coding? . . . But then after awhile, it was just, ok, this is easy. I get it. Just type in this and type in that. Make this do that. So like you are the controller. You make it do what you want it to do.
>
> (Interview, 12/15/10)

We can see in this reflection that Kyra shifted how she saw herself and began to see herself as someone who was comfortable with basic programming. In doing so she also developed a better understanding of what programming is—telling the computer exactly what to do and in what order. Even more important, Kyra was always capable—she just initially lacked confidence. Crossing into domains of electronics and programming through her predispositions toward crafting and sewing, Kyra became more confident in her abilities and began to own a "techie" identity as something to be proud of. While not all of the girls in our study were as comfortable with taking on a "techie" identity, almost all of them expressed satisfaction at knowing about circuitry and how to write computer code. Many girls' opinions changed simply through having the opportunity to learn about something technical and, most importantly, to do so through a medium that felt comfortable for them—crafting and sewing. E-textiles possibly provided girls a bridge to new identities and ideas about what they were capable of and what they might be interested in. In this way, e-textiles helped to disrupt traditionally gendered notions of "high-tech" materials and practices.

Lucas

In contrast to the experiences of Kyra and other girls in our study, boys tended to see sewing as a means to an end—a skill they would continue to use insofar as it allowed them to do "techie" stuff. Only one boy found sewing "addictive"; the others tolerated it at best in the beginning. Lucas, a 14-year-old Caucasian male in the 9th grade, could always be found at the "gamer" table at lunchtime, where students talked to one another as they played online games on their laptops. Within this lunchtime social group, Lucas was widely acknowledged as an expert by his peers. Lucas participated in two of our workshops. In his first workshop, Lucas constantly asked if he could work with a different programming language (Scratch) that he had been introduced to earlier in the year instead of working on e-textiles. He disparagingly proclaimed sewing to be "a girl's sport." In his first workshop, Lucas attempted to make a hat but was unable to complete it because of his difficulties with sewing. For a novice sewer, sewing through the stiff backing of the baseball hats we had available for student use proved quite difficult. In his second workshop, Lucas returned to the idea of making a hat but this time chose a more personally relevant design, electing to make an anime-based hat for his brother. Asked to describe how he developed the idea for his project, Lucas explained:

> Okay, well, originally I was going to make a hat with two big eyes on it, but then I realized that that would be really hard and the eyes didn't look very good when I put them on and, oh so, I stopped and made a new one where it has two, well, a plus and X on the other side . . . And then I have the yellow star because that's my brother's anime symbol. . . . So I'm making this hat for [my brother]. Hopefully he likes it.
>
> (Interview, 5/26/11)

While Lucas still struggled with sewing quite a bit in the second workshop and received crafting help from a female friend and the instructors, it is worth noting his persistence with the project. We attribute this, at least to some degree, to the personal significance of Lucas's project. He noted that "Mainly I really don't create stuff physically but I like to do stuff on the computer" (Interview, 5/26/11). However, in the end he was most proud of the yellow star he had cut out from a sheet of felt and affixed to his hat using iron-on transfer paper. Lucas also reconsidered his thoughts on sewing as a girl's sport when he reflected on the idea of creating circuitry by sewing, saying, "I'd never actually think that a thing that I thought was a woman's sport until now would actually be a pretty fun thing" (Interview, 5/26/11). This change in attitude toward sewing demonstrates the new value he found in that domain, even if he still saw it as primarily something for girls and women.

For us as researchers, as well as for Lucas and his classmates, there was never any doubt about Lucas's identity as a gamer and, by extension, as someone who was good at programming in our workshops. What is notable is that Lucas was able to renegotiate what he saw as "male" and "female" activities within engineering, programming, and crafting. Rather than viewing sewing as a "girl's sport," Lucas began to like the challenge of sewing and crafting, reflecting, "Well, it's not that it's fun—it's more tedious—but I like a challenge most of the time, so the more challenging it is, the funner it gets" (Interview, 5/26/11). This new awareness of different technologies—not just digital technologies—is an important step in opening up new, more inclusive spaces for making. Lucas was able to recognize that there were other dimensions to creating a functional e-textile artifact and he began to respect those skill sets as part of maker culture. Still, we recognize the tensions students face between comfortable, familiar gendered positionings, such as Lucas's fondness for more abstract programming in Scratch, and newer, less comfortable positionings that may break traditional bounds of gendered dispositions.

Reshaping Gendered Positionings In and Through Making

Returning to the questions that started this chapter—How did gender play a role in the way youth engaged in e-textile maker activities? What shifts, if any, could we observe in students' positionings in regard to crafting, engineering, and coding?—we found that students negotiated and changed their own positionings within the conflicting gendered cultural histories embodied in hybrid activities like e-textiles. We argue that the hybrid, domain-crossing nature of e-textiles facilitated students' reshaping of the gendered cultural histories surrounding engineering, programming, and craft practices. As we observed, many students began the workshops with stereotypical associations with the different gendered histories embedded in e-textiles: feeling more comfortable in domains such as computing and engineering that were historically masculine or domains such as crafting that have been traditionally considered more feminine regardless of their prior experience (or lack thereof) in these domains. The domain-crossing nature of e-textiles allowed for multiple points of entry into the making activities, valuing different kinds of expertise and ideas that students may bring from outside of school (e.g., Moll, Tapia, & Whitmore, 1993; Sefton-Green, 2006), and opening up a space for students to explore their gendered identities in these contexts.

Beyond just providing an initial starting place for students, making with e-textiles provided a context in which many students developed new knowledge and ideas of what they were capable of and interested in. Most students, especially girls, recognized that computing could be relevant in multiple realms that extended beyond the screen that many saw as a primary context of computing. Further, some students like Lucas who earlier had seen crafting and sewing as the domain of women began to see the challenges and value inherent in those skills. In later iterations, we found a number of boys who embraced e-textiles as providing a legitimate "excuse" to sew in public areas like classrooms, welcoming the opportunity to transgress perceived gender boundaries in a sanctioned way (see Searle, Fields, Lui, & Kafai, 2014). These observations suggest that combining contradictory traditions into a single hybrid enterprise, such as crafting and computing in e-textiles, provide not only different starting points but also promising pathways towards helping learners to broaden their own perceptions of computing. Their contradictory hybridity may provide directions to broaden maker culture writ large.

What is different about e-textiles compared with other more prominent maker activities? We point to the role of handcrafts in e-textiles as relatively unique. In contrast to 3D printing and laser cutting, e-textiles begin off the screen and in the hands with needle, thread, and fabric. Unlike robotics, they include materials that are historically more familiar to women. More broadly than sewing, however, a variety of handcrafts have long histories in many cultures that are worth considering in opening up more equitable making spaces. We suggest also examining other sociohistorical constructs that influence participation in making activities. Hybrid activities like e-textiles can provide pathways for students to value the cultural histories of their families and communities while broadening their skill sets with new expertise in relevant domains. For instance, recent research has shown that in a community with different cultural histories related to crafting, e-textiles have provided a legitimate point of entry for American Indian female and male youth to take up making activities that involve computing and engineering (Searle & Kafai, 2015a, 2015b). These kinds of investigations into the intersectional nature of crafting and computing complicate our often binary understandings of low and high technologies, masculine and feminine positionings, and traditional and new forms of making. Ultimately, we want to provide multiple entry points into making and value the different expertise and ideas that aspiring and experienced makers bring to maker activities to develop and enhance learning while making for all.

References

Buechley, L. (2006). A construction kit for electronic textiles, In *Wearable Computers, 2006 10th IEEE International Symposium* (pp. 83–90), October 11–14, Montreux, Switzerland. doi:10.1109/ISWC.2006.286348

Buechley, L. & Eisenberg, M. (2008). The LilyPad Arduino: Toward wearable engineering for everyone. *Wearable Computing Column in IEEE Pervasive, 7*(2), 12–15.

Buechley, L. & Hill, B. (2010). LilyPad in the Wild: How hardware's long tail is supporting new engineering and design communities. In *Proceedings of the 8th ACM Conference on Designing Interactive Systems (DIS)* (pp. 199–207), August 16–20, Aarhus, Denmark.

Buechley, L., Peppler, K., Eisenberg, M., & Kafai, Y. (2013). *Textile messages: Dispatches from the world of e-textiles and education.* New York: Peter Lang.

Ensmenger, N. (2010). *The computer boys take over.* Cambridge, MA: MIT Press.

Fields, D. A. & Enyedy, N. (2013). Picking up the mantle of "expert": Assigned roles, assertion of identity, and peer recognition within a programming class. *Mind, Culture, and Activity: An International Journal, 20*(2), 113–131.

Halverson, E. R. & Sheridan, K. (2014). The Maker Movement in education. *Harvard Educational Review, 84*(4), 495–504.

Kafai, Y. B., Fields, D. A., & Searle, K. A. (2014). Electronic textiles as disruptive designs in schools: Supporting and challenging maker activities for learning. *Harvard Educational Review, 84*(4), 532–556.

Moll, L. C., Tapia, J., & Whitmore, K. (1993). Living knowledge: The social distribution of cultural resources for thinking. In G. Salomon (Ed.), *Distributed cognitions: Psychological and educational considerations* (pp. 139–163). Cambridge: Cambridge University Press.

Oldenziel, R. (1999). *Making technology masculine: Men, women, and modern machines in America.* Amsterdam: Amsterdam University Press.

Parker, R. (1986/2011). *The subversive stitch.* New York, NY: I.B. Tauris.

Pascoe, C. J. (2007). *Dude you're a fag.* Berkeley: University of California Press.

Rusk, N., Resnick, M., Berg, R., & Pezella-Granlund, M. (2008). New pathways into robotics: Strategies for broadening participation. *Journal of Science Education and Technology, 17*(1), 59–69.

Searle, K., Fields, D. A., Lui, D., & Kafai, Y. B. (2014). Diversifying high school students' views about computing with electronic textiles. In *Proceedings of International Computing Education Research* (pp. 75–82). New York, NY: ACM.

Searle, K. A. & Kafai, Y. B. (2015a). Culturally responsive making with American Indian girls: Bridging the identity gap in crafting and computing with electronic textiles. In *Proceedings of the Third ACM Conference on Gender and Information Technology (GenderIT)* (pp. 9–16). Philadelphia, PA: ACM.

Searle, K. A. & Kafai, Y. B. (2015b). Boys' needlework: Understanding gendered and indigenous perspectives on computing and crafting with electronic textiles. In *Proceedings of the Eleventh Annual International Conference on International Computing Education Research* (pp. 31–39). Omaha, NE: ACM.

Sefton-Green, J. (2006). Youth, technology, and media cultures. *Review of Research in Education, 30,* 279–306.

Yin, R. K. (2008). *Case study research: Design and methods* (4th ed.). Thousand Oaks, CA: Sage Publications.

CHAPTER 6

Motivation for Making

NATALIE RUSK

Introduction

One of the most promising aspects of the Maker Movement is the opportunity to change people's understanding of what motivates learning. While many educators, parents, and developers continue to focus on extrinsic rewards—such as points and prizes—to motivate learning (Usher & Kober, 2012), the growing engagement of youth in making projects shows that interest-based motivation is also possible (Honey & Kanter, 2013).

In makerspaces and other creative programs, young people are choosing to spend time creating projects in art, design, music, and other interest areas using a range of physical and digital tools (Peppler & Bender, 2013). These programs build on intrinsic motivation, that is, interest and enjoyment of an activity itself and the desire to participate with others engaged in that endeavor (Larson & Rusk, 2011).

In today's complex and changing world, helping young people develop intrinsic motivation for learning is more important than ever before. Researchers have found that intrinsic motivation is particularly suited for creative endeavors and learning in complex situations (Nakamura & Csikszentmihalyi, 2009; Ryan & Deci, 2000).

What sparks and sustains young people's motivation to create projects? In this chapter, I explore what motivates making by examining how youth describe their reasons for using Scratch. Scratch (scratch.mit.edu) is a creative coding environment that young people (ages eight and up) use to design and program interactive stories, animations, and games—and share their creations with others in an online community (Resnick et al., 2009). Scratch was launched in 2007, and participation has grown rapidly, with

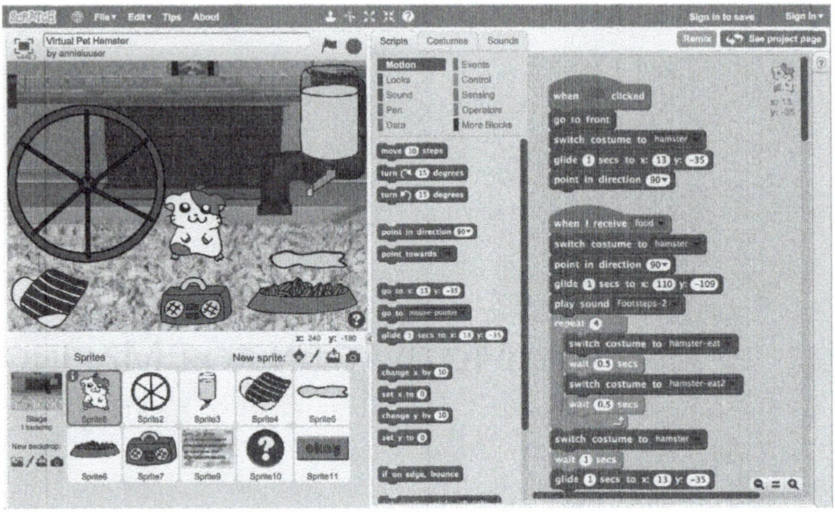

Figure 6.1 An example of a project created within the Scratch creative coding environment.

thousands of youth from around the world making and sharing projects in the Scratch online community each day.

Although maker projects typically involve building physical creations, the process of computer programming can also be considered a form of making (e.g., see chapters 4, 9, and 12 in this volume). The design of Scratch is inspired by LEGO building bricks: in Scratch, young people create programs by snapping together colorful blocks on the screen, combining them to program images, text, music, and sounds (Figure 6.1). Scratch is designed to be "tinkerable"—the blocks are designed to support the process of learning through experimenting (Resnick et al., 2009; Resnick & Rosenbaum, 2013).

Young people in makerspaces often create with Scratch, either on its own or with connections to sensors and other physical devices. For example, many children and teens have designed and programmed video games in Scratch, and then built game controllers using physical materials, such as paper plates, modeling clay, wires, and sensors (e.g., Davis, Kafai, Vasudevan, & Lee, 2013; Millner, 2010). Similarly, young people have created puppets and other animated characters using a combination of craft materials and sensors connected to Scratch (see Figure 6.2). In these projects, they are learning to create projects that bridge physical and digital worlds.

The design of Scratch is grounded in constructionist learning philosophy, which argues that people learn best when creating projects that are

Figure 6.2 An example of a puppet made from physical materials connected with a sensor to interact with an animated Scratch program.

Braafladt, 2009.

personally meaningful (Papert, 1993). People build ideas and knowledge in their minds by building things in the world, whether a sand castle, a computer program, or a poem (Kafai & Resnick, 1996; Papert & Harel, 1991). Constructionist philosophy recognizes that individuals do not only build knowledge by themselves, but learn from participating in a creative community (Papert, 1980; Zagal & Bruckman, 2005). Scratch enables youth to develop their ideas by creating, sharing, and revising projects in the Scratch online community (Resnick et al., 2009).

Making and Motivation Theory

What motivates people to work on projects despite challenges, setbacks, and frustrations? A key tenet of the Maker Movement is that people inherently enjoy making things. As stated on the first page of the Maker Movement Manifesto: "Making is fundamental to what it means to be human. We must make, create, and express ourselves to feel whole" (Hatch, 2014, p. 1). At the same time as emphasizing an intrinsic desire to make, the Maker Movement also recognizes the importance of other people, particularly the sense of satisfaction that comes from sharing one's projects and skills with others.

Though it may sound idealistic to think of making as intrinsically motivated, children from a young age often have an interest in making things—such as building with blocks, sculpting with clay, and painting pictures. John Dewey (1900/1915) referred to making things and artistic expression as two of children's natural interests: "the interest in conversation, or communication; in inquiry, or finding out things; in making things, or construction; and in artistic expression" (p. 45). He referred to these as "natural resources" which, when supported and nurtured, lead to the active growth of the child.

Self-determination theory provides a framework for understanding intrinsic motivation (Ryan & Deci, 2000). Self-determination theory is based on the idea that people are, by nature, curious creatures who like to explore, learn, and actively engage in their environment. The theory suggests that this active engagement in the environment is more likely when three key human needs are satisfied: *autonomy* (a sense of agency over one's actions, rather than feeling controlled by others), *relatedness* (a sense of connection with other people), and *competence* (a sense of effectiveness in dealing with one's environment). Self-determination theorists have found that when these three needs are satisfied, people are more likely to take initiative, to express creativity, and to experience satisfaction and a sense of well-being. Within educational research, these three factors have also been shown to support persistence and deeper learning (see reviews by Niemiec & Ryan, 2009; Vansteenkiste, Lens, & Deci, 2006).

A common misunderstanding of the concept of intrinsic motivation is that it comes only from within an individual, in isolation from other people. In fact, within self-determination theory, a core concept is that a feeling of connection with others fuels intrinsic motivation to learn and grow (Furrer & Skinner, 2003; Ryan & Deci, 2000).

Self-determination theory has been applied to understanding what helps (or hinders) people to feel motivated to engage actively within a variety of contexts, including workplace and educational environments. A core aspect of the theory is that an individual's subjective experience of an environment influences whether that person will feel engaged and motivated to participate.

In this chapter, I explore how young people's reflections on their own motivation for making and sharing projects relates to ideas explored by researchers of motivation, with a focus on self-determination theory. I chose to discuss self-determination theory after looking at young people's descriptions of their reasons for using Scratch and seeing themes that related to those discussed by researchers of self-determination theory.

Youth Responses Through Projects

Many youth choose to actively participate on the Scratch website and work hard to create projects that reflect their diverse interests (such as games, animation, art, math, science, fantasy, and storytelling). Youth participate in a variety of ways, such as creating projects (on their own or with others), organizing contests, playing with others' projects, and posting comments. To better understand why young people choose to participate on the site, our team at the MIT Media Lab (which develops and manages Scratch) decided to ask youth on the website to describe why they use Scratch.

Rather than asking them to respond to a survey, we invited them to create and post Scratch projects. We chose this approach because it fits with authentic practices within the Scratch online community, as creating projects is the primary way that participants express their ideas on the site. We also anticipated that the invitation to create projects would provide for a rich range of responses. Open-ended questions have been used by other researchers to investigate individuals' motivation for participating in other pursuits (e.g., Csikszentmihalyi, 1997; Seifert & Hedderson, 2010).

In April 2013, our team posted the question, "Why do you use Scratch?" and invited youth to create projects and share them online. Specifically, the prompt said:

> What do you like to do in Scratch, and why? The Scratch Team is interested to know. We're interested in learning more about what motivates Scratchers. Make a project about why you like Scratch (the program and/or the online community).

Although this question was new, the format of calling for youth to post projects on a theme is integrated into the ongoing activities on the website. Within the three weeks that this call for projects was highlighted on the Scratch home page, 119 projects were posted in response. (Two projects that appeared to have been made by adults were excluded from this analysis.)

The projects that youth posted ranged widely in style (Figure 6.3). Some projects were all text, while others incorporated drawings, animations, and music.

The dozens of youth who responded to the call for projects were all engaged in creating and sharing projects on the online community. So, they are not necessarily representative of all youth who use Scratch or who become involved in making. However, they do represent a range of ages on Scratch and describe a variety of interests and different ways of participating on the site.

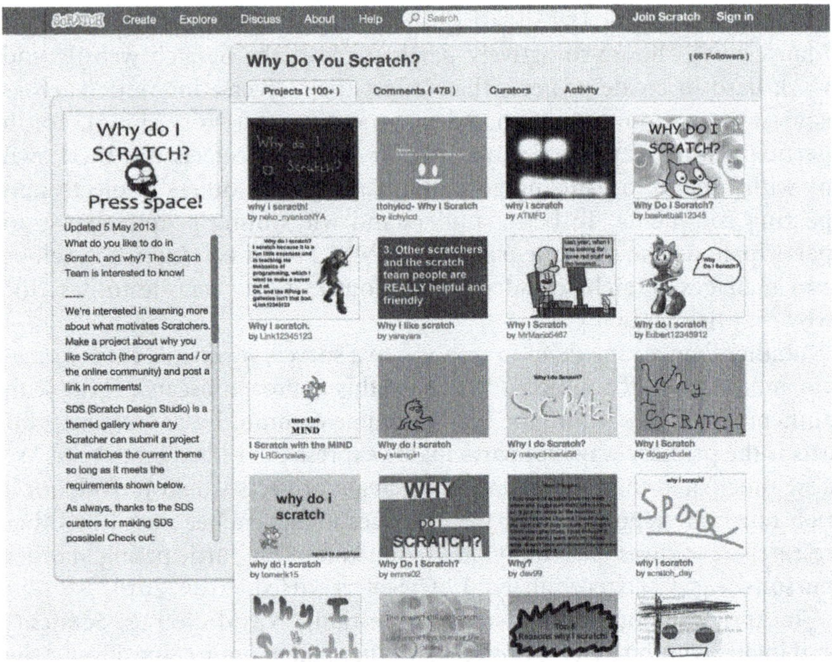

Figure 6.3 Screenshot from the collection of youth projects on why they use Scratch.

Multiple Reasons for Participating

When our team announced this call for projects, we had anticipated that each youth might respond by naming one or two aspects of Scratch that they liked best. So, we were surprised to find that most listed multiple reasons for using Scratch, with many numbering the reasons. For example, one wrote:

1. It's simple fun free programing
2. Sharing with friends is REALLY easy!
3. Other scratchers and the scratch team people are REALLY helpful and friendly
4. It gives people who wanted to make a cool project or game simply and easily their wish
5. It can be educational
6. Scratch is just plain COOL!

   :D

Here is another example of a young person who wrote a numbered list of reasons for using Scratch:

> These are the reasons I SCRATCH
> Reason number 1: Scratching is educational
> Reason number 2: I get to show off projects to school friends!
> Reason 3: I think it's cool to think that I can make my own games instead of playing games that someone else has made, such as "Minecraft"!
> Reason 4: It gives me something to do in my free time
> Reason 5: I do it for fun! I think Scratch is fun!!!

While many responded in the form of lists, others wrote long narratives describing the history of their experience with Scratch. These narratives typically included how they first learned about Scratch, the types of projects they created over time, their friends and role models on the Scratch site, and their plans for the future.

The projects were visible to all, so some of the projects the youth created were likely influenced by others' projects. Yet each was different in wording, length, and style. Although the youth expressed their responses in different formats, we identified many common themes. We identified the following five themes as the reasons for using Scratch most frequently mentioned by the youth:

1. To **create** projects based on their ideas and interests;
2. To **connect** with friends and the online community;
3. To **share** projects and receive feedback;
4. To **learn** skills they can use;
5. To **have fun.**

The first two reasons, to *create* and to *connect*, were identified with equal frequency, appearing in almost two-thirds of the projects (63% each). Two other frequently mentioned reasons, to *share* and to *learn*, were identified in more than one-third of the projects (41% and 43%, respectively). In addition, youth often stated that they use Scratch to *have fun*, with one-third of the projects (33%) specifically using the word "fun" to describe their experience.

The following sections examine what supports and sustains youth motivation for participating, based on a closer look at specific responses from youth within each of these themes. The youth names are pseudonyms in place of the Scratch usernames. Because participants' ages are not made public on Scratch, they are not reported with the quotes.

I first discuss the ideas expressed by these youth who participate on the Scratch website, and then explore how each of these ideas relate to what other researchers have observed about motivation and making. Finally, I suggest what we might learn from these youths' perspectives about ways to support motivation for learning through making in both physical and online environments.

Motivated to Create

Most of the participants wrote that they like using Scratch because it gives them the ability to make their own projects. Because Scratch was designed for this purpose, the focus on creating projects is not surprising. Yet, the desire to create is not often recognized as a source of motivation in educational settings. Even within self-determination theory, creativity is typically seen as an outcome of feeling intrinsically motivated rather than as a source of motivation. By taking a closer look at the young people's responses, we can see several different facets to their motivation to create.

Ability to Make Anything You Want

Aurorazz, who had joined Scratch six months earlier, made a project called, "The Top 5 Reasons I Love Scratch More Than Anything in the World." Because her list of reasons clearly articulated the main themes identified within the youth responses overall, I include the full text of her reasons (beginning here and then as relevant when discussing the other main themes).

The first reason Aurorazz listed in her project was that Scratch allows people to be creative (see Figure 6.4). As she wrote:

> AN OUTLET: Scratch allows people to be creative on so many different levels. on scratch, you can be anything, an artist, a programmer, a musician, a writer, and so much more! The world is really your oyster, and whatever you want to make, you can.

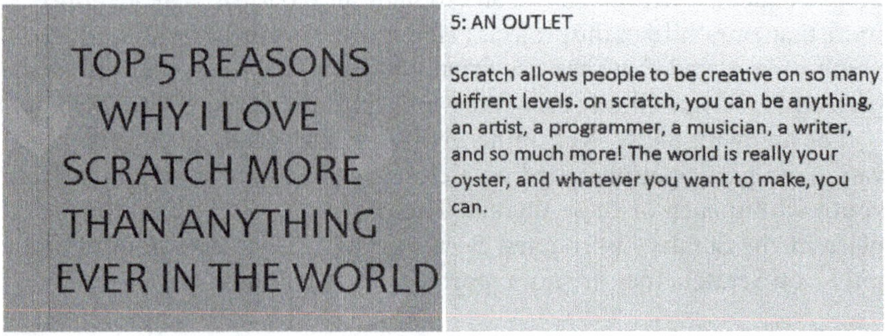

Figure 6.4 The first two pages of the project by Aurorazz.

Like Aurorazz, many other youth also emphasized not only the ability to create, but specifically the ability to create whatever you want. For example, one wrote, "I just make games. Animations. Logos. Requested Projects. Or just anything I feel like doing." Another exclaimed, "I love Scratch, because you can make ANYTHING YOU WANT!"

Some youth expressed surprise as well as excitement about the broad range of projects that Scratch made possible. For example, one youth described, "I tried it the very night my teacher told us about it. I was immediately amazed at all I could do with Scratch! I could make games, movies, music videos, all sorts of stuff!"

Building on Interests

While some youth emphasized this ability to make *anything*, others expressed interest in making particular types of projects. RubyDaisy explained: "I play and love Scratch because I can create games and video clips. As I love games myself, creating them is beyond." Davy99 wrote, "It allows me to make video games, which I thought was impossible before scratch."

Several youth described having wanted to make games before they had encountered Scratch. For example, RaccoonTop explained that before Scratch he would draw out his ideas for games on paper. "There was one game I made with a paper character that I could take out of a case and play with, but I still wasn't satisfied." He described how he learned about Scratch from his father, and then listed the different types of projects he had made since that time, as well as the friends he had made on the site.

Similarly, SonicMan wrote about his initial efforts to make games before finding Scratch:

> Well, I have wanted to make a video game for pretty much my entire life. That became my reality when I first discovered Microsoft Powerpoint. I would use the "custom animation" toolbar to make boxes and circles fly around the screen. Then I'd program a trigger to make an "if clicked, disappear" sort of thing. This was using software not meant for programming, and so, there were strict limitations.

He goes on to describe his introduction to Scratch:

> Then, as a birthday present, I got to take a beginner's programming class. The teacher introduced Scratch. This looked to be the thing I had been waiting for all this time. Simple enough to quickly put blocks together to make a program that made sense just by looking at the code, combined with small limitations, letting one's creativity be one of the only boundaries. Scratch is awesome because of just that, it's so easy to whip up a quick test program that looks and feels however you want.

Another popular area of interest was creating animations. As one youth wrote, "I can always go on Scratch and make animations! I love drawing, so animating them really cheers me up!" Other popular areas of interest that youth described included art, storytelling, and music.

Self-Expression

While we had anticipated that youth would describe specific project areas, we were surprised how many young people also wrote at a more abstract level about how they like to use Scratch to express their ideas and creativity. For example, one wrote, "It's an awesome way to express creativity." Another young person wrote, "I can show my createtivity [sic] everywhere." Others also wrote about using Scratch to express their ideas, for example:

- I scratch because I feel like I can truly express myself and try new things.
- I can make animations based on my comics to show everyone what goes on inside my head.
- I get epic ideas and this place is the best place to express them.
- Well, it's official: I've been on Scratch for nearly four years now, and I still post things. Why, you may ask? Well, let me explain. I Scratch because I like to. It helps me express myself and show others my creations.

These youth articulated the desire to express their ideas through creating and sharing projects.

Supporting Identity as a Creator

As mentioned above, Aurorazz described Scratch as allowing people to be creative in a variety of ways. Interestingly, she states these abilities in terms of roles: "you can be anything, an artist, a programmer, a musician, a writer, and so much more!" Similarly, another youth wrote, "I Scratch because I'm an artist, a programmer, an animator, a creator." Another wrote, "It's just so easy to use Scratch to express your abilities in whatever field you specialize in (games, animations, art) and that's really nice and useful." These descriptions suggest that youth are developing identities as creators, often across multiple domains.

Motivation to Create Builds on Interests and Ideas

These young people's enthusiasm for making a wide range of projects aligns with Dewey's ideas about children's natural desire to make things, communicate, and express themselves artistically. In addition, their emphasis on making "whatever you want" can be seen as satisfying the fundamental need for autonomy. As defined by self-determination theory, autonomy refers to the sense of volition: the feeling that you are deciding what to do, rather than having your actions controlled or coerced by others (Ryan & Deci, 2000). For these youth, the ability to express and represent their ideas is motivating.

Scratch has been critiqued by some educators as too open-ended, in contrast to coding software that gives students step-by-step puzzles to solve. Yet it is precisely this open invitation and opportunity to create a range of projects and express one's own ideas that the youth highlighted as a primary reason they like to use Scratch.

The invitation and opportunity to create projects based on one's own ideas and interests is also valued in physical makerspaces. Participants in makerspaces may participate in structured workshops, yet even within workshops they are often focused on learning skills that they can apply in self-directed projects (Sheridan et al., 2014). Wilkinson, Anzivino, and Petrich (chapter 10 of this volume) suggest ways to support learners exploring their own ideas through the process of tinkering, such as providing whimsical materials, encouraging quirky ideas, and offering projects that invite narrative. The value of connecting with learners' interests and supporting personally meaningful projects is at the core of constructionist learning philosophy, on which Scratch is based.

Motivated to Connect

Another reason youth frequently listed for using Scratch was the ability to connect with other people on the Scratch website. For example, Aurorazz described her online friends as another of the reasons she likes Scratch:

> FRIENDS: Scratch is, although it is sad to admit, the place on earth where I feel as though I belong and fit in. I thought for a while before making this project why that is, and I realized that it is your friends that make your world, and I have more good friends on scratch than anywhere else. I love all my friends, and scratch would not be scratch without them.

Many other youth also emphasized the importance of friends for motivating their ongoing participation. TopSpark, who has participated on Scratch for more than five years, made a strong statement about the role of friends on the site:

> I would not have been here today if it wasn't for all my great friends. Every day, I chat, role-play, joke, and do other stuff with my closest friends. I feel like I belong here. People actually like and care about me. I'm not treated like I'm not a human being with emotions and problems. So I thank all of you who I enjoy to call my friends. You helped me stay on Scratch all these years, and you're still helping me stay.

In this statement, TopSpark articulates a feeling of belonging and connection to others and says this has motivated continued participation on the site. TopSpark's statement can be seen as well aligned with the idea in self-determination theory that satisfying the need for connection can motivate learning and active participation.

Other youth also wrote about how much they appreciate the friends they connect with on Scratch. For example, Sandwich111 wrote:

> It's a way to express myself and meet up with new Scratch Friends. Whenever someone adds me to their friends list, it always makes my day. I keep all of my messages about when someone adds me. It makes me feel so happy to know someone out there, in a different state or even country considers me a friend.

Other youth also mentioned valuing making friends with people in other countries.

Importance of Community

Young people not only discussed the importance of making friends on the site, but also the importance of the broader community. Aurorazz listed community as her number one reason for loving Scratch:

> COMMUNITY: The very best thing about scratch to me is the amazing, amazing community of people to work with. I love doing all sorts of collabs with people, and I love seeing what others do as inspiration. The whole website and the ability to post projects and look at others easily is what really makes scratch different from all other programming languages out there.

Aurorazz's description reveals several different aspects of the community that she values. She enjoys seeing what others create, the ability to share her own projects, and collaborating with others (in self-organized teams known by Scratchers as "collabs").

Many youth emphasized the importance of having a friendly and welcoming community. For example, one wrote:

> First, Scratch is a community. Everyone appreciates and celebrates each other's work. If someone says something hurtful, everyone stands up for the person who has been put down. We also welcome new Scratchers and eventually, who knows? They could become the best programmer ever.

One of the participants wrote:

> Ever since i got scratch i have loved it for so many things like, friends, program[ming], and more but the thing that is the most helpful is the

> community why? because if everyone was mean then we would have no friends and scratch would be horrible and other stuff.

A participant of several years wrote, "The community was the first proper online community I got involved with and I loved how everyone was friendly and constructive."

Connection Through Collaboration

One way that young people make connections with other people on Scratch is by collaborating on projects. For example, WarriorFan described how friends in the community helped with learning to create projects in Scratch:

> I gave it a try and found it very hard to create something worthwhile. I would've quit earlier, but then I made friends. I commented on one of TLB's projects (an anime styled RPG) and he commented back, and found out he had the same interests as me. After that led me to join his "company" TeamAnime, with lots of other people with similar interests, so I made friends. Of course I had friends in real life, but having friends in other countries with the same interests kept me coming back to talk to them.

Self-determination theory identifies a sense of connection as an essential human need which, when satisfied, makes it more likely for people to be motivated to learn and participate in activities. The youth were articulate about ways in which the feeling of connection and belonging motivated and sustained their ongoing desire to participate in Scratch. Friendships were important, but also important was the overall sense of a friendly community.

As noted in the introduction, constructionist learning philosophy recognizes the importance of participating in a creative community to support creative learning. Within constructionism, the emphasis is often on learning from and creating with others, while within self-determination theory the emphasis is on the feeling of belonging and connection with others.

The young people's emphasis on the importance of community and connections resonates with sentiments expressed by participants in the broader Maker Movement. As in Scratch, participants in physical makerspaces connect by sharing skills and by collaborating on projects. For example, Sheridan and colleagues (2014) highlight the importance of community within one of the makerspaces they studied, where participants indicated that the people (rather than tools, materials, or equipment) were the most valued aspect of the space. They found that this makerspace was designed to support people sharing projects and skills and to foster a sense of belonging.

Motivated to Share

While most youth expressed the importance of friends and other community members for connection, many also described participating in the Scratch online community because they enjoyed having an audience for their work. For example, MoonKnight wrote:

> I discovered sharing my projects could bring recognition. I love views and approval of my work! Because of my love of game making and programming, I work hard to make my best. I hope that people will enjoy it and figure out how to make stuff like I do.

As MoonKnight describes, having an audience can motivate working hard. MoonKnight's goal is not just approval, but helping others to enjoy and learn from his projects.

This desire to have an audience can be seen as an extension of the desire to express one's ideas. As one Scratcher wrote, when describing reasons for liking Scratch:

> The Fact I can Bring My Ideas to Life: Never before could I do this. I could have ideas for TV shows and stuff that would never get noticed by anyone, so I would be stuck with 'em. Scratch gives me the opportunity to share my ideas with people from around the world; maybe not hundreds, but a lot more than if I never shared them to begin with!

Several youth expressed a desire to become "famous" on Scratch, while also recognizing and reconciling themselves to other goals. For example, one wrote:

> Although I'm not what you might call "famous" I like creating entertainment for the community. (If they happen to stumble upon me . . .)

Another youth, whose project was written with a question and answer format, wrote:

> Do you want to become a famous Scratcher? Oh yes! I want to be like Aster123 or Canzo one day, but I know the possibility of that happening is 0/0. : (But I have many friends to keep me going and maybe, with a little more practice, I will one day become a Scratching master. :D

Interestingly, this statement shows a young person who wants to be famous, but also expresses other motivations to keep going, including connection with friends and developing competence. Self-determination theory views motivation on a continuum, from seeking extrinsic goals (such as fame and money) to more intrinsic goals (such as personal growth, health, and friendship) (Vansteenkiste et al., 2006). Some of the youth can be seen as holding both of these goals, or as shifting from extrinsic goals to more intrinsic ones.

Appreciating Feedback

Many youth wrote about how much they appreciated receiving positive feedback and attention for their projects. For example, one wrote:

> I love the feeling of when you log on and that "1 message" sign shows up. Somehow, there is satisfaction behind knowing someone saw your project and cared.

Although most were focused on positive feedback, some also mentioned appreciating suggestions for improvement. As Aurorazz explained:

> FEEDBACK: What makes scratch even better as an outlet, is not only can you make whatever you want, you can also get opinions from others on what you made. Whether it's just a comment saying "I love it!!!" or some great suggestions on how to improve it, every comment I get on my projects make[s] me smile.

Some wrote about how feedback motivates their participation. For example, one wrote:

> I can get comments and feedback - that is what really keeps me going as a Scratcher. It's you people! The honesty and pure feedback of Scratch.

Magnifico (2010) writes about the importance of an authentic audience and feedback to motivate students to write. The youth descriptions in Scratch suggest that having an audience is also motivating for youth to learning to write computer programs. Their perspectives contribute to a growing body of research on the role of the online community for motivating participation (e.g., Kafai & Burke, 2014).

Many of the youth appeared to be motivated to share by an intrinsic desire to express one's ideas with others, aligned with Dewey's idea of communication as a natural interest. Others saw sharing primarily as a way to attract attention or become famous, which is a more extrinsic rather than intrinsic goal (Vansteenkiste et al., 2006). Yet even those seeking fame also expressed appreciation for more intrinsic forms of connection, such as making friends or helping or entertaining others.

The broader Maker Movement recognizes that a major motivation for making projects is the desire to share one's creations with others.

Community and local events, such as Maker Faires, provide opportunities for sharing and motivation for completing or improving a project based on feedback from others (Hlubinka, 2011).

Motivated to Learn

Another major theme identified in the youth responses was their motivation to learn programming and other skills. Aurorazz described how she was drawn to Scratch initially to learn to program:

> EXPERIENCE: Before I was on Scratch, I didn't really know anything about programming. One day I decided I wanted to learn some programming, and I found Scratch. Now, my dream in life is to be a programmer when I grow up, and after only half a year of Scratch I am already finding it easier to learn other programming languages, such as Java, just because I learned Scratch first.

She goes on to describe how she also gained drawing skills, and how she developed a passion for both drawing and programming:

> It is the same with art. I didn't know how to draw before Scratch, but the amazing artists here inspired me to start drawing, and now it is one of my passions. I learned so much from Scratch, and it wasn't hard. I learned it in one day, and made my first game. Ever since then I knew what I wanted to do with my life, and I will never forget Scratch for giving me that (in fact I think I want to work on the scratch team as a programmer when I grow up :D).

About one-third of the youth wrote about learning to program as one of the reasons that they liked Scratch. They also mentioned other skills too, particularly drawing or animation skills. Here are three other examples:

- I LOVE programming animating remixing and drawing . . . so basically I LOVE everything on scratch!!!! XD
- When I scratch I often have programming sessions of around three hours and art sessions of even longer!
- I had fun using the blocks to program sprites and animations. Simple and complex. I like the way you can do that in Scratch. It taught me how to program and it's how it got me to learning Python right now. I enjoyed drawing and animating. I got better at it through the months! and making games as well.

Some youth, like Aurorazz, came to the site already wanting to learn how to program. Others were not previously aware of programming, and found out about it through participating on Scratch, as one youth wrote, "Scratch has opened up a world that was hidden to me. Before I started Scratch I had no idea that programming even existed. Now, it's my favorite thing to do all the time."

Youth also wrote about how Scratch has influenced them in other ways, including influencing their plans for the future. For example, these youth described different areas of interest influenced by Scratch:

- Thanks to you Scratch, I have set my dream to be a programmer!
- Scratch really changed my perception of life . . . and especially my perception of my own abilities. <3 Besides simple games and even animations, besides what I've learned (I could apply trigonometry before the schools ever taught it!), I have discovered that Math is Art!
- I think Scratch is a place where you can create foundations for epicness and a possible career. I want to get into independent game developing in the future, and I think Scratch has paved a way for that.

Learning From Others

Many young people wrote about learning Scratch by interacting with others' projects. For example, PathTrader, who has participated for more than three years, wrote:

> When I used the website, I got interested in the projects of others. This is largely how I learned scratch; through remixing and sharing and creating . . . I made many friends here, who remix my projects, give comments, and have taught me new things.

Scratch is designed to make it easy for youth to see inside others' projects, view the scripts to see how the project works, and remix the project to create their own variations. Youth also wrote about being inspired by others' projects to improve their own abilities.

Social-Emotional Learning

In addition to talking about learning skills related to programming and creating, some youth wrote about learning social skills. For example:

> There are lots of goals to meet, some as simple as being a good friend. Some goals are as complex as making a game something no one has ever seen before.

A young person named Tola12 writes about gaining confidence from participating in Scratch:

> Before I started programming, I didn't know who I was (Not literally.). I didn't really know what my passion was, I thought no one liked me,

> I didn't know what clothes I liked. . . . I was just confused and insecure. I still don't know a lot of these things, but I feel so much more secure and confident. I connected with people who programmed as well and learned so much more about myself by finding something I really like to do, and the awesome people that came with it. This isn't supposed to be a "sob story." It is supposed to let you guys know to be yourselves and try new things.

Tola12's statement can be seen as connecting the three needs described by self-determination theory: finding something you like to do (autonomy), connecting to other people with similar interests (relatedness), and gaining confidence in the process (competence). Tola12 encourages others to also pursue being themselves and trying new things to find their passion.

The motivation to learn and develop one's abilities aligns with the emphasis on learning from others and on improving one's projects in the Maker Movement. The Maker Movement Manifesto states that makers are continually seeking to learn new materials, tools, and processes, and sharing what they learn with others (Hatch, 2014). Learning can be motivated by seeing what others are making or by having an idea for a project or encountering a problem to solve.

Motivated to Have Fun

The other main theme identified in the youth projects was that they use Scratch to have fun. This theme can be seen as overlapping with the idea of intrinsic motivation, as it involves pursuing an activity based on enjoyment. However, because some youth included fun as a distinct reason for participating, it seems worth considering how this related to their other reasons.

Some wrote about having fun as their main reason for participating; for example, one wrote, "I mostly scratch because it's fun. But not only that, I love the community and people's projects." Another wrote, "I scratch because I have fun and I have friends."

NorthernMo, who made his project in the form of a story about himself, wrote, "He knew scratch was meant for him because of the amazing and nice community, how you can communicate with friends, and especially, have fun."

Some specified that it was fun making projects or games. Most spoke generally about Scratch or the Scratch website as fun. It seems that it was the overall experience, rather than one specific aspect that they considered fun.

Several youth described Scratch as both educational and fun. One wrote, "It's fun, and entertaining. It's also educational, and inspiring. You can make friends of all ages all around the world! You can make anything!" Another explained:

> I like scratch because it is fun! You can do so much with it (role-play, school projects, games, art, meeting new people, etc.). I also like how it is easy to use and teaches basic programming. Because of Scratch, I discovered what I wanted to do when I grow up!

Their statements again can be seen as touching on all three needs described by self-determination theory: autonomy to choose what you want with it, connecting to other people, and developing competence.

The Scratch site itself does not use the word "fun" as a description. However, it is designed to encourage a playful approach to creating projects. The Scratch programming language, made of colorful blocks that snap together, is designed to support learning through tinkering and experimenting. The images and examples also model a spirit of playfulness. This playful spirit is reflected in the Maker Movement more generally, with an approach to making which Dale Dougherty refers to as "experimental play" (Dougherty, 2013, p. 7). As Peppler and Bender (2013) recommend to educators starting makerspaces: "Think less about the products youth create and allow more time for experimentation and play with the materials. Projects will begin to emerge from this type of exploration, as will innovative ideas" (p. 25).

The finding that these youth talked about Scratch as fun and educational as part of their experience on Scratch contrasts with the assumption that the only way to make learning fun is by framing it as a game. It fits with Dewey's idea of tapping into children's natural desire to make things, express themselves, and communicate, as opposed to trying to make learning more interesting by trying to "cover it with sugar coating" (Dewey, 1902/2008, p. 30).

Supporting Young People's Motivation for Making

The youth who responded to the call for projects wrote expressively about why they use Scratch. Their descriptions revealed that an interest in creating art, games, or animations often drew them to Scratch. However, getting to know people in the online community was important for ongoing involvement. Many appreciated learning new skills, which influenced their plans for the future. Many also described the experience of participating in Scratch as fun.

The community fueled motivation in several ways: by providing a sense of connection with other people, giving an audience for one's work, offering encouraging and helpful feedback, and displaying projects by others that inspired and sparked new ideas.

Although these young people's responses were focused on reasons for using the Scratch creative coding environment and community, the ideas they expressed may provide some insights for educators and others seeking to spark and sustain young people's motivation for learning through making. Table 6.1 summarizes the key ideas identified in the youth responses and suggests ways to support young people's motivation for learning through making. Each of these categories is described further, below.

Table 6.1 Practices to support motivation for making

Motivation	*Aspects Youth Discussed*	*Practices to Support Motivation*
Create projects based on your ideas and interests	- Ability to create your own games, animations, art, and more - Make whatever you want - Express your ideas - Pursue interest areas - See self as artist, programmer, animator, and more	- Provide tools and opportunities to create projects in open-ended way - Share examples that suggest a diversity of potential projects (both playful and practical) - Build on existing interest areas (such as animation, art, games, music, sports) - Respect youth as creators (not only learners)
Connect with others in a friendly community	- Keep coming back because have made friends here - Supportive community helps you feel like you belong - Make friends by collaborating - Find others with similar interests - Meet people from around the world	- Support the development of an inviting learning environment where people can create together - Help connect people with shared interests and across countries - Arrange events and structures that encourage collaboration with friends and others with shared interests
Share creations and receive feedback	- Motivating to know others will see your creations - Highly motivating to receive positive feedback - Constructive criticism can help you improve - Appreciate the friends you have (don't just focus on becoming popular)	- Organize community to support sharing projects - Model and mentor providing constructive feedback - Dedicate time and resources to modeling and maintaining a friendly tone throughout the community

Learn skills you can use	- Learning programming skills - Improving art and drawing skills - Inspiring to see and learn from others' projects - Opens up other opportunities - Prepares and inspires you for a career	- Design tools and community to encourage peer learning - Engage community members with diverse skill levels - Make visible the skills youth can learn in the process of creating - Offer ways to learn about future steps and opportunities
Have fun as you create and share	- Having fun is a reason to participate - Making projects can be seen as both fun and educational - Ability to choose from a variety of activities adds to sense of fun - Connecting with friends often mentioned along with fun	- Making itself can be fun, without turning it into a game - Support playful tinkering - Support a variety of projects and activities - Support social interaction as well as creating

Supporting Youth as Creators: Many of the young people spoke of themselves as creators across a variety of domains (including art, animation, game making, music, and programming). Physical spaces for making can also highlight diverse types of projects to engage young people with diverse interests. For example, the book *The Art of Tinkering* (Wilkinson & Petrich, 2014) suggests a broad and intriguing range of project ideas, from practical to playful.

Although most tools can be used to create a wide variety of projects, just being introduced to the tool may not suggest the variety of creative possibilities, particularly for young people new to making. Too often, tools are introduced with a focus on learning the technology itself (e.g., Intro to Laser Cutting), without suggesting how the tool can be used to make projects that connect with a learner's interests (e.g., design your own lantern, make a cell phone case, or laser cut your food). When offering workshops or other opportunities for learning, particularly for newcomers, we suggest highlighting a theme and project examples that participants may find interesting or useful, rather than overemphasizing the technology (e.g., within robotics, see Rusk, Resnick, Berg, & Pezalla-Granlund, 2008). In addition, treating youth first and foremost as creators (rather than as learners) may help them see themselves in new ways and make connections to related fields.

Supporting Connection and Community: Youth emphasized that what motivated them to continue participation was the connection with friends and others in the community. Creating and maintaining a welcoming, helpful, and supportive community requires time, thought, and ongoing effort by program leaders as well as community members. Developing community guidelines that promote a friendly, respectful, and welcoming environment can provide an important basis for ongoing conversations. To help people make connections and friendships, organize community events and program structures that encourage collaboration (such as Scratch Day gatherings or Mini-Maker Faires), or developing projects to improve the space or neighborhood. When possible, help connect people with shared interests to work together on projects or exchange ideas. Encourage and help participants to connect to others not only in the local community, but also across other sites. *The Computer Clubhouse* book (Kafai, Peppler, & Chapman, 2009) provides examples of how program structures (such as mentoring roles and collaborative events) can help develop and sustain a supportive creative community, both online and offline.

Supporting Sharing and Constructive Feedback: The Maker Movement Manifesto states: "Sharing what you have made and what you know about making with others is the method by which a maker's feeling of wholeness is achieved" (Hatch, 2014, pp. 14–15). A physical space can be set up to encourage sharing. Dedicate time and resources to modeling and maintaining a culture that encourages sharing of ideas, materials, and work in progress. Provide a context in which participants learn to give each other encouraging and constructive feedback. For example, the *Creative Computing* guide (Brennan, Balch, & Chung, 2014) suggests ways to organize "unfocus groups" in order to provide youth an opportunity to give each other constructive feedback as they develop their projects.

Supporting Motivation to Learn and Develop Skills: Learning through making is often motivated by the experience of working on a project, encountering obstacles, and iterating to improve the design. In order to support motivation for making, you can organize opportunities for peer learning, engage community members with diverse skill levels, and make visible the skills youth can learn in the process of creating. In addition, you can help learners connect to further opportunities and see how they could apply these skills in a variety of fields.

Supporting Having Fun: The process of making and sharing projects can be seen by youth as both fun and educational. Supporting exploration and tinkering can help make the experience enjoyable and give youth a sense of agency within the creative process (see chapter 10 of this volume). Providing opportunities for youth to make friends as they are making projects can help make the experience more enjoyable and meaningful.

By looking at opportunities for making through the lens of self-determination, we can better understand what can motivate young people to take initiative, persist, and learn new skills in the process of making. First, we can arrange opportunities that allow young people to feel a sense of agency, for example, by enabling them to choose which projects they work on and to express their ideas and interests when creating projects. Second, we can help them develop a sense of connection by working hard to develop and maintain a friendly and collaborative community of fellow makers. Third, we can help them recognize the skills and competence they are building by providing them opportunities to share their work, get feedback, and reflect on their own development. By improving our understanding of young people's motivation for making, we can provide more opportunities and support for young people to create, connect, share, learn, and have fun in physical as well as online communities.

References

Braafladt, K. (Photographer). (2009). *Talking sandwich project from a workshop exploring Scratch and LEGO WeDo* [Photograph]. Retrieved on July 25, 2015 from scratched.gse.harvard.edu/stories/lifelong-learning-interview-keith-braafladt-about-science-museum-minnesota

Brennan, K., Balch, C., & Chung, M. (2014). *Creative computing: An introductory computing curriculum using Scratch.* Retrieved on July 20, 2015 from http://scratched.gse.harvard.edu/

Csikszentmihalyi, M. (1997). *Flow and the psychology of discovery and invention.* New York: Harper Perennial.

Davis, R., Kafai, Y., Vasudevan, V., & Lee, E. (2013). The education arcade: Crafting, remixing, and playing with controllers for Scratch games. In *Proceedings of the 12th International Conference on Interaction Design and Children* (pp. 439–442). New York: ACM Digital Library.

Dewey, J. (1900/1915). *The school and society.* Chicago: University of Chicago.

Dewey, J. (1902/2008). *The child and the curriculum.* New York: Cosimo.

Dougherty, D. (2013). The maker mindset. In M. Honey & D. E. Kanter (Eds.), *Design, make, play: Growing the next generation of STEM innovators* (pp. 7–11). New York, NY: Routledge.

Furrer, C. & Skinner, E. (2003). Sense of relatedness as a factor in children's academic engagement and performance. *Journal of Educational Psychology, 95,* 148–162.

Hatch, M. (2014). *The Maker Movement manifesto: Rules for innovation in the new world of crafters, hackers, and tinkerers.* New York, NY: McGraw-Hill.

Hlubinka, M. (2011). New models for education: Maker Faire and the young makers program [Web log post]. Retrieved on July 12, 2015 from www.edutopia.org/blog/education-maker-faire-young-makers-program

Honey, M. & Kanter, D. E. (Eds.). (2013). *Design, make, play: Growing the next generation of STEM innovators.* New York, NY: Routledge.

Kafai, Y. B. & Burke, Q. (2014). *Connected code: Why children need to learn programming.* Cambridge, MA: MIT Press.

Kafai, Y. B., Peppler, K., & Chapman, R. (Eds.). (2009). *The computer clubhouse: Constructionism and creativity in youth communities.* New York: Teachers College Press.

Kafai, Y. B. & Resnick, M. (1996). *Constructionism in practice: Designing, thinking, and learning in a digital world.* Hillsdale, NJ: Lawrence Erlbaum.

Larson, R. & Rusk, N. (2011). Intrinsic motivation and positive youth development. In R. M. Lerner, J. V. Lerner, & J. B. Benson (Eds.), *Positive youth development: Advances in child development and behavior, Vol. 41* (pp. 89–130). New York: Academic Press.

Magnifico, A. M. (2010). Writing for whom? Cognition, motivation, and a writer's audience. *Educational Psychologist, 45*, 167–184.

Millner, A. (2010). *Cultivating and sustaining communities of youth as designers of tangible user interfaces.* PhD dissertation, MIT Media Lab, Cambridge, MA.

Nakamura, J. & Csikszentmihalyi, M. (2009). Flow theory and research. In C. R. Snyder & S. J. Lopez (Eds.), *Handbook of positive psychology* (2nd ed.) (pp. 195–206). New York: Oxford.

Niemiec, C. P. & Ryan, R. M. (2009). Autonomy, competence, and relatedness in the classroom: Applying self-determination theory to educational practice. *Theory and Research in Education, 7*, 133–144.

Papert, S. (1993). *The children's machine: Rethinking school in the age of the computer.* New York, NY: Basic.

Papert, S. & Harel, I. (1991). Situating constructionism. In S. Papert & I. Harel (Eds.), *Constructionism* (pp. 1–12). New York: Ablex Publishing.

Peppler, K. & Bender, S. (2013). Maker Movement spreads innovation one project at a time. *Phi Delta Kappan, 95*(3), 22–27.

Resnick, M., Maloney, J., Monroy-Hernandez, A., Rusk, N., Eastmond, E., Brennan, K., . . . Kafai, Y. (2009). Scratch: Programming for all. *Communications of the ACM, 52*(11), 60–67.

Resnick, M. & Rosenbaum, E. (2013). Designing for tinkerability. In M. Honey & D. Kanter (Eds.), *Design, make, play: Growing the next generation of STEM innovators* (pp. 163–181). New York: Routledge.

Rusk, N., Resnick, M., Berg, R., & Pezalla-Granlund, M. (2008). New pathways into robotics: Strategies for broadening participation. *Journal of Science Education and Technology, 17*, 59–69.

Ryan, R. M. & Deci, E. L. (2000). Self-determination theory and the facilitation of intrinsic motivation, social development, and well-being. *American Psychologist, 55*, 68–78.

Seifert, T. & Hedderson, C. (2010). Intrinsic motivation and flow in skateboarding: An ethnographic study. *Journal of Happiness Studies, 11*, 277–292.

Sheridan, K., Halverson, E. R., Litts, B., Brahms, L., Jacobs-Priebe, L., & Owens, T. (2014). Learning in the making: A comparative case study of three makerspaces. *Harvard Educational Review, 84*, 505–531.

Usher, A. & Kober, N. (2012). *Can money or other rewards motivate students?* Retrieved on July 20, 2015 from www.cep-dc.org

Vansteenkiste, M., Lens, W., & Deci, E. L. (2006). Intrinsic versus extrinsic goal contents in self-determination theory: Another look at the quality of academic motivation. *Educational Psychologist, 41*, 19–31.

Wilkinson, K. & Petrich, M. (2014). *The art of tinkering.* San Francisco: Weldon Owen.

Zagal, J. P. & Bruckman, A. S. (2005). From samba schools to computer clubhouses: Cultural institutions as learning environments. *Convergence: The International Journal of Research into New Media Technologies, 11*, 88–105.

Section 2
The Tools and Materials of Makers

CHAPTER 7

From a Movie to a Movement

Caine's Arcade and the Imagination Foundation

MIKE McGALLIARD

A Chance Encounter

On the last day of summer, a filmmaker named Nirvan Mullick drove along Mission Boulevard in East Los Angeles in search of a new door handle for his 1996 Toyota Corolla. Mission Boulevard, speckled with numerous auto parts and repair shops, runs alongside the Los Angeles River through a somewhat industrialized part of the city. Nirvan randomly selected one stop, a small shop set up against the street, thinly walled and colored with bright swatches of yellow and red.

Nirvan stepped inside Smart Parts and there he met 9-year-old Caine Monroy. Wearing a simple blue T-shirt with the word "staff" stenciled in black, the boy was proudly stationed in front of an elaborate display of old-style arcade games made from cardboard and other recycled materials. Hand-painted cardboard signs decorated the store and announced, "Caine's Arcade."

Caine asked Nirvan if he wanted to play the games. Curious and entertained by the potential of this encounter, Nirvan asked, "How much to play?"

"You get four turns for a dollar," Caine answered, "but for $2 you can buy a Fun Pass."

"How many turns do I get for a Fun Pass?"

"You get 500 turns for a Fun Pass."

Nirvan bought the Fun Pass and played the games. One was a mini basketball-themed game made from a cardboard box, tiny basketball hoop (acquired from a prize drawer at Shakey's Pizza, Caine's favorite restaurant), and wadded up pieces of paper used as tiny basketballs. Another was a soccer game; the top of the box was lined with repurposed Army Men blockers.

If Nirvan would win points after playing a game, Caine would crouch down and crawl into the back of the box, and there, hidden inside, he would push out a string of prize tickets through a slit on the front side.

Setting foot inside Smart Parts, it was evident that Caine was working to make and share a deeply engaging vision of something he was passionate about. As his dad George Monroy later explained, Caine loved arcades. He would always stop to play when he came across one. So he wanted to make his own, and to share it with customers. With the limited resources available—mainly cardboard boxes that his father would use to ship and receive auto parts and his own recycled toys for prizes—Caine built his own arcade.

A cash register, piles of hand-drawn Fun Passes, repurposed Hot Wheels and various other prizes, even a homemade security system that would test the validity of any Fun Pass by using the square root button of calculators taped onto the front of each game; Caine had designed and built an immersive experience.

But despite Caine's efforts, no one stopped to play at this arcade, not one customer. At least, not until Nirvan stopped by that day, on the last day of summer, to replace his car door's broken handle. Amazed by the boy's creativity, and a bit heartbroken by the fact that he was Caine's only customer, Nirvan was determined to make Caine's day. He set out to bring a flash mob

Figure 7.1 Filmmaker Nirvan Mullick and Caine Monroy on the steps in front of Caine's Arcade.

of customers to come and play at Caine's Arcade and to make a film about it all. Using Facebook, Reddit, and other social media platforms, Nirvan invited Los Angeles to come play at Caine's Arcade on October 2, 2011.

This flash mob marks the climactic end to the short film titled *Caine's Arcade*, which tells the story of Nirvan's chance encounter. The film ends with the flash mob greeting a surprised and joyfully giddy Caine and chanting together, "We came to play!"

From a Movie to a Movement

In April of 2012, the 11-minute short film *Caine's Arcade* was released on social media and was an immediate viral sensation. Within a few days of its release, it was viewed over 8 million times, and over 30,000 contributors had given over $134,000 to Caine's scholarship (today, that fund is worth slightly more than $240,000).

Media outlets heralded the film as telling a "great American story" (Goodale, 2012), and a statement about child creativity and the "amazing" things "children can do when left to themselves" (Banks, 2012). The film was widely celebrated, cited by numerous sources as one of the most inspirational stories of 2012. Caine himself appeared in Forbes on at least seven different occasions since the film was released.

Perhaps the most unexpected and inspiring aspect of the *Caine's Arcade* phenomenon is the response the film elicited from children and communities around the globe. Within days of the film's online release, children from multiple parts of the world were uploading pictures and videos of their own cardboard games and artifacts and posting them to the *Caine's Arcade* Facebook page.

Early in the film's release, commentators realized the potential impact of *Caine's Arcade* on education, calling it a model for "connected learning" and "a kind of crowdsourced education," an example of how social media can work "as a way for kids to link up with peers and mentors" (Melby, 2012).

Caine's Arcade fandom quickly grew, becoming a large and sociable network extending around the world. Active fans got involved in making cardboard games (not only children, but adults too), hosting a variety of large- and small-scale *Caine's Arcade*–themed events, and even participating in discussions online and in real life around topics like project-based learning, DIY activities, making, entrepreneurship, and other forms of hands-on learning. This fan culture remains grounded in a strong ethic of sharing news and information together, creating and commenting on each other's ideas, and celebrating inspirational stories of creative kids.

It's from this fan culture that the Global Cardboard Challenge was born.

Global Cardboard Challenge

The launch of the Imagination Foundation followed the viral success of *Caine's Arcade*. With the foresight of the film's director, Nirvan Mullick, the support of an entrepreneurial Los Angeles–based donor (the Goldhirsh Foundation), and a mission statement Nirvan scribbled on the back of a napkin (literally), the Foundation was born. The mission read, "To find, foster and fund creativity and entrepreneurship" in more kids like Caine. A primary motivation for starting the Foundation was to engage and fuel what appeared to be a growing movement ignited by the film.

The Foundation's first program, the Global Cardboard Challenge (GCC), was designed to leverage and grow the movement that sprung from Caine's Arcade. Through GCC, children are encouraged to take cardboard and recycled materials and build whatever they can dream up. The program leverages the popularity of Caine's Arcade, the ubiquity of cardboard, and a simple "just build it" mentality to celebrate children's creativity and the simple things adults can do to foster it. GCC activities have taken place in more than 60 countries and, by 2015, had reached a total of over 350,000 participants.

From community to community, Cardboard Challenge activities are characterized by significant diversity. Some are single events with hundreds of people engaged in a frenzy of daylong cardboard making; others

Figure 7.2 A photo of a "high five parade" at the one of the first Cardboard Challenge events in Boyle Heights in Los Angeles.

are extensive multiweek projects (in and out of the classroom) focused on more elaborate design and construction. Many of the challenges culminate in what we call "a day of play"; a specific date in early October each year, the day of play is reminiscent of the flash mob that came out to make Caine's day in the short film. Communities come together on this day in various numbers and places to play and build together in the form of community arcades, mazes, play structures, robot parades, and other unique creative expressions.

To some extent, it was expected that many of the partners engaging in GCC would be teachers using the Cardboard Challenge to enrich classrooms and engage students through project-based learning. But the appeal of GCC reaches far beyond classrooms, into homes, parks, libraries, community centers, and even places like store parking lots and shopping malls. Businesses have gotten involved, donating recycled cardboard and lending employees to join in the fun (for example, a national mattress retailer hosted cardboard building activities at their retail stores in select cities, and in multiple locations, the company's trucks and drivers delivered recycled mattress boxes to local schools and community events).

Re-Imagine Learning Through Creative Play

In late 2014, the Global Cardboard Challenge was named Champion (along with nine other entries) in the LEGO Foundation's competition to "Re-imagine Learning" (LEGO Foundation, n.d.). This global challenge, coordinated in partnership with Ashoka, reviewed 632 program submissions from organizations worldwide. The ten Champions are celebrated as "some of the most innovative, impactful and sustainable projects aimed at transforming the way the world learns" (LEGO Foundation, n.d.).

Though GCC was named Champion in this challenge, it's important to note that GCC is less a formally designed program and more a natural outgrowth of children's response to the *Caine's Arcade* short film. The team at the Imagination Foundation gave GCC a name, provided some definition and scope, and compressed it in time (making it a fall event to correspond with important story points from the film). We created resources to help GCC organizers and utilized online social networks for them to share their experiences with each other and the public at large. But what's most significant about GCC is that it's based on children's *natural response* to the film.

GCC is an attempt to construct a coherent programmatic framework around an unexpected but compelling grassroots response to the *Caine's Arcade* film—a delicate task to be sure, because we wanted to grow the movement around *Caine's Arcade*, not burden it with obtrusive structures. But we felt it was important to connect the activity of GCC to a larger conversation about education and how children learn best. Although teachers and schools have always played a major role in leading the movement, much of the activity has been initiated by noneducators within informal environments. The Foundation's goal was to create a teaching and learning model from GCC that would capture the most educationally significant elements of *Caine's Arcade* fandom, but simplify them enough so that educators and noneducators alike could understand them.

We call the pedagogical model that emerged from GCC "Creative Play." In its simplest expression, it's a process of physically constructing ideas and then sharing these constructs in a meaningful public context. Because cardboard play is low tech and because *Caine's Arcade* is universally appealing, our hope was that this educational model could proliferate in and outside of school, as a way for everyone to understand the value and simplicity of teaching and learning creativity and other next-generation skills.

The Creative Play Spiral

Creative Play begins with inspiration and culminates in the sharing of an original artifact made by children using whatever tools and materials are available. In this process, kids open up their minds to what's possible, take chances, solve problems, collaborate, and become better creative thinkers and doers.

As a theory of teaching and learning, Creative Play draws inspiration from a number of sources. At Imagination Foundation, we're big fans of Seymour Papert, of course, and constructionism, which promotes the construction of physical artifacts and self-directed inquiry as the best ways to build knowledge: "children will do best by finding for themselves the specific knowledge they need." We also like how Papert expands and shifts the role of the teacher, from one who supplies knowledge to one who accompanies a learner on their own journey of self-discovery. "Organized and informal education," he writes, "can help most by making sure [children] are supported morally, psychologically, materially, and intellectually in their efforts" (Papert, 1993).

Most influential to our model is what MIT professor Mitch Resnick (2007) calls the "'kindergarten approach to learning'—characterized by a spiraling cycle of Imagine, Create, Play, Share, Reflect, and back to Imagine," an approach that, he writes, "is ideally suited to the needs of the 21st century" (p. 1).

We adapted the Resnick spiral to represent better the behaviors we were observing during GCC; mainly, that children's cardboard creativity was kicked off with inspiration, often with the viewing of *Caine's Arcade*. We observe that stories and experiences help trigger a child's passions and interests. Therefore, our spiral starts with "inspire." We also chose the word

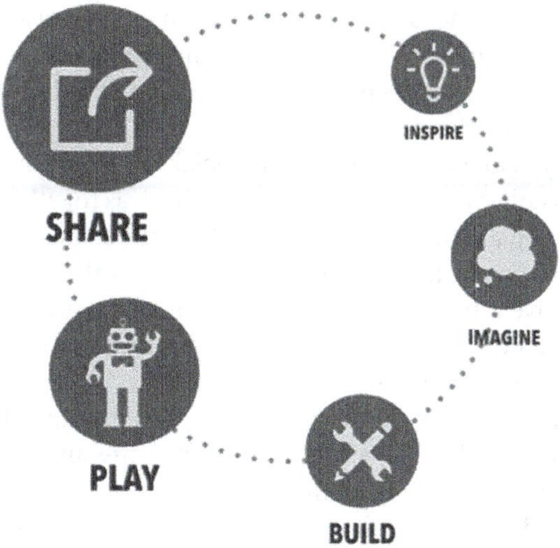

Figure 7.3

"build" as opposed to "create," because it signifies a process that's more physical and concrete, emphasizing the hands-on nature of making.

"Play" is time to tinker and test one's creations, and "share" is about presenting one's work in a meaningful public context. Through GCC, sharing is done both online (as kids post photos and videos)and also physically, often in the form of public events in which community members come out to interact with the various games, toys, and other kid-made artifacts.

The following diagram outlines the five major components of our Creative Play spiral:

The "kindergarten approach to learning" is at times disorderly. For example, it may not be until a child "plays" with available materials that they get "inspired" to make something. Additionally, components in the spiral can be repeated numerous times in a cycle (e.g., a child may repeat "build" and "play" and in the process "imagine" new possibilities). In other words, it can be a messy process, which is reflected in most typical Cardboard Challenge activities. But the experience does escalate as children build upon their ideas over time. This is why we represent the process as a spiral.

We have observed that through Creative Play kids practice a comprehensive set of next-generation skills. For example, they practice traditional creativity-aligned skills like creative fluency (as kids generate different ideas and stretch their imaginations), flexible thinking (as they think of lots of different ways to use the same materials and ideas), and problem finding (an ability to identify problems that others might not know exist). We also talk about "creative self-efficacy," a combination of skills and attitudes that help a child persist in the face of challenges with optimism and imagination, trying and retrying without the crippling concerns of failure (for more on making and self-efficacy, see chapters 3, 4, and 6 in this volume, and Regalla, 2016, in volume 1 of this series).

Creative Play also engages numerous social and emotional skills, as kids work in playful collaboration to build out their ideas together. They practice patience, empathy, and kindness. Further still, kids engage in a set of talents we call "entrepreneurial thinking and innovation" as they make artifacts and ventures that have a real-world impact. This is one reason why the "share" piece of Creative Play is so critical: through sharing, children recognize that their creations have value in the world.

These skills align to the latest research and thought-leader opinion about the most valuable skills for 21st-century life and work. For example, 17 countries in OECD (Organisation for Economic Cooperation and Development) identify "creativity and innovation" as a core competency so important it calls for the realignment of national educational priorities (Ananiadou & Claro, 2009). And, a popular survey of 1,500 CEOs from 60 countries and 33 industries identified creativity as the "most crucial factor for future success" (Bronson & Merryman, 2010).

It's important to note that though there is a lengthy theoretical basis for Creative Play, we intend our model to be simple, requiring little facilitation because it taps into children's natural creative talents. It would be a mistake to overly design a Creative Play experience. Adults (teachers, parents, and others) can step out of the way a bit and watch as Creative Play leads to some surprising outcomes.

Unexpected Outcomes: Creative Play Unites a Divided Town in Bosnia

What has been most inspiring for us at Imagination Foundation are the unexpected outcomes of GCC, how organizers have used Creative Play to address community and regional-specific problems in ways that we frankly did not imagine. Take, for example, the inspirational story of Bosnia and Herzegovina:

> At first glance, the picturesque town of Mostar in Bosnia and Herzegovina looks as if it's been plucked right out of a fairy tale. Stone houses with orange rooftops dot the lush green hillsides, and towering medieval structures stand sentry at each end of the Stari Most, a breathtaking 500-year-old limestone bridge. Next to the emerald green waters of the Neretva River, below the Stari Most, a gray cobblestone walkway bustles with vendors and shopkeepers.
>
> When you look a bit closer though, you can see what lies underneath.

Buildings and homes are dented from gunfire, and a small chunk of the bridge sits in a quiet corner on top of the Stari Most. In thick black lettering, the tombstone-like monument reads: "Don't Forget '93."

That year, the people of Mostar went through something unthinkable. The community was on the front lines of the brutal Bosnian war, and for weeks at a time, bloody battles between the Catholic Croats and Bosniak Muslims raged in the streets. For nine months, the town was under siege, and residents were left without electricity or food. In the fighting, the Stari Most was destroyed.

Before the war, the Bosniaks and Croats lived peacefully alongside one another in Mostar. Today, 19 years after the war's end, the 100,000-person community has become the most ethnically divided town in all of Bosnia. Croats live on the west side of the river while the Bosniaks live on the east. Rarely do they cross paths.

Each side of the Neretva River has its own postal system, schools, language, phone networks, and even its own electricity providers. Though most signs point toward the continuation of this sharp ethnic divide, a glimmer of hope for reconciliation lies within the youth of this community.

This was apparent at the first ever Cardboard Challenge in Bosnia. Matea Peric, a 27-year-old economist born and raised in Mostar, saw *Caine's Arcade* and learned about the Global Cardboard Challenge. That's when the idea struck her: could a day of play and making with simple materials reunite the children of Mostar?

Peric reached out to Association Plus (Plus), a local organization working to improve society through education and community-building initiatives, to help her plan the event. The first thing they did was send letters to principals at every school in Mostar requesting their participation. She

Figure 7.4 Children at the Mostar Imagination Foundation make Rube Goldberg Machines using cardboard and various items.

wasn't sure what to expect, but 17 out of the 22 schools actually said yes. Peric and Plus continued to prepare, and recruit local businesses. And on the day of the Challenge, 260 Croat and Bosniak fifth, sixth and seventh graders came together for a day of imagination, creativity, and play.

"It was a special moment when I saw them coming into the place where we organized the event," she says. "They were all smiling, carrying boxes, and my heart was, how do you say . . . as a big as a house."

The kids broke into teams, collaborated on ideas in different building stations, and made an assortment of artifacts: a cardboard stove, chess game, basketball game, a few castles, a robot, vending machine, train, some musical instruments . . . One of the teams, a collection of Bosniak and Croatian children, built the famous Mostar bridge which divides their two communities.

Peric says that something like this is unimaginable to Bosnian politicians. They say bringing Croats and Bosniaks together under one roof is impossible. "This proves that it can happen," she declares.

Peric not only wanted to bring communities together; she also wanted to help kids explore their imaginations.

There has been so much political and economic strife in the area that creativity and critical thinking in education have fallen by the wayside, she says. This is why next year, she is set on hosting another Cardboard Challenge in her town and bringing this day of creativity and imagination to schools across all of Herzegovina—the southern region of Bosnia and Herzegovina.

"We want to engage every school, and continue to bridge the ethnic divide. The children need hope," she says, "and then everything after that is easy."

(Inglee, 2013)

Imagination Chapters: A "Pop Up" Model for Creative Play

Led by community member Matea Peric, Mostar also became home to one of the world's first Imagination Chapters.

Like Matea, GCC organizers from around the world wanted to drive longer engagement with children through activities like the Cardboard Challenge. In response to this desire, we designed an educational model we call Imagination Chapters—a context for consistent and repeated engagement in Creative Play. We define Chapters as "pop-up" learning spaces that foster creativity, entrepreneurship, and 21st-century skills through Creative Play. The Chapter model is an agile one that works with a specific cohort of children over time, within numerous contexts.

Chapters are community organized and volunteer led. They are designed to launch in a variety of locations and can accommodate whatever resources are available, low tech or high (especially and including recyclables). Many Chapters launch in classrooms and operate as part of the regular school day. Others launch in homes, libraries, and community centers and alongside afterschool programs or other nonprofits. Professional educators. as well as other adults, from all walks of life, can start and lead an Imagination Chapter. Consistent with the simple pedagogical framework of Creative Play, the Chapter model is straightforward and works like this:

A cohort of approximately 20 children gather weekly for 2 hours in places like homes, classrooms, parks, and other spaces. Sessions are facilitated by teachers or adult volunteers from all walks of life.	During the meet-up (or over a series of meet-ups), children make something using available resources. Projects are as diverse as children's imaginations and can escalate from simple to highly advanced materials.	Children share their creations in a meaningful public context, with parents, friends, and the local community or online. Sharing can be as simple as show-and-tell, or it can involve the whole community through an event.

The focal point of a Chapter meet-up is a Creative Play session. Sessions can align to different themes, disciplines, or content standards, and the most engaging sessions will follow from child interest. Sessions can be simple or complex depending on participant age, context, materials, and facilitator experience. Simple projects may take two hours to complete; others may take weeks.

In 2014, Chapters were piloted at 30 sites in 6 countries, in contexts that range from Pre-K through early high school. And, in 2015, 100 additional sites were added. *Caine's Arcade* fandom remains a prominent driving factor in the proliferation of Chapters, and Cardboard Challenges remain a favorite exercise. But because Chapters offer repeated engagement for children, opportunities exist for the introduction of additional tools and materials and the advancement of more complex skills.

Chapters conduct their activities in "real life" within their local communities, but they participate in a global network as well, sharing their ideas, artifacts, stories, and experiences with other Chapters around the world. This exchange is facilitated by popular social media platforms, like Facebook Groups, Google Hangouts, and Skype sessions, and works to build the capacity of Chapter Leaders as well as enrich child experience.

Chapters demonstrate an enormous variety of characteristics depending on age of participants, location of sessions, experience level of facilitators, and the various materials, themes, and skills explored. The following are some intriguing examples of the wide range and versatility of Chapters:

Building a DIY Playground with Cardboard

In Lincoln, Nebraska, preschoolers at the Nature Explore Imagination Chapter experiment with tools by Makedo (reusable plastic connectors that increase the complexity of build projects using cardboard and recyclables). Kids work together to build life-size habitats and play structures out of cardboard in an outdoor classroom setting.

Making with Code and Electronics

Denver's Imagination Chapter dives into coding. In one session, with the help of Chromebooks and Scratch programming, kids use MaKey MaKey circuit boards (supplied by Imagination Foundation sponsor, SparkFun) to turn Play-Doh into working keyboard controllers. Sessions are hosted every weekend at the school district's technology center.

Re-Engineering Old Technology

For the Hornung Elementary Imagination Chapter's Take Apart Day, kids dismantle items like VHS players and old remote controls, examine their inner workings, and then repurpose spare components and turn them into robots and other inventions. The Chapter meets weekly after school.

Designing Solutions for Real-World Problems

Following their motto, "We make the world more awesome," Allisonville Imagination Chapter fifth graders work with local organizations to solve problems in their community. In a collaboration with Indy Humane, an animal shelter, kids design beds for animals. The Chapter meets in class as well as takes field trips to local sites.

Conclusion

In our work to unpack the unexpected and even surprising educational impact of *Caine's Arcade*, there is a clear through line—that creativity is universally present among children, and sometimes the best thing adults can do is step back a bit and give children space to unleash their creative genius. The Global Cardboard Challenge (GCC) has provided numerous opportunities to observe this point.

Our Creative Play pedagogy was designed in close observation of GCC activities in an attempt to give a coherent framework to all that creative frenzy, but also to attach it to a larger conversation about education, the value of play and "making," and how children learn best.

Imagination Chapters emerged as a new child-centered and highly agile model for consistent and repeated engagement in Creative Play. Today there are over 125 Imagination Chapters in 23 countries; another unexpected outcome of an 11-minute short film about a 9-year-old boy and his cardboard arcade.

What can we further say about the impact of *Caine's Arcade*? For example, how does this film (and the programs that have followed) impact traditional education and the role of schools and teachers? Or informal education and the role of parents and community members? How is *Caine's Arcade* changing the conversation around labels we give to children like "gifted" or "genius"?

Or what it means to prepare kids for 21st-century jobs? Or the tools and tactics we need to get kids STEM ready? With hundreds of teachers, volunteers, and leaders from around the world, we are in the process of answering these questions. For now, we can offer a few compelling conclusions:

1. Schools are only one part of a vast educational ecosystem. Creative Play is a way to unlock the potential of informal learning environments and align them to 21st-century needs.
2. STEM and 21st-century skills don't have to be taught with 21st-century technology. In fact, by focusing more on Creative Play and less on modern tools (e.g., 3D printers) or explicit STEM-related content (e.g., robotics), we can engage groups that are underrepresented in STEM fields (like girls and children of color). Cardboard is ubiquitous, and playing with it is universally appealing. We can build on that (so to speak) to proliferate STEM learning more widely.
3. Start with a "low floor" but have a "high ceiling." Creative Play exercises can escalate from cardboard to more complex materials and advanced skills. For example, by introducing different tools to cardboard (e.g., MakeDo, which is a set cardboard-focused construction tools) artifacts become more intricate. And by introducing circuits to cardboard (e.g., via LittleBits), children can make their artifacts light up, or move and make noise. Experienced educators can effectively layer a wealth of additional content and skills onto a Creative Play exercise. However, there's a lot to be said for kids figuring things out for themselves as they tinker and play with new materials. Inexperienced educators or parents can also tinker alongside their kids as co-learners.
4. Anyone anywhere can help foster child creativity. Whether it's by hosting a GCC-like activity, or starting an Imagination Chapter, Creative Play is rather simple to facilitate. Its value is in the experience of the Creative Play spiral, using whatever resources are at hand. It avoids a reliance on heavy training, cost-prohibitive materials, or expensive infrastructures. In this sense, it's an educational model that's at once cutting edge and egalitarian.

References

Ananiadou, K. & Claro, M. (2009). 21st century skills and competences for new millennium learners in OECD countries. *OECD Education Working Papers*, No. 41. OECD Publishing. doi:10.1787/218525261154

Banks, S. (2012, April 21). The secret of the cardboard arcade. *Los Angeles Times*. Retrieved on September 12, 2015 from articles.latimes.com/2012/apr/21/local/la-me-banks-20120421

Bronson, P. & Merryman, A. (2010, July 10). The creativity crisis. *Newsweek*. Retrieved on September 12, 2015 from www.newsweek.com/creativity-crisis-74665

Goodale, G. (2012, April 13). Why 'Caine's Arcade' moves grown men to tears (+video). *The Christian Science Monitor*. Retrieved on September 12, 2015 from www.csmonitor.com/USA/Society/2012/0413/Why-Caine-s-Arcade-moves-grown-men-to-tears-video

Inglee, J. (2013). Imagination reunites a divided town in Bosnia. *Imagination Foundation*. Retrieved on September 12, 2015 from imagination.is/storybook/imagination-rebuilds-a-war-torn-bosnian-town/

LEGO Foundation. (n.d.). The LEGO Foundation and Ashoka announce 10 champions of the re-imagine learning challenge. *LEGO Foundation*. Retrieved on September 12, 2015 from www.legofoundation.com/en-us/newsroom/articles/2014/champions-reimagine-learning-challenge/

Melby, C. (2012, April 12). 9 reasons why the 9-year-old founder of Caine's Arcade will be a billionaire in 30 years. *Forbes*. Retrieved on September 12, 2015 from www.forbes.com/sites/calebmelby/2012/04/12/9-reasons-why-the-9-year-old-founder-of-caines-arcade-will-be-a-billionaire-in-30-years/

Papert, S. (1993). *The children's machine: Rethinking school in the age of the computer*. New York: Basic Books.

Regalla, L. (2016). Developing a maker mindset. In K. Peppler, E. Halverson, & Y. Kafai (Eds.), *Makeology: Makerspaces as learning environments* (Volume 1) (pp. 257–272). New York, NY: Routledge.

Resnick, M. (2007, June). All I really need to know (about creative thinking) I learned (by studying how children learn) in kindergarten. In *Proceedings of the 6th ACM SIGCHI Conference on Creativity & Cognition* (pp. 1–6). Washington, DC: ACM Press. doi:10.1145/1254960.1254961

CHAPTER 8

Electronics Meets Textiles

Sewing the Way to Powerful New Ideas About Technology

SOPHIA BENDER

Introduction

Many of the "big-name" maker toolkits, like 3D printers and robots, tend to be considered "masculine" and are primarily used by men, as discussed in chapter 5 of this volume. This chapter explores e-textiles—electronics embedded into clothing and other soft wearables—which exemplify a different, "softer" way of "doing" technology and making, one that women tend to find more attractive (see, for example, Buechley & Hill, 2010). This means that the act of creating e-textiles has the potential to engender "powerful ideas" that make historical, cultural, domain, personal, and epistemological connections related to how we think about technology, what it can and should do, and who should be involved in it (Bers, 1995; Papert, 1980). This chapter will profile several e-textile toolkits and show how they can be a source of powerful ideas.

Textile crafts have a long history, of course, and, in our culture, at least, they tend to be viewed as traditionally feminine and undervalued (Burman, 1999; Green, 1996). Many modern textile crafters are part of an indie DIY craft movement that espouses many of the same values as the Maker Movement, but, according to Levine and Heimerl (2008), predates it. These values include dignity in creation, making as activism, and personal production rather than mass production (Levine & Heimerl, 2008). Despite this shared commitment, the two communities rarely intersect. *MAKE* magazine rarely if ever features crafts or textiles (Buechley, 2013), and our personal experience at Maker Faires shows us that they tend to relegate traditional crafts to small, out-of-the-way areas. Meanwhile, it's the Maker

Movement that's receiving all the big press and accolades, while traditionally feminine crafts remain on the margins.

E-textiles, by incorporating electronics into textile crafts, represent a site where these two communities intersect on a material level. Thus, they help us to rethink the separation between maker technology and craft.

The next section will focus in on several sets of e-textile tools: the LilyPad Arduino, Adafruit FLORA, and Aniomagic kits. Parts in the LilyPad Arduino toolkit all have large sew holes for easy wrapping of conductive thread, are well marked with information pertinent to the circuitry and programming of the parts, and are easy to get to work, as well as allowing for highly advanced, elaborate projects—in other words, LilyPad parts have a "low floor and wide walls" (Resnick & Silverman, 2005). The Adafruit FLORA toolkit is very similar to the LilyPad—also Arduino compatible, but with some different options for parts. The Aniomagic kits (now retired) also featured LEDs, sensors, and controller boards designed to be sewable, but they greatly simplified programming with a web interface that reprograms "over the air." All these toolkits bring their own unique affordances to the table.

E-Textile Construction Kits

The LilyPad Arduino (Figures 8.1–8.4) was a trailblazer in e-textile technology. The first LilyPad came into being when designer and computer scientist Dr. Leah Buechley became frustrated with the lack of options for

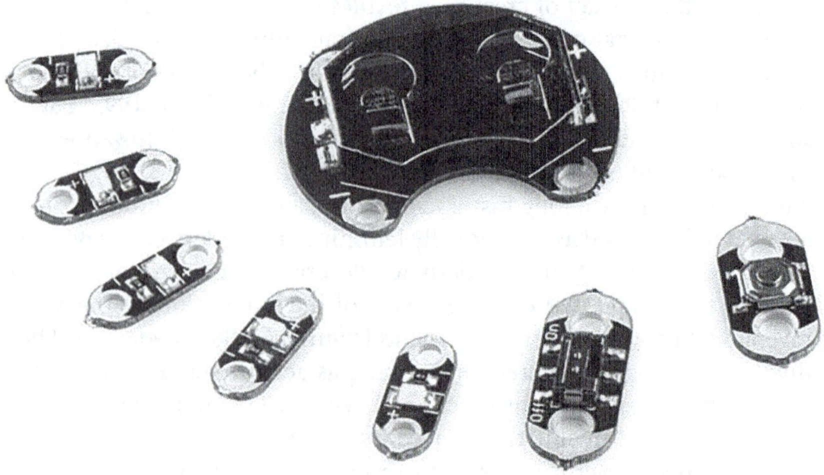

Figure 8.1 LilyPad LEDs, battery holder, and switches.

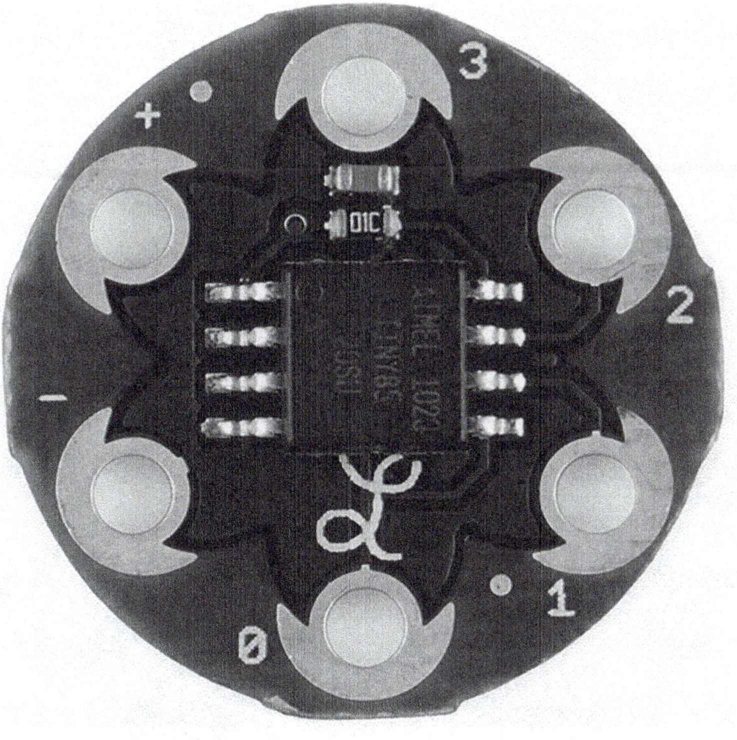

Figure 8.2 LilyTiny.

wearable computing. Her first prototype of the LilyPad Arduino microcontroller involved attaching the main chip of an Arduino microcontroller to a piece of fabric, with conductive fabric leading from the programmable pins of the microcontroller outward in a flower shape (Buechley, Peppler, Eisenberg, & Kafai, 2013). Today, the LilyPad Arduino, as pictured below in Figure 8.4, is made with plastic to facilitate mass production, but it still retains its round flower shape. The Arduino microcontroller is one of the most popular platforms for physical computing, but, for most Arduino boards, you need to connect parts with wires, breadboards, and solder. The LilyPad was revolutionary in being the first Arduino board that easily facilitated a soft approach, involving sewing with conductive thread directly onto fabric.

Buechley, as part of her work at the MIT Media Lab, developed several additional sewable components to go along with the LilyPad Arduino. The simplest LilyPad parts (Figure 8.1) are LEDs (light-emitting diodes) that

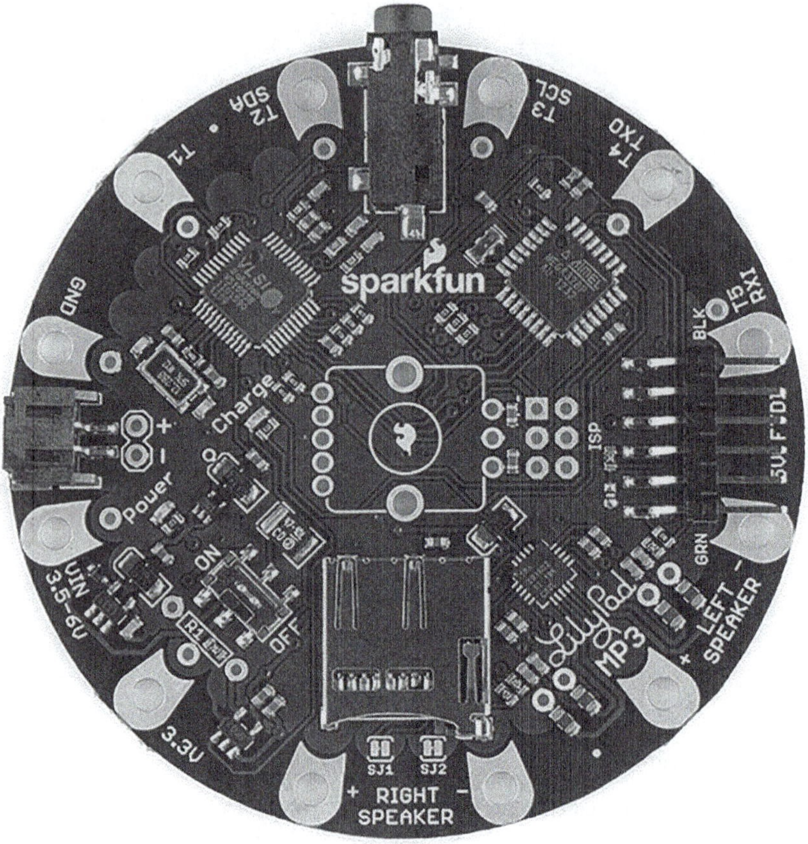

Figure 8.3 LilyPad MP3.

come in an array of colors, all clearly marked with a positive or negative sign near each of the two sew holes, to indicate polarity. Sew a loop with conductive thread from an LED to a Lilypad 3V coin cell battery holder (also clearly marked for polarity), and you will have created the simplest possible circuit with e-textile parts. You can add a switch to the circuit, either a slide switch or push button.

Computational parts can make your circuit more complex. The LilyTiny (Figure 8.2) and LilyTwinkle both contain small microcontrollers that come preprogrammed to allow LEDs sewn to their pins (the holes) to flash in different patterns. The LilyPad MP3 (Figure 8.3) comes preprogrammed to allow you to play up to five MP3 files that you load to it with a MicroSD card, if you also attach switches and speakers or headphones. Essentially,

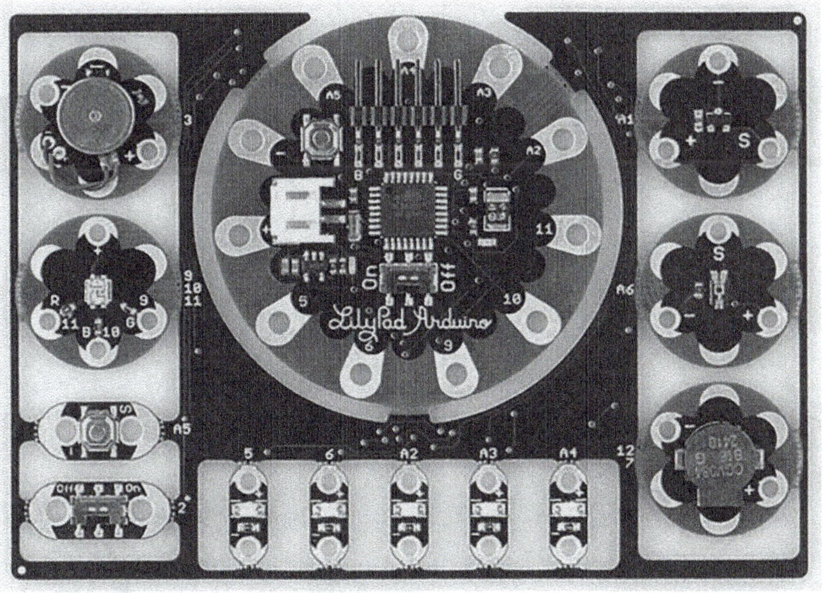

Figure 8.4 The ProtoSnap LilyPad Development Board, with LilyPad Arduino Simple Board along with LEDs, switches, buzzers, and sensors, all connected on a single board for easy programming and easily snapped apart to be sewn onto your project.

Image courtesy of SparkFun Electronics, licensed as CC BY-NC-SA 3.0.

it allows you to have a wearable music player. All of these preprogrammed parts can be reprogrammed with a little bit of hacking and coding.

If you want to do your own programming from the start, then the original LilyPad Arduino and a simplified version with fewer pins called the LilyPad Simple allow you to do so. They can be programmed with the well-known Arduino programming language, or with simpler block-based interfaces such as Modkit or ArduBlock. There is no difference between the way you program a LilyPad and the way you program other, more conventional Arduino boards such as the Arduino Uno, because the basic microcontroller chip is the same.

You can program the LilyPad to control the flashing of LEDs, to play music notes with the LilyPad Buzzer, and to interact with light sensors, temperature sensors, and myriad other sewable parts. All you need to do is sew with conductive thread to the pins of the boards, located on the petal-shaped sewable pads.

Buechley and her collaborators at the online retailer SparkFun continue to develop new parts for the LilyPad set and to promote continued education through these materials (Buechley et al., 2013; Buechley, Qiu, & de Boer, 2013; Peppler, Gresalfi, Salen Tekinbaş, & Santo, 2014; Peppler,

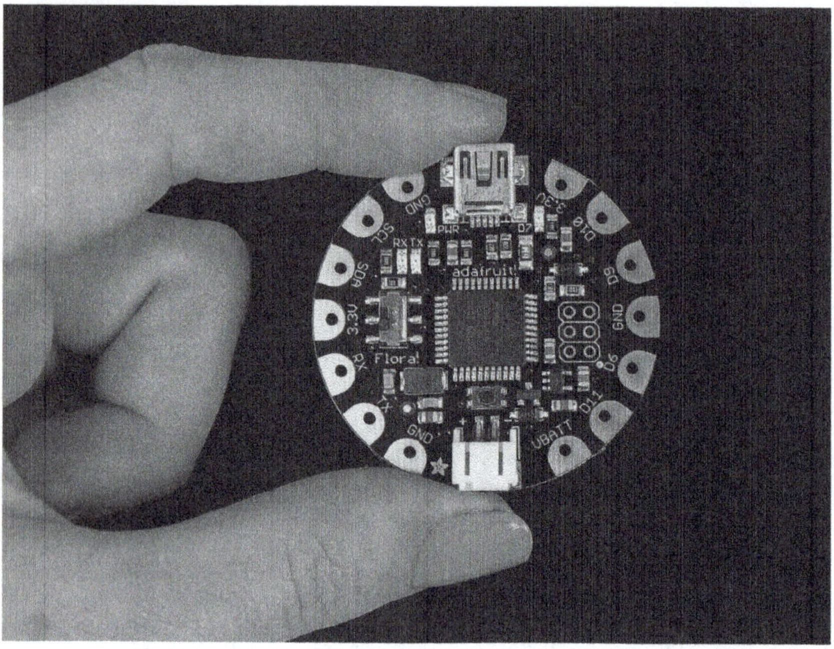

Figure 8.5 Adafruit FLORA board.

Salen Tekinbaş, Gresalfi, & Santo, 2014). More information can be found at lilypadarduino.org.

Adafruit's FLORA board (Figure 8.5) is very similar to the LilyPad—round, sewable, powered by the same sorts of batteries, and programmable through Arduino. The Adafruit e-textiles set contains many of the same parts as the LilyPad set, including LEDs (called "LED sequins"), a light sensor, and an accelerometer. But it also includes additional modules such as a color sensor, UV sensor, and even a GPS module (Figure 8.6). The focus of the FLORA set appears to be on programming, because it tends to promote its programmable NeoPixels (Figure 8.7) that can shine in any color, rather than the static LED sequins. NeoPixels must be programmed and attached to a board in order to work (unlike LilyPad LEDs, which will light up when just attached to a battery), and the mini version of the FLORA, called the GEMMA (Adafruit's version of the LilyTiny) (Figure 8.7) does not come preprogrammed. The result is the FLORA kits may be harder for novices to use, but, on the other hand, the possibilities for interaction with the outside world through sensors are far more numerous than with the LilyPad. Online retailer Adafruit also continues to develop new parts for this set and regularly posts example FLORA projects on its site to inspire users.

Figure 8.6 Adafruit FLORA GPS Module connected to a battery and a FLORA board.

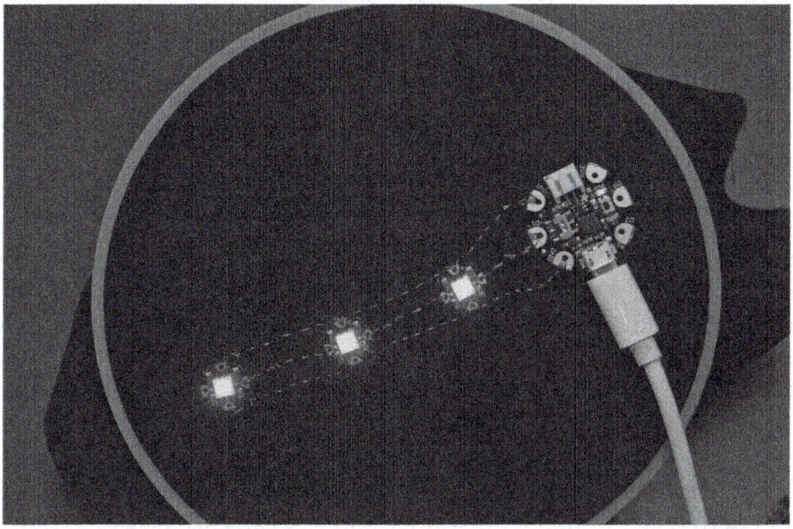

Figure 8.7 Adafruit GEMMA, a smaller version of the FLORA. Does not come preprogrammed like the LilyTiny, but has a built-in mini USB port for easy connection to a computer. Attached to RGB Smart NeoPixel LEDs. The NeoPixels can be programmed to shine in any color, unlike most LilyPad LEDs, which come with a predetermined color.

Dr. Nwanua Elumeze's Aniomagic set was born out of his collaboration with Buechley and Dr. Mike Eisenberg at the University of Colorado, Boulder. Elumeze's innovations address his frustration with having to drag around several accoutrements, such as USB cords, to reprogram even the simplest of computational textile projects. He introduced a very straightforward online or mobile programming interface that can send programs to the Aniomagic boards "through the air" (Elumeze, 2013), just by waving the board in front of the screen. No physical connections are needed. This makes these kits novice-friendly, introducing computational concepts such as if–then logic without need for any technical knowledge.

Aniomagic's several kits each fulfilled a different purpose. The Sparkle kits allowed for simple sensing interaction—a touch switch, a tilt switch, or a sound-triggered switch, along with LEDs that you could program to flash in two patterns: one for when the circuit is "at rest," and one for when the switch is triggered. The Colorwell was a sewable, programmable RGB LED that could flash in any of 10 colors and did not need to be connected to any additional boards, though it could be incorporated into a circuit with one of Aniomagic's other sensors. The Chiclet board allowed for more advanced sensing interactions, including light, temperature, sound, and touch sensors, accelerometers, magnet switches, infrared switches, and motorboards. Though no longer commercially available, the Aniomagic kits represented a unique approach to communication between computers and e-textiles through ambient programming, an approach that has many implications for the growing Internet of Things trend, in which it is envisioned that many "smart objects" in the home will be able to communicate in an ambient manner.

E-textile creators, like others in the DIY handcrafting movement, are also known for creating their own parts to add to their projects, parts that can be made from easily accessible materials but cannot be found in commercially available kits. Designer Hannah Perner-Wilson, a former student of Leah Buechley's at MIT Media Lab, went on to form the design collaborative Kobakant. With her collaborator Mika Satomi, she has explored numerous computational interactions that question our traditional notions of electronics as hard, blocky, and wiry by incorporating traditional crafts. Many of her innovations involve textiles. For instance, her "stroke sensor" (Figure 8.8) consists of several short conductive "hairs" that, when stroked, flatten out and complete a circuit between patches of conductive fabric sewn on the back. Besides conductive thread, there are types of fabric, yarn, and Velcro that are conductive as well, and you can curl the legs of regular two-pronged LEDs to make them sewable. All can be creatively incorporated into e-textile projects.

This description of various e-textile materials should already help to demonstrate how e-textiles differ from typical tools used to engage with

Figure 8.8 Hannah Perner-Wilson's stroke sensor made with conductive fabric and thread.

www.kobakant.at/DIY/?p=792

technology. In contrast with the blockiness, sharp edges, and hard plastics and metals of other popular DIY technologies such as robotics, e-textiles offer softness, malleability, and, often, beauty. In contrast with practices such as wiring, soldering, and bolting, e-textiles can involve sewing, embroidery, and knotting. Instead of a purely functional object such as a robot meant to win competitions or an Arduino-powered "smart house" full of sensors, e-textiles are intensely personal and personally meaningful, worn in public as a statement about the self, just as ordinary clothing is. They marry high and low tech and not only bring traditionally devalued "feminine" crafting practices to the domain of computing and electronics, but also do so in such a way that the crafting and electronics cannot be meaningfully separated. As such, e-textile creation is a fruitful means of engaging in critical making and triggering powerful ideas about how and who can "do" technology.

E-Textile Creation as Sites for Powerful Ideas

How can e-textiles become a foundation for "powerful ideas" in the tradition of constructionism (Papert, 1980)? Constructionism, an extension of Piaget's constructivism, posits that learning occurs best when learners can construct shareable, personally meaningful artifacts that represent (and help facilitate) the mental constructions they are building (Harel & Papert, 1991). Papert takes this to be about more than just the learning of content domains. Sufficiently powerful "objects to think with" can also help us change the way we think about history, culture, the personal, and even the epistemological—to change the way we think about learning and knowledge itself (Bers, 1995; Papert, 1980). As Bers (1995) puts it, "powerful ideas afford new ways of thinking, new ways of putting knowledge to use, and new ways of making personal and epistemological connections with other domains of knowledge" (p. 23). From a constructionist perspective, helping children encounter powerful ideas is one of the primary goals of education. By making historical, cultural, domain, personal, and epistemological connections, powerful ideas bring about a fundamental reorganization of thinking, knowledge, and action (Bers, 1995). In terms of technology, we need new ways of thinking about it so that it will seem more accessible to women and others who feel shut out from it (Margolis, 2008; Margolis & Fisher, 2003). The construction of e-textiles provides the connections necessary to bring about this powerful shift in thinking about and with technology.

Historical Connections

The connection between textiles and computing goes almost as far back in the history of computing as it is possible to go. The first programmable machine was the Jacquard loom, which made use of punched cards to "program" the loom to weave patterns into silk (Essinger, 2007). Essinger's book *Jacquard's Web* shows how, through a complex series of circumstances, this eventually led directly to computing as we know it today. During the Victorian period, Charles Babbage worked on conceptualizing and building the first modern computer by adapting the punched card system of the Jacquard loom (Essinger, 2007). His associate Ada Lovelace—a woman—saw the potential of Babbage's creation to "*weave [. . .] algebraical patterns* just as the Jacquard loom weaves flowers and leaves" (Menabrea, 1843, p. 697, as cited in Whitson, 2015, emphasis original). In fact, it was she and not Babbage who wrote the first computer program, one that could generate Bernoulli numbers (Whitson, 2015).

Critical making involving historical precedent allows makers to "repurpose history and imagine alternatives" (Whitson, under contract, p. 4). Whitson discusses this in the context of steampunk artifacts, which imagine an alternative Victorian history that can in turn question the inevitability of how history has played out. The process of creating e-textiles can be similarly historically critical, by recovering connections to textiles and the feminine in computing that the dominant cultural narrative has suppressed.

It is important to note that making these historical connections is not inevitable. Just as there can be unreflective steampunk making that does not attempt critical engagement with history, there can also be unreflective e-textile making. But, at the least, e-textiles involve makers in a long tradition of textiles and the feminine in computing. With appropriate facilitation of reflection, e-textile creation can help us start to change the way we view the history of computing, as inextricably interwoven with traditionally feminine textile crafts.

This new view of history is a powerful idea that can start to break down gender barriers in computing and other technological fields, as well as help us rethink the way we "do" technology. With time, perhaps this historical view of the pervasive role of textiles and the feminine in computing will become prevalent in our culture and persist over the generations, rather than remaining forgotten and obscured. This is what Bers (1995) says is necessary for a powerful idea to make historical connections. Getting e-textiles to reach a broader audience can help to facilitate this process.

Cultural Connections

The dominant cultural narrative around technology and computing is stereotypically masculinized. E-textiles *can* represent a more feminine approach to computing, but do they really in practice? Do women in fact identify with e-textiles more than they tend to do with more traditional forms of electronics? And, if so, what implications does this have for the cultural narrative surrounding technology and computing? Recent work suggests that women are more likely than men to engage in the e-textile community. For instance, Buechley and Hill (2010) found that, as compared to projects posted online made with conventional Arduino microcontrollers, more online LilyPad projects were created by women. The difference was striking; 86% of the conventional Arduino projects they located were made by men, while 65% of the LilyPad projects were made by women. This has the exciting implication that e-textiles appear to be the first computing field dominated by women.

The LilyPad kit is also perceived by youth to be generally more feminine than other circuit kits are. When youth are asked to sort five circuit kits into bins labeled with "Boys," "Both," and "Girls," youth are more likely, on average, to sort e-textiles more towards the "Girls" side of the spectrum (Peppler, Thompson, Bender, & Wohlwend, 2015). They did not do the same with the other circuit kits, one of which involved pieces that snap together, one that had magnetic pieces, one that used Play-Doh as "wires," and a conventional circuit kit with alligator clips and nonpolar bulbs similar to the one used in many schools.

So, e-textiles seem to have been taken up more by women than by men and are perceived as more feminine (for more on gender in e-textiles, see chapter 5 of this volume). But in order for this new, different approach to technology to become a powerful idea that subverts the masculine narrative around technology, Bers (1995) says the culture needs to reach "consensus about its importance and relevance for the culture itself. At the same time, once installed in society, a powerful idea naturalizes itself and appears as if it was always there" (p. 25). As e-textiles become more pervasive in our culture, perhaps they will be able to achieve this. Perhaps, one day, no one will assume that a radio *must* be controlled by hard buttons and knobs, but will understand that it could also be controlled by textile-based interactions like wrapping and twisting, as in Ramyah Gowrishankar's Soft Radio (vimeo.com/68115876). Perhaps no one will question that a pillow can softly sing you to sleep, like Hannah Perner-Wilson's pillow with an embroidered speaker (Figure 8.9). When many different approaches to technology become acceptable in our culture—approaches that appeal to all different kinds of people so that the gender gaps in technology fields close—then, perhaps, no one will ever again question the presence of women in technology fields. Pervasive use and wearing of e-textiles may help to accomplish this.

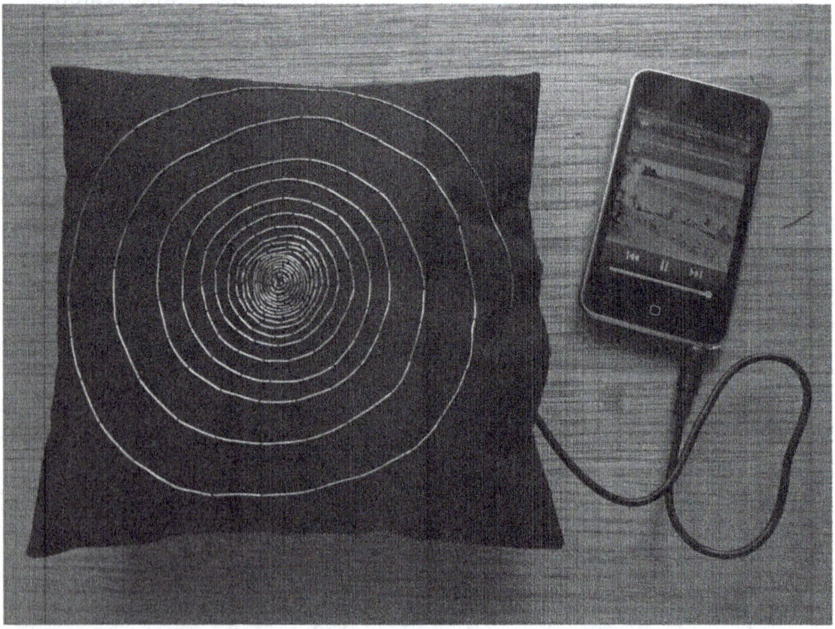

Figure 8.9 Hannah Perner-Wilson's embroidered speaker.

www.flickr.com/photos/plusea/8310204975/in/album-72157632347234398/

Domain Connections

When making connections to a domain of content knowledge, powerful ideas must do more than just help increase learning in that domain. According to Bers (1995), "Powerful ideas serve as organizing principles for rethinking a whole domain of knowledge and connecting it with others" (p. 26). For e-textiles, then, the questions become, do e-textiles help organize the domains of electronics and computation? And do they connect to any other domains of knowledge?

Misconceptions about circuitry abound in our society, including misconceptions about polarity, the necessity for tight connections between points in a circuit, current flow, and causes of short circuits (Evans, 1978; Fredette & Lochhead, 1980). These misconceptions—especially the one about polarity—are exacerbated by traditional circuit kits used in schools that make use of nonpolar light bulbs. In fact, our recent work has shown that, when compared to students who played with other circuit kits including e-textiles, students who played with a traditional nonpolar bulb kit, on average, actually had *decreased* polarity scores on their posttests (Peppler, Tan, Thompson, & Bender, 2015). Anecdotally, we have found that elementary school teachers who regularly teach circuitry to their students with nonpolar bulbs have trouble when confronted with polar components such as LEDs. Continuing to teach with materials like nonpolar bulbs in which polarity doesn't matter clashes with the reality that most electronic components must take polarity into account. Additionally, Kafai and Peppler (2014) reported on a large-scale e-textile workshop that Peppler and her colleagues did with women involved with computing at the university level, ranging from undergraduate novices to tenured professors. Here they found that even those already steeped in the domains of electronics and computing ran into the same problems in their e-textile circuits that youth with no experience did in other workshops, such as causing shorts, reversing the polarity of the LEDs, and not making tight enough connections with the thread around conductive sew holes. This seems to point to a lack of transparency in the types of electronics these women were used to working with, which in turn made transfer of concepts difficult to the new domain of e-textiles (Kafai & Peppler, 2014). Indeed, today's popular electronic devices seem to intentionally black-box how they work, hiding their "guts" beneath sleek exteriors and voiding warranties when curious customers try to poke under the case to figure out the internal mechanisms.

In contrast, e-textiles make circuitry concepts such as polarity, connections, current flow, and short circuits highly visible. LilyPad and Aniomagic parts, in particular, are very clear about their polarity. Connections become salient when you must wrap your conductive thread several times around a sew hole in order to make a tight connection that will communicate with the rest of the circuit. Current flow becomes clear in the closed loop you must sew between all the components. Finally, conductive thread is uninsulated, unlike most wires, which are coated in plastic. This means it is easier to create short circuits, and thus it is easier to learn about what causes shorts and how to fix them. As for computing, the programming process becomes visible to users when they can directly see the connections between their coding and the behavior of their LEDs, sensors, and other components.

With this visibility, it should come as no surprise that youth who sew e-textile projects significantly increase their understanding of circuitry concepts (Peppler & Glosson, 2013) and are better able to transfer this understanding to other circuit kits (Peppler, Tan, et al., 2015). As for computing, Buechley, Eisenberg, and Elumeze (2007) and Kafai et al. (2014) both found that engaging in workshops that involved programming the LilyPad with the Arduino language helped youth to learn more about programming and to see coding as more personally relevant and attainable. Therefore, the process of making e-textiles seems to help organize the domains of circuitry and computing by making concepts visible, so that learners can transfer their understanding to other materials and see the relevance of computing to their everyday lives.

Finally, e-textiles make a connection to traditional textile crafts, a domain that is not often associated with electronics and computing, despite the history behind these fields, as outlined above. With sewable e-textile parts, at least, this connection is impossible to disentangle. Sewing properly with conductive thread is just as integral to the function of the e-textile circuit as the electric components are. Failing to stitch, loose loops, and improperly tied knots are weaknesses in craft that have a direct impact upon the function of the circuit (for more on the connections between craft and electronics in e-textiles, see chapter 13 of this volume). What this domain connection means is that those who have a preexisting interest in the domain of textile crafts can use e-textiles as a bridge into the domains of electronics and programming and vice versa, which they may not have done otherwise, as discussed in chapter 5 of this volume. This is an especially salient point given the rich history of sewing and other forms of crafting that are often passed down generationally (Gonzalez, Moll, & Amanti, 2005). E-textiles, especially with the toolkits outlined in this chapter, privilege all of these domains equally.

Personal Connections

Clothing decisions tend to be intensely personal. After all, clothing is external and visible to everyone we interact with visually. Many people see garment choices as an expression of self. All this is acutely present in the creation of e-textiles. When makers sew an e-textile project, they are actively aware of the fact that they are creating something to be worn, so they take care to make it something they would want to wear—or if it is to be a gift, something that the recipient of this gift would want to wear.

In our lab's many experiences with e-textile workshops, we have never seen two projects turn out looking exactly the same. Even when the workshop is short and youth are given only a single choice of circuit design, they find a way to personalize with their choice of color of fabric and LEDs, with the decorative materials we provide, and sometimes even in the way they choose to stitch their conductive thread. This is a marked contrast to other circuit kits such as the traditional one used in schools. If you are simply hooking alligator clips between a battery and a bulb, your circuit will look no different from anyone else's. In those situations, there is no invitation to personalization and little opportunity for making personal connections,

Figure 8.10 These diverse e-textile projects all came from the same workshop, where youth were asked to sew a LilyPad LED into a felt cuff.

except perhaps in the delight at getting something to light up. But when you must uniquely craft around the circuit and, indeed, incorporate the craft directly *into* the circuit, while remaining aware that you're going to wear this for all the world to see, the potential for making personal connections increases exponentially.

E-textile workshop attendees always tend to leave thinking e-textiles are "cool," but it is more exciting and gratifying when interviews or surveys show that the attendees have come to perceive technology and programming as something they are capable of, something they are more interested in than they were before, and something that is directly relevant to their everyday lives (Buechley et al., 2007; Kafai et al., 2014). These attendees have created a personal connection to the e-textile artifact in the way they personalized it, but they also made a personal connection to the circuitry, the craft, and (if applicable) the programming, because all of these elements are integrated in e-textile projects.

Powerful ideas make personal connections when people can "establish personal relationships with the ideas" (Bers, 1995, p. 25). E-textile creators can establish a personal relationship with this new and unusual way of approaching technology, one that may inspire them to continue approaching technology in this way, which could lead to widespread societal change in the way we "do" technology.

Epistemological Connections

Turkle and Papert (1990) explore how an abstract, formal, and logical epistemology is overprivileged in approaches to computing and in society in general. The problem with this is that the abstract and distant tends to be associated with masculinity, while the more concrete and personal is viewed as not only less mature (as in Piaget's stages), but also more feminine (Turkle & Papert, 1990). Unfortunately, programming even today tends to be taught in an abstract, formal manner that many women do not find approachable (Margolis & Fisher, 2003). Turkle and Papert argue that there is no reason not to approach programming in a more concrete and personal fashion, as it allows people who are used to thinking that way to feel more comfortable in that domain. Programming in itself allows a connection between the abstract code one writes to the concrete effects that can be seen on the screen when a command is carried out, and this connection to the concrete is further strengthened in graphical user interfaces (Turkle & Papert, 1990).

E-textiles—and physical computing in general—take this one step further by taking code one writes on the computer and having it display itself in and interact with the real world. Coders can make a concrete and personal connection with the program they wrote and the lights flashing on their shirts, as the youth did in the study described in chapter 13 of this volume. Additionally, as argued above, clothing is particularly personal. Also, as presented above, the nature of e-textiles helps to make the way they work very visible and transparent to anyone who makes them.

Here we see computing manifested in a tangible and concrete artifact that can be intensely personal and makes visible the way it works. E-textiles encourage an epistemology of computing and technology that shows the importance of the tangible, visible, concrete, and personal. If we as a society valued these things more than the abstract, the hidden, the intangible digital, and the distant, then perhaps we would shut fewer people out of technology fields and would feel freer to approach technology in entirely new ways. The field of e-textiles can help to effect this change, by showing how electronics and coding can be integral parts of our everyday lives, not just in devices that others have designed for us in factories, but in objects in our lives that we have designed, that we choose to wear, and are thus important to us. This can also be a critical process that questions the dominant abstract epistemology and dominant design narratives of mass production. Therefore, e-textile creation really can engender epistemologically powerful, critical ideas.

Conclusions

Despite these promising powerful connections, some challenges remain before e-textiles can become pervasive and before they can help change the dominant narrative around technology. One obvious barrier is cost. Whether working with the LilyPad, FLORA, or Aniomagic kits, the cost of materials can really add up, especially when buying for an entire classroom. This makes it harder for these materials to reach populations with lower incomes, which could just serve to exacerbate existing class-related gaps in technology access and entry into technology fields (see Margolis, 2008, for an exploration of these class- and ethnicity-based technology gaps). Some costs can be defrayed by forgoing the prefabbed parts and creating your own battery holders, switches, and sewable LEDs from less expensive raw materials, but this is impossible with programmable components and also significantly adds to the workload. It seems the problem of expense may not be solved unless further market competition drives costs down.

Another challenge is the Arduino interface itself. It may seem just as unapproachable as any other text-based programming interface, especially to younger children. Fortunately, there are other options. Programming Aniomagic parts requires no specialized knowledge and can be done with just a web browser or smartphone—though functionality is limited. Additionally, the LilyPad can be programmed on block-based, visual programming interfaces such as Modkit and Ardublock, which youth seem to be able to pick up easily. E-textiles may also provide sufficient motivation to overcome misgivings about programming and learn conventional Arduino coding. Certainly this was the case for the youth in Buechley et al. (2007) and Kafai et al.'s (2014) studies. But, there is also the possibility that e-textiles may inspire us to change our programming interfaces entirely. Nwanua Elumeze, founder of Aniomagic, envisions a future where tangible programming is the norm, and simply walking past certain patterns in the environment will reprogram your electronically enhanced garment (2013).

Additionally, e-waste from e-textiles may present a significant environmental challenge in the future, if e-textiles become common. E-textile wearers should be able to keep their garments for as long as possible, pointing to a need for these materials to improve their machine washability. Parts should be reusable—and, in fact, the LilyPad now has a version with snaps, allowing you to easily detach it from one project and snap it to another. Recycling programs should also be set up.

There are in fact ways to overcome all these challenges, and working towards them helps us to envision entirely new, different approaches to technology. Snappable computers, programming your dress through the air, and wearing your smartphone on your sleeve are just the beginning. But e-textiles are more than just tools for making flashy outfits and devices; the process of e-textile creation can help makers make historical, cultural, content domain, personal, and epistemological connections that fundamentally change the way we think about technology. Historically, they can help reconnect us to the role of women and textiles in computing from the very start. Culturally, they can show us a computational field that is dominated by women and approachable for them. In terms of learning circuitry and programming, e-textiles make these concepts visible, as well as connecting inextricably to the domain of textile crafts. E-textile projects can be intensely personal, as makers design something unique that they plan to actually wear. And e-textiles suggest the valuing of a concrete, personal epistemology toward technology, one that welcomes all genders. Together, these powerful ideas of a softer, more concrete, more personal, more transparent approach to technology that marries high and low tech, the masculine and the feminine, and technology with craft suggest an entirely different way of "doing" technology from what we are used to in today's world, a way that can overcome challenges and that opens up new vistas of possibility so far unimagined.

References

Bers, M. U. (1995). *Blocks to robots: Learning with technology in the early childhood classroom.* New York, NY: Teachers College Press.

Buechley, L. (2013, October). *Thinking about making.* Closing Keynote Talk Presented at Fablearn 2013, Stanford, CA.

Buechley, L., Eisenberg, M., & Elumeze, N. (2007). Towards a curriculum for electronic textiles in the high school classroom. *ACM SIGCSE Bulletin, 39*(3), 28. doi:10.1145/1269900.1268795

Buechley, L. & Hill, B. M. (2010). LilyPad in the wild: How hardware's long tail is supporting new engineering and design communities. In *Proceedings of the 8th ACM Conference on Designing Interactive Systems* (pp. 199–207). New York, NY: ACM. doi:10.1145/1858171.1858206

Buechley, L., Peppler, K. A., Eisenberg, M., & Kafai, Y. B. (Eds.). (2013). *Textile messages: Dispatches from the world of e-textiles and education*. New York: Peter Lang.

Buechley, L., Qiu, K., & de Boer, S. (2013). *Sew electric*. Cambridge, MA: HLT Press.

Burman, B. (1999). *The culture of sewing: Gender, consumption and home dressmaking*. New York, NY: Bloomsbury Academic.

Elumeze, N. (2013). Traveling light: Making textiles programmable "through the air." In L. Buechley, K. A. Peppler, M. Eisenberg, & Y. B. Kafai (Eds.), *Textile messages: Dispatches from the world of e-textiles and education* (pp. 43–51). New York, NY: Peter Lang.

Essinger, J. (2007). *Jacquard's web: How a hand-loom led to the birth of the information age*. Oxford, UK: Oxford University Press.

Evans, J. (1978). Teaching electricity with batteries and bulbs. *The Physics Teacher, 16*(1), 15–22. doi:10.1119/1.2339794

Fredette, N., & Lochhead, J. (1980). Students' conceptions of simple circuits. *The Physics Teacher, 18*(3), 194–198. doi:10.4324/978141061346

Gonzalez, N., Moll, L. C., & Amanti, C. (Eds.). (2005). *Funds of knowledge: Theorizing practices in households, communities, and classrooms*. Mahwah, NJ: Routledge.

Green, N. L. (1996). Women and immigrants in the sweatshop: Categories of labor segmentation revisited. *Comparative Studies in Society and History, 38*(3), 411. doi:10.1017/S0010417500020004

Harel, I. E. & Papert, S. E. (1991). *Constructionism*. New York, NY: Ablex Publishing.

Kafai, Y. B., Lee, E., Searle, K., Fields, D., Kaplan, E., & Lui, D. (2014). A crafts-oriented approach to computing in high school: Introducing computational concepts, practices, and perspectives with electronic textiles. *ACM Transactions on Computing Education, 14*(1), 1–20. doi:10.1145/2576874

Kafai, Y. B. & Peppler, K. A. (2014). Transparency reconsidered: Creative, critical, and connected making with e-textiles. In M. Boler & M. Ratto (Eds.), *DIY citizenship* (pp. 179–188). Cambridge, MA: MIT Press.

Levine, F. & Heimerl, C. (2008). *Handmade nation: The rise of DIY, art, craft, and design*. New York: Princeton Architectural Press.

Margolis, J. (2008). *Stuck in the shallow end: Education, race, and computing*. Cambridge, MA: MIT Press.

Margolis, J. & Fisher, A. (2003). *Unlocking the clubhouse: Women in computing*. Cambridge, MA: MIT Press.

Papert, S. (1980). *Mindstorms: Children, computers, and powerful ideas*. New York: Basic Books, Inc.

Peppler, K. & Glosson, D. (2013). Stitching circuits: Learning about circuitry through e-textile materials. *Journal of Science Education and Technology, 22*(5), 751–763. doi:10.1007/s10956-012-9428-2

Peppler, K., Gresalfi, M., Salen Tekinbaş, K., & Santo, R. (2014). *Soft circuits: Crafting e-fashion with DIY electronics*. Cambridge, MA: MIT Press.

Peppler, K., Salen Tekinbaş, K., Gresalfi, M., & Santo, R. (2014). *Short circuits: Crafting e-puppets with DIY electronics*. Cambridge, MA: MIT Press.

Peppler, K., Tan, V., Thompson, N., & Bender, S. (2015, April). *New tools for circuitry learning: Evaluating the efficacy of circuitry construction kits.* Paper Presented at the Annual Meeting of the American Educational Research Association, Chicago, IL.

Peppler, K., Thompson, N., Bender, S., & Wohlwend, K. (2015, April). *"Nothing really for girls": Examining actionable "gendered-ness" of circuitry learning toolkits.* Paper Presented at the Annual Meeting of the American Educational Research Association, Chicago, IL.

Resnick, M. & Silverman, B. (2005). Some reflections on designing construction kits for kids. In *Proceedings of the 2005 Conference on Interaction Design and Children* (pp. 117–122). New York, NY: ACM. doi:10.1145/1109540.1109556

Turkle, S. & Papert, S. (1990). Epistemological pluralism: Styles and voices within the computer culture. *Signs*, *16*(1), 128–157.

Whitson, R. (2015). Critical making in the digital humanities. In J. Wolfrey (Ed.), *Introducing criticism in the twenty-first century*, pp. 157–177. Edinburgh, Scotland: Edinburgh University Press.

Whitson, R. (under contract). Making steampunk, or how to theorize with a hammer and an oven. In B. Croxall & R. Bowser (Eds.), *Like clockwork: Essays on steampunk.* Minneapolis, MN: University of Minnesota Press.

CHAPTER 9

Bridging Crafting and Computing in Making

Designing Interactive Touchpads and Board Games With MaKey MaKey

VEENA VASUDEVAN AND YASMIN B. KAFAI

Introduction

Today's makerspaces include many materials and tools that fall into the categories of either crafts or electronics. MaKey MaKey offers a bridge between crafting, circuitry, and computing. It is a circuit board that gives aspiring makers a way to supplant a traditional keyboard without any programming by using everyday conductive materials. MaKey MaKey's successful Kickstarter campaign in 2012 fueled makers' imaginations to transform everyday conductive things like foil, fruits, and Play-Doh into objects to think and tinker with. Now, three years after the toolkit's initial launch, projects using MaKey MaKey continue to proliferate; even a mobile version is being developed. A quick web search reveals many videos, blog posts, and sites that are devoted to tinkering and making projects with MaKey MaKey. The range and breadth of projects is impressive, including many musical instruments such as guitars and tiny drum sets, remixes of popular children's games like Operation©, and interactive art displays such as touch-sensitive paintings. These projects illustrate the many ways that crafting and computing materials can be brought together to make new things and find new ways of interacting with everyday objects.

In this chapter, we examine this bridge between everyday and craft materials and electronics in context of making games for learning (Kafai, 1995; Kafai & Burke, in press) and consider the affordances of expanding game design activities into the material plane. Play-Doh, paper, and aluminum foil stickers are all easy and accessible materials for making. Add MaKey

MaKey to the mix and it creates many opportunities for youth to make, code, and play their own controllers and games. We present the outcomes of two workshops in which middle school youth used the programming environment Scratch (Resnick et al., 2009) to code and remix games and MaKey MaKey and different conductive materials to expand their designs. In one workshop, middle school youth in small groups designed touchpad game controllers for Scratch video games. In the second project, a different group of middle school youth designed augmented board games with components like digital dice and playing cards. In addition to presenting example projects from these studies, we also examine how youth navigated challenges at the intersection of tangible and digital designs and how they reflected on their efforts and experiences. Using MaKey MaKey for tangible design and Scratch for game programming on the screen in both workshops, we asked first, How do aspiring makers deal with the complexities of coordinating the virtual and tangible designs of their games and controllers? and second, How does designing tangible aspects of digital games impact their overall design process?

These two workshops illustrate how the computational construction kit MaKey MaKey can broaden the boundaries of game design and create more entry points for youth to participate by blending craft and computing. MaKey MaKey "allow[s] children to combine traditional arts and crafts such as sewing and sketching with computation and electronics" (Grover & Pea, 2013, p. 41). While these construction kits have been successful in making participation in computational activities more accessible, there is still significant work to be done. Design projects like the ones we will describe in this chapter help to broaden opportunities to participate in computation by creating more entry points, in this case through the use of craft materials that connect to electronic materials. These activities also give young people opportunities to engage with computational concepts, practices, and perspectives (Brennan & Resnick, 2012; chapter 12 of this volume) through design activities that are facilitated by MaKey MaKey and Scratch programming.

Background

Computational construction activities have long been used to introduce programming to novices (Kelleher & Pausch, 2005; chapter 13 of this volume; Fields & Lee, 2016, in volume 1 of this series). Scratch is a multimedia programming environment (Resnick et al., 2009) where youth can create animations, games, stories, art, music, and more. The concept of remixing is an important aspect of Scratch and other digital media design activities. In Scratch, remixing means that you can take an existing game, story, animation, or other program and put your own twist on it by changing the aesthetics, sounds, or actual functionality. Remixing programs is an accessible activity for beginners because they can tinker with existing designs to make them their own. Anyone can create a game and upload it to the Scratch environment. Once it is shared, others can remix it in any way they see fit. There is an extensive collection of projects with Scratch and other programming environments where youth of all ages have made their own games for learning (for an overview, see Kafai & Burke, in press) and engaged in learning various computational concepts and practices (Kafai & Burke, 2014).

MaKey MaKey is part of the larger family of physical computational construction kits, such as the popular LEGO Mindstorms that provide motors and sensors to bring traditional LEGOs to life (Martin, Mikhak, Resnick, Silverman, & Berg, 2000). Unlike Lego Mindstorms and other computational construction kits such as the LilyPad Arduino (Buechley, Peppler, Eisenberg, & Kafai, 2013; chapter 8 of this volume), MaKey MaKey does not require extensive setup or deep technical knowledge and thus has widened opportunities to tinker, particularly for younger children. This is facilitated by MaKey Makey's function of turning anything conductive into a tangible user interface, simply by using alligator clips as the connective link. The use of these simple connections and everyday materials lowers significantly the barriers to computational prototyping (Silver, Rosenbaum, & Shaw, 2012).

The MaKey MaKey gives users the ability to use conductive objects to replace traditional keyboard inputs, e.g., up, down, right, left, and space bar keys, and in the process learn about conductivity of everyday objects like fruits, Play-Doh, and aluminum foil (see Figure 9.1). It plugs into the

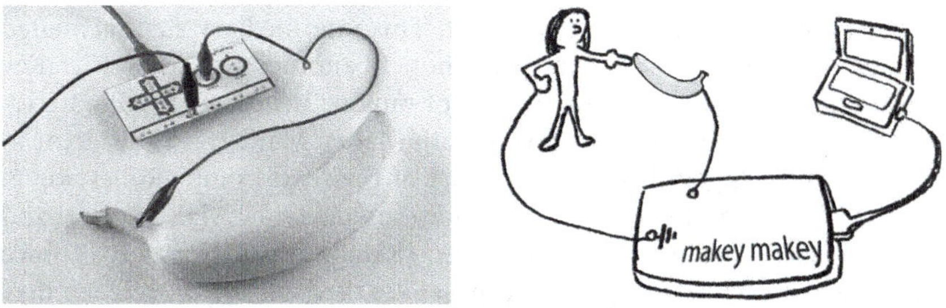

Figure 9.1 (Left) MaKey MaKey with a banana space bar. The upper (red) USB cable connects the MaKey MaKey to the computer, while the left (black) cable is the connection to the earth and the right (blue) cable is connected to the conductive object, in this case the banana that functions as a space bar. (Right) A cartoon setup with the banana illustrating the continuous flow of electricity from person to banana to MaKey MaKey.

Left: sparkfun.com.
Right: ahimsa on flickr.com.

computer using a simple mini-USB to USB cord (in this example, the upper red cable). Another cord (the left black cable) is a connection to earth, which is a way to ground the circuit. Finally, there are cords that connect to the conductive objects (the right blue cord connected to a banana).[1] When a user holds the black wire connected to earth in one hand and touches the banana, the circuit is complete, and thus enables electricity to travel from the computer, through the MaKey MaKey to the banana, and back around. This allows the computer to interpret touching the banana as touching the space bar. Given that many Scratch video games use the basic key controls like up, down, right, left, and the space bar, beginning programmers can easily replace these keys by designing new touchpads and controllers using many conductive materials. These features render MaKey MaKey particularly well suited for tinkering and prototyping for beginning makers (Resnick & Rosenbaum, 2013). The designs work with easy-to-find materials, do not require a great deal of setup, and provide immediate feedback.

Much of the current research using MaKey MaKey has been in informal learning spaces like afterschool programs or summer workshops. In these settings, MaKey MaKey has been used to facilitate prototyping within larger design projects. For instance, in one study 25 youth aged 5–13 from largely underprivileged communities in Mexico blended their cultural knowledge of *alebrijes*—fantastical Mexican folk art creatures meant to protect one from nightmares—with digital augmentation in the form of small LED lights (Hamidi, Saenz, & Baljko, 2014). MaKey MaKey was used in this workshop to help children learn what a simple circuit was, so when it was time to digitally augment their *alebrijes* designs, they could replicate these relationships. Youth were able to work together to create a simple sound effect when they completed the circuit. This intermediary step facilitated further work with circuits in the workshop. In another case, MaKey MaKey was used to facilitate the construction of musical instruments with at-risk youth, with the immediate feedback from MaKey MaKey as a key factor in keeping youth engaged in the early part of their workshop (Robertson & Bertelli, 2014). In our own work, we have used MaKey MaKey to expand game design activities beyond the screen (Kafai & Vasudevan, 2015), since we know that rich learning opportunities are available to youth when they design their own games (Kafai, 1995). Using MaKey MaKey, middle school youth have learned to make wearable game controllers (Vasudevan, Kafai, & Yang, 2015) and designed their own augmented board games (Vasudevan & Kafai, 2015) to learn about crafting, circuitry, and computing. In all of these studies, MaKey MaKey was used to model concepts such as conductivity and circuitry and nurture comfort with technology and amongst children without any extensive prior computing and engineering experience.

In the sections that follow, we look at examples from two pilot studies where middle school youth used MaKey MaKey to enhance their game designs: in the first pilot, youth used Play-Doh and MaKey MaKey to create game controllers for remixed Scratch programs; in the second pilot, youth designed tangible board games that were augmented with digital components like dice and playing cards via MaKey MaKey. Both of the workshops took place with youth aged 11–13 years old at a K–8 public school with an ethnically and economically diverse background located in a northeastern city in the United States. The workshops were part of course electives that include offerings as far reaching as chess, digital photography, and kickball. Each of the five-week long workshops were held twice a week for about 50 minutes. We collected detailed field notes, images of students' artifacts along the process (e.g., draft sketches of board games), youth's final Scratch code, and planning materials. In addition, we conducted interviews with all the participants.

Moving Game Design Beyond the Screen

The Controller Design Workshop: Creating Touchpads With MaKey MaKey

In the winter of 2012–2013, we held a workshop during which seven youth (three boys, four girls) created Scratch video games and extended them with tangible controllers made out of Play-Doh facilitated by MaKey MaKey. The games that youth in our workshop designed were in service of a culminating arcade, where 4th and 5th graders came to play each of the games. In the workshop, youth spent the first few sessions learning the basic Scratch concepts by receiving instruction on how to design a simple game. Youth also had the opportunity to play and tinker with other starter games available on the Scratch website. They eventually selected a game to remix and made changes to the aesthetics (e.g., colors, background, characters) and functionality (e.g., adding scores, adding levels, adding bad guys). By the end of this process, youth had remixed a starter project to create their own video game in Scratch. Then, they learned about MaKey MaKey and designed and tested their own controllers. Finally, they participated in an arcade where 4th- and 5th-grade students visited in small groups (of about 20) to play their games. The youth in our workshop acted as guides and facilitators to explain how to play their games and resolved technical difficulties in real time.

Youth were given Play-Doh, foil tape, and foil as options to create their controllers, but we observed that they gravitated towards Play-Doh because it is easy to work with and familiar. It is also easy to mold and shape, and

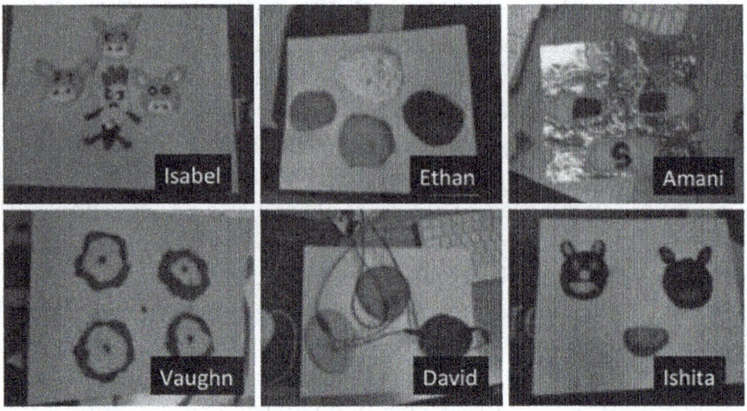

Figure 9.2 MaKey MaKey Touchpads with Play-Doh.

its colors gave those youth interested in aesthetics more opportunities to create controllers that matched their game in some way. When we analyzed the controller designs youth made, we observed two distinct approaches: one group of controllers matched the theme of the Scratch games while the other seemed purely functional. In this first group, some youth crafted controllers to make physical instantiations of sprites (or characters) that they also had created in their Scratch games, while in the second group, youth created buttons to simply play their games—aesthetics were not the primary goal for them (see Figure 9.2).

We now highlight the case of Amani, a 6th-grade student who participated in a previous workshop in which she designed a zombie game in Scratch. We selected Amani because she iterated on her on-screen and tangible controller designs and we felt this was one of the more successful examples we observed in the workshop, in that she engaged in a cohesive design in her on-screen and tangible components, remixed an original design, and improved it to make the game more complex and iterated in real time on the usability of her game upon observing others playing the game. In this workshop, she decided to upgrade her zombie video game. In the original game, the object was to get a zombie to consume brains complete with Michael Jackson's *Thriller* as her background music. In her remix of the zombie game, she kept her original zombie character and the music but added a score, and made the game more complex by adding both good (pink) and poisonous (green) brains that contributed to or took away points respectively. She also correlated the size of each of the brains to a point value so the brains with higher point values were larger and those with lower point values were smaller (see Figure 9.3). Amani then had a chance to expand her game design activities to incorporate controller design. This was an opportunity for her and other students to experience the interplay between her on-screen design (or the digital) and the off-screen (or tangible) design.

We saw above how Amani iterated on her original Scratch program to make changes that made the game more challenging. Her controller design went through a few iterations (see Figure 9.4). She designed the first version

Figure 9.3 Amani's video game: Game (1) only pink brains exist; Game (2) includes good (pink) and bad (green) brains with point values.

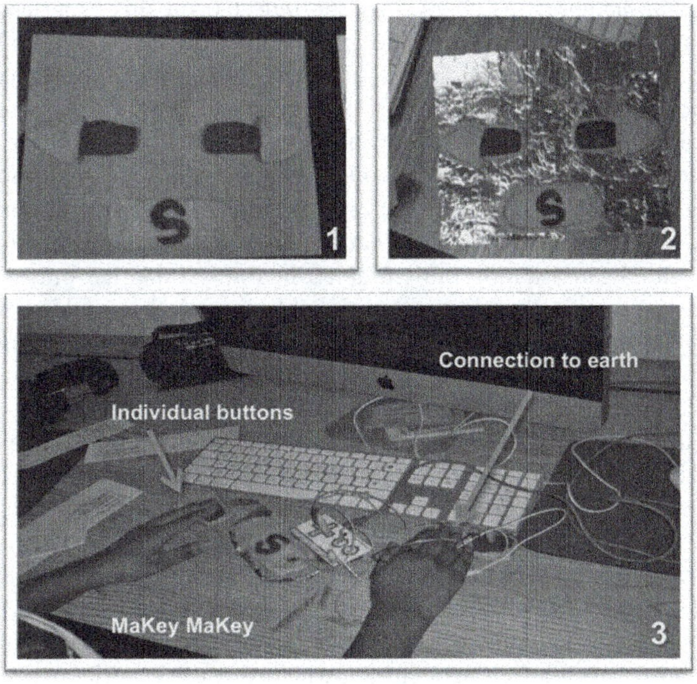

Figure 9.4 Shifts in Amani's interface design: (1) initial design, (2) more detailed design that short-circuited, and (3) final design with touchpad pieces separated.

to have two arrows and a space bar to match the zombie's left, right, and jump movements. One challenge with keeping the entire touchpad on one surface was that the moisture from the Play-Doh began to seep into the paper, thus causing short circuits and stopping her controller from working. In the next iteration, she added a thin orange outline and placed the pieces on foil tape. When she tested this second version of her controller, it also did not work because it was short-circuiting; in this case, the entire surface became conductive. In her final version, Amani created individual buttons for the right, left, and spacebar keys. To do so, she took the controller design and cut out each button. That way, each Play-Doh button still was reinforced by foil tape on the bottom. Then she set each button: space bar in the middle, right arrow key to the right of space, and left arrow key to the left.

On the last workshop day, during the arcade, each youth created a sign to identify their game and set up their station with their controller on the table and the video game on the screen. During the arcade, Amani had a large crowd gathered around her game. After the first group of 4th- and 5th-grade youth had visited, Amani decided that she needed to add a high score so the game had a definitive ending and more customers could come through her line. In between groups of visitors, she updated her Scratch code to implement this change. As she reflected on this experience, she explained what she might have done differently before the arcade began: "Like I should make a score, and I should um . . . like attach those pieces [her interface components] to an actual piece of paper cuz they got, like when one point they all fell on the floor and it got disconnected and everything. So I should have like put it on one piece of paper and . . . um . . . move the keyboard, maybe." Here, we see her reflecting on the challenges she encountered during the arcade, noting what might have made her controller and overall video game station more usable. She noticed that her buttons were not staying in one place like a traditional keyboard, thus making it more challenging to maintain the integrity of the controller. Her reflections illustrate Amani's thoughtful attention to usability and coherence between the tangible and digital aspects of game design.

All the youth in this workshop participated in cycles of iterative design that, without a MaKey MaKey and familiar materials like Play-Doh, could have seemed like a daunting task. Instead, once they understood the basics, they were able to navigate the game and controller design processes. Moreover, through practice, play, and tinkering, youth had a chance to engage with concepts like conductivity and basic circuits, as well as to see how the digital and tangible might intersect and connect. Making touchpad game controllers for their Scratch games helped youth experience prototyping, debugging, and user testing on and off the screen. First, the controller design situated youth's thinking about the logistics of their Scratch video game designs, how it felt to actually play their games using controllers, and what adjustments needed to be made in the tangible or digital realm. Moreover, being able to quickly create controllers allowed youth to run back to their computers to test the controllers out and troubleshoot. Play-Doh is flexible enough that it can handle everything from small tweaks to major reconstruction. Finally, we observed that youth were able to iterate in real time during the student arcade, moving alligator clips around, repositioning their buttons after someone had played, or even tweaking the buttons to make sure the clips stayed in the Play-Doh.

The Board Game Workshop: Augmenting Board Games With MaKey MaKey

We extended the game design activities in the winter of 2013–2014 to the digital augmentation of board games. Many popular commercially available board games such as Monopoly, the Game of Life, and others have recently broadened their gameplay with digital augmentations like electronic banking. In the workshop, we asked youth, working in small groups of two to three, to design their own board games and augment them with digital components like digital dice and playing cards, using MaKey MaKey and Scratch. Working in their small groups, youth moved through a process of conceptualizing their game ideas, developing prototypes for their boards (play-test boards), identifying and testing what elements to digitize (e.g., digital dice), and building out their final digitally augmented board games. To support their augmented game development, we provided teams with sample Scratch code for digital dice and playing cards, which they could then remix (or change) to align with the aesthetic and theme of their board games. Youth also had an opportunity for peer feedback when groups played each other's play-test boards prior to augmentation. This peer feedback helped youth to observe what components of their games worked and what needed to be clarified or reimagined.

To construct their final boards, we provided a wide range of materials for youth to create with, some that were conductive, like aluminum foil tape and Play-Doh, and others that were not, like markers, crayons, decorative tape, and construction paper. Having these materials at their disposal gave groups an opportunity to work collaboratively and with their hands in embellishing their games. During the board game design process, we transformed the classroom space by taking advantage of a central set of desks that were clustered together. We used this cluster as a makeshift makerspace by situating the craft materials in the middle, so teams could share and also observe other teams. Having visibility to each other's work made it not only easier for youth to focus on their designs but also possible to be inspired by others' board game designs.

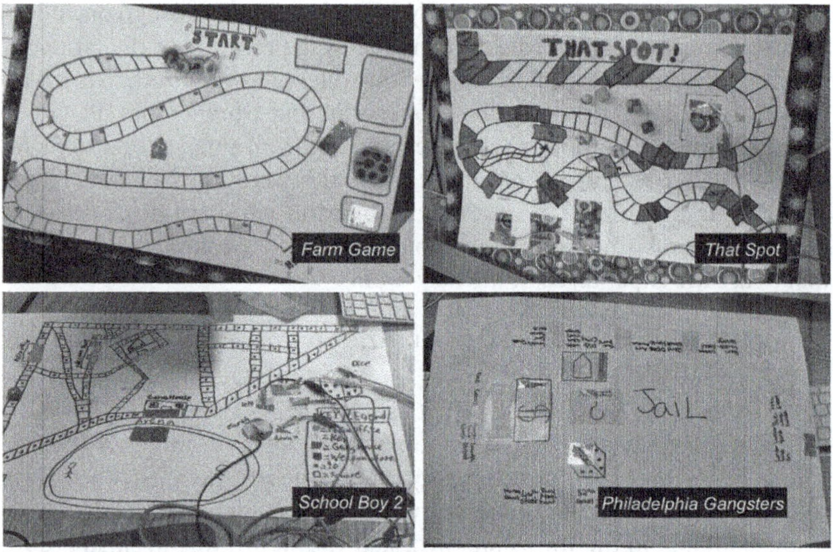

Figure 9.5 Examples of augmented board games.

The five design teams in the workshop came up with distinct themes for their augmented board games (see Figures 9.5 and 9.6): *Road Trip*, a game where players travel across the country; *The Farm Game*, a trivia game with a country aesthetic; *That Spot*, named for the red and green spots that indicate good or bad luck in the game; *School Boy 2*, which allows "gangsters" and "good guys" to battle for money; and *Philadelphia Gangsters*, a city-specific themed gangster game similar to Monopoly. The board games could be categorized into start-to-finish-style games ($n = 3$) and Monopoly-style games ($n = 2$). Start-to-finish games are won by who gets to the end first, whereas Monopoly-style games are defined as those that do not have a definitive end, but rather require players to survive or acquire the most resources (e.g., money) to win. Three teams, comprised of all girls, focused more on aesthetic design and composition of their games, playing with color, images, and use of materials.

The following case study of one team, a group of three girls who designed the *Road Trip* board game (see Figure 9.6), illustrates the many ways in which teams navigated the demands of tangible and digital design. We selected this game because the three 6th-grade girls—Evie, Kimberley, and Alanna—built the most successful game. We identified this as the most successful because their team's board game most clearly responded to the design challenge. First, the team maintained coherence between their boards and their on-screen Scratch code in terms of aesthetics and content.

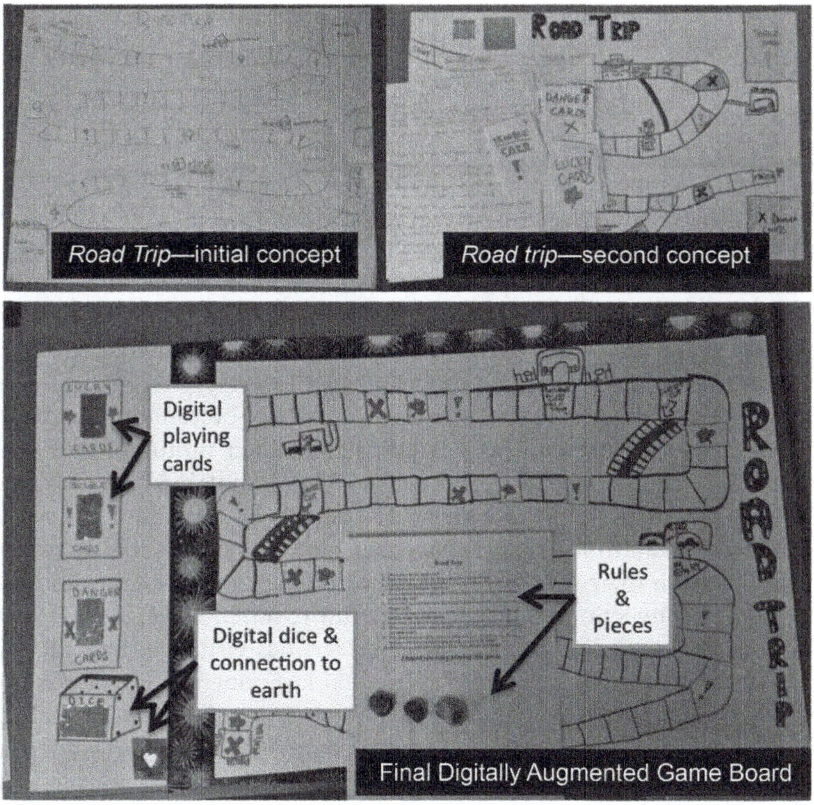

Figure 9.6 Road Trip: Initial concept (top left), second concept (top right), and the final augmented board game (bottom).

Second, the team had all of the components in place for a full game, including a completed final board that integrated digital components, functioning Scratch code for dice and playing cards, playing pieces, and finally a set of rules. Ultimately, their code and augmented board worked together and was fully playable.

Road Trip was a start-to-finish game that required players to navigate challenges in order to get to the end of the road trip. To operationalize these challenges, they had three kinds of cards: Trouble (yielding a bad consequence), Danger (trivia questions), and Lucky (yielding a good consequence). If a player landed on a space marked with the symbols for Trouble, Danger, or Lucky, she or he would have to pick a card and deal with the consequences.

During play testing, the girls observed that their board was too simple and a little too short in terms of the number of actual spaces on their board (which they determined because their peers were able to "win" or "lose" the game quickly), so they chose to make their final game board both longer and more complex (see Figure 9.6, bottom image). Originally, on their play-test board (or the second board), the only element they had digitized was a die. After play testing and talking through the possibilities for digitizing certain components, the girls opted to digitize the playing cards (e.g., trouble, danger, lucky) that were originally handwritten paper cards. In order to make this switch from paper to screen version, they had to determine where to add new hotspots on their board game and how to remix the code for playing cards. They also had to generate additional content for the digital playing cards that was theme specific, which the girls mentioned was extremely time consuming and challenging.

For the final augmented board game version (see bottom of Figure 9.6), the girls were intentional about building from their prototype and adding more spaces to make the game longer. They maintained their original symbols for danger ("X"), trouble ("!"), and lucky cards (a picture of a shamrock) and also made sure that the hot spots were aligned. They also made space on their final game board for their dice and a connection to earth (or a connection to ground the circuit required by MaKey MaKey), drawing an actual dice and the image of earth as visual cues for each of these features. In doing so, the player could keep one hand on earth and put the other on one of the other outcomes (e.g., rolling the dice, selecting a card). They used decorative tape to embellish their board game and eventually printed their rules (see bottom of Figure 9.6). In reflecting on what they were most proud of, Evie said quite simply, "We did a good job." Alanna responded, "Well . . . Well I just think it's cool that we got to make a digital game. Like, we got—we made a board game and then transferred it onto the computer. And I think . . . probably the way we—like we really worked on the cards the most and when you draw a card it comes up on the screen and it reads it to you and we have it down. And so I thought that was pretty cool."

In this workshop, the team of *Road Trip* game designers and those in other groups were able to innovate on a common artifact: the board game. Youth experienced the iterative nature of the making process, moving from a sample idea, to a prototype, to play testing, and eventually to a final augmented board game. In addition, participants learned basic aspects of Scratch programming and about conductivity and usability. They used their knowledge of board games and familiar materials such as markers, tape, cardboard, and Play-Doh and meshed them with unfamiliar materials like sticky foil tape, alligator clips, and MaKey MaKey to produce a digitally augmented board game. In doing so, they were able to connect craft, circuitry, and computing.

Discussion

With construction kits like MaKey MaKey, everyday materials such as foil and Play-Doh can interface with computer programs and help youth to become not just the extensive consumers of technology they already are, but also producers of their own media, creating controllers and augmenting board games. In our research we found that game design in the digital and tangible realms widened youths' understanding of conductivity and computation, gave them opportunities to practice debugging and iterative design, and, finally, provided a bridge between craft and electronics. Below, we describe how these ideas pertained to youth maker experiences made playful participation essential to the game design process in each workshop.

First, we consider youth's experiences with the expanded game-making context. In the game controller workshop, youth were able to design or remix their own games and make their own controllers to play those games. They also tested their designs in an authentic context and with a real audience—an arcade for younger students. For instance, Amani had to make changes on the fly in her Scratch game and had to be vigilant in keeping the controller components in place so her game was playable and her controller usable by younger students. In her post-workshop interview, Amani was able to draw on this experience to inform how she might navigate future controller designs; in her case, trying to keep her entire controller anchored so the buttons didn't go flying after just a few rounds of game play. She was also able to explain how the different components of her touchpad controller and the MaKey MaKey worked. In programming the Scratch game and crafting her touchpad controller, she not only engaged with computational concepts and practices (Brennan & Resnick, 2012), but also furthered her understanding of conductivity.

In the board game workshop, youth augmented traditional board games with digital components and, in doing so, had to think about usability and coherence of their game designs. In our case study about *Road Trip,* we saw how Evie, Kimberley, and Alanna were able to execute their original vision for their game while iterating to incorporate additional digital components in each round of prototyping. They had a chance to further their understanding of conductivity when they were laying out the digital components on their board and needed to make sure to avoid short circuits. In tweaking Scratch scripts and designing rules and logic of their board game, they also engaged with computational concepts and practices (Brennan & Resnick, 2012). Some of these insights were facilitated by peer feedback and the playing-while-making approach to design that was embedded within the workshop design.

Our research also illustrated the ways in which these expanded game design projects lead to debugging and thoughtful decision making around usability and design, aided by what we characterize as playful participation. The debugging process was facilitated by the immediate feedback available to youth when working with both Scratch and MaKey MaKey. If a circuit was shorted or the code was buggy, the youth were able to assess and make changes and retest. Youth were only able to glean these insights through actually playing their games and using the controllers. As youth played their own or other's games or observed peers playing their games, they came across small and large issues in their designs that deviated from their intentions. In the board game design workshop, playing their games gave youth not only insights into whether their rules and board logic made sense, but also into the usability of their boards. For instance, youth had to negotiate where their hotspots were located, where the computer was positioned, and how everyone could participate in the game play on and off the board. In the controller design workshop, youth had to think about the configuration of their controller pieces, how the pieces were anchored, and what it actually felt like to use the buttons versus the keyboard to play. Both workshops situated game play within social contexts: in the controller workshop, student designers were situated in an arcade, and in the board game workshop, the game itself became a social space. Thus, the debugging and iterative design that youth were able to experience was mediated by social interactions that are playful and fluid in nature.

Finally, MaKey MaKey, and other computational construction kits, can provide bridges between craft and electronics. Workshop projects like augmented board games and Play-Doh touchpads were brought to life through the imaginations of youth, coupled with the easy-to-use technical features of MaKey MaKey. Thus, the workshops created opportunities to integrate science, engineering, and design. Such interdisciplinary projects are important given the shrinking spaces for creative work in K–12 schooling (Honey & Kanter, 2013). With heavy emphasis on testing and STEM disciplines, arts and crafts are often considered less important. With MaKey MaKey and similar construction kits, arts and crafts can become intertwined with technology. This both provides an entry into more technical topics for youth who are more comfortable with arts and crafts and allows those who might not have seen themselves as creative makers to enter this design space.

Given that educators are looking for opportunities to bring prototyping and inventing into traditional classrooms, MaKey MaKey is an ideal introductory tool because getting acclimated to it takes little time, allowing youth to focus more on their designs (Martinez & Stager, 2013). Since MaKey MaKey is easy to set up, it has also been seen as a key resource in mobile FabLabs (fabrication labs), giving educators opportunities to bring maker projects into their classrooms (McKay & Peppler, 2013). By expanding what counts as game design and by having youth create controllers and augment board games, we also create more entry points into computational concepts and practices, engineering, and how the two intersect. MaKey MaKey helped to create a bridge between computing, circuitry, and crafts and broadened an already rich learning activity—game design—to give young people an opportunity to see themselves as makers, designers, and tinkerers.

Note

1 The cord colors are only referenced for clarity. As long as the alligator clip is functioning, any color can be used to connect to any of the spots on the MaKey MaKey. There are no restrictions.

References

Brennan, K. & Resnick, M. (2012). *New frameworks for studying and assessing the development of computational thinking.* Paper Presented at the Annual Meeting of the American Educational Research Association, Vancouver, BC, Canada.

Buechley, L., Peppler, K., Eisenberg, M., & Kafai, Y. B. (Eds.). (2013). *Textile messages: Dispatches from the world of electronic textiles and education.* New York, NY: Peter Lang.

Fields, D. A., & Lee, V. R. (2016). Craft technologies 101: Bringing making to higher education. In K. Peppler, E. Halverson, & Y. Kafai (Eds.), *Makeology: Makerspaces as learning environments* (Volume 1) (pp. 121–137). New York, NY: Routledge.

Garcia, A. (Ed.). (2014). *Teaching in the connected learning classroom.* Irvine, CA: Digital Media and Learning Research Hub.

Grover, S. & Pea, R. (2013). Computational thinking in K–12: A review of the state of the field. *Educational Researcher, 42*(1), 38–43.

Hamidi, F., Saenz, K., & Baljko, M. (2014). Sparkles of brilliance: Incorporating cultural and social context in codesign of digital artworks. In *IDC '14 Proceedings of the 13th International Conference on Interaction Design and Children* (pp. 77–84). New York, NY: ACM.

Honey, M., & Kanter, D. (Eds.). (2013). *Design, make, play: Growing the next generation of STEM innovators.* New York, NY: Routledge.

Kafai, Y. B. (1995). *Minds in play: Computer game design as a context for children's learning.* Hillsdale, NJ: Lawrence Erlbaum.

Kafai, Y. B. & Burke, Q. (2014). *Connected code: Why children need to learn programming.* Cambridge, MA: MIT Press.

Kafai, Y. B. & Burke, Q. (in press). *Connected gaming: What making video games can teach us about learning and literacy.* Cambridge, MA: MIT Press.

Kafai, Y. B. & Vasudevan, V. (2015). Constructionist gaming beyond the screen: Middle school students' crafting and computing of touchpads, board games, and controllers. In *WiPSCE '15 Proceedings of the 10th Workshop in Primary and Secondary Computing Education* (pp. 49–54). New York, NY: ACM.

Kelleher, C. & Pausch, R. (2005). Lowering the barriers to programming: A taxonomy of programming environments and languages for novice programmers. *ACM Computing Surveys, 37*(2), 83–137.

Martin, F., Mikhak, B., Resnick, M., Silverman, B., & Berg, R. (2000). To mindstorms and beyond. In A. Druin & J. Hendler (Eds.), *Robots for kids: Exploring new technologies for learning* (pp. 10–33). San Diego, CA: Academic Press.

Martinez, S. L., & Stager, G. S. (2013). *Invent to learn: Making, tinkering, and engineering the classroom*. Los Angeles, CA: Constructing Modern Knowledge Press.

McKay, I. & Peppler, K. (2013). *MakerCart: A mobile fab lab for the classroom*. Presented at the 13th International Conference on Interaction Design and Children. New York, NY: ACM. Retrieved September 17, 2015 from www.peppler.com

Resnick, M., Maloney, J., Hernández, A. M., Rusk, N., Eastmond, E., Brennan, B., . . . Kafai, Y. B. (2009). Scratch: Programming for everyone. *Communications of the ACM, 52*(11), 60–67.

Resnick, M. & Rosenbaum, E. (2013). Designing for tinkerability. In M. Honey & D. Kanter (Eds.), *Design, make, play: Growing the next generation of STEM innovators* (pp. 163–181). New York, NY: Routledge.

Robertson, E., & Bertelli, E. (2014). Conductive music: Teaching innovative interface design and composition techniques with open-source hardware. In *Proceedings of the international conference on New Interfaces for Musical Expression (NIME)* (pp. 517–520). London, UK.

Silver, J., Rosenbaum, E., & Shaw, D. (2012). MaKey MaKey: Improvising tangible and nature-based user interfaces. In *Proceedings of the Sixth International Conference on Tangible, Embedded and Embodied Interaction* (pp. 367–370). New York, NY: ACM.

Vasudevan, V. & Kafai, Y. B. (2015). Hi-Lo tech games: Crafting, coding and collaboration of augmented board games by high school youth. In *IDC '15 Proceedings of the 15th International Conference on Interaction Design and Children* (pp. 130–139). New York, NY: ACM.

Vasudevan, V., Kafai, Y. B., & Yang, L. (2015). Make, wear, play: Remix designs of wearable controllers for scratch games by middle school youth. In *Proceedings of the 15th International Conference on Interaction Design and Children* (pp. 339–342). New York, NY: ACM.

CHAPTER 10

The Big Idea Is Their Idea

KAREN WILKINSON, LUIGI ANZIVINO, AND MIKE PETRICH

Introduction

The Big Idea Is Their Idea: this phrase sums up our connection to constructionist pedagogy. Seymour Papert coined this phrase which asserts that understanding is actively constructed in the mind of the learner through the construction of a physical artifact (Papert, 1980), a fundamental tenet of what we do in the Tinkering Studio at the Exploratorium in San Francisco. Since the learner is front and center in our process, the phrase may also help illuminate some of the defining ideas or characteristics behind our approach to experience design.

Tinkering is an age-old practice of mending and repairing household objects with whatever the *tinker* had on hand, including an expanding repertoire of knowledge that developed over time and through experience. Tinkering has been a part of the Exploratorium since its inception, but the emphasis on having visitors involved directly in the process of tinkering and bringing their ideas into physical reality started with the Tinkering Studio in 2007—first as a small and temporary space, then as a permanent space on the floor in 2010 (for more on the history of the Tinkering Studio, see Petrich, Bevan, & Wilkinson, 2016, in volume 1 of this series). It's currently located within a larger gallery that emphasizes "thinking with your hands" as a valid way of coming to understand science, art, and technology.

Learning that happens in the Tinkering Studio feels qualitatively different from more formal settings or other museum experiences, and because of this we've been faced with the challenge of describing this learning to people who are not as deeply immersed in the work as we are. We find that we need a common language to do this, one that more fully describes the learning and allows us to reflect on the work, describing what we value in it.

Figure 10.1 The Tinkering Studio.

Exploratorium

Through a 2-year-long process, in collaboration with our Visitor Research and Engagement (VRE) group, we identified four broad Dimensions of Learning along with Learning Indicators based on observable behaviors we were able to recognize in our tinkering activities: (1) Engagement; (2) Initiative and Intentionality; (3) Social Scaffolding; and (4) Development of Understanding (see the Learning Dimensions Framework below).

But tinkering is nuanced, and although the dimensions of learning are visible as people are engaged in these explorations, the purpose of this chapter is to describe the choices we make in designing and facilitating tinkering activities to meet these learning dimensions. We describe them below and discuss what we do in order to create the conditions that allow tinkering to happen.

Interest and Motivation

In order for these tinkering experiences to be meaningful, learners have to be interested in what they're doing. In the Tinkering Studio, choice is a definitive factor. Activities are done on a drop-in basis and are not timed; learners decide when to begin and determine when their projects are complete or they're ready to stop. They may not be automatically drawn to an activity when they first arrive, but once they begin working with something

Table 10.1 Learning Dimensions Framework

Learning Dimension	*Indicators*	*Description of Learners' Interactions*
Engagement	Spending time in tinkering activities	• playing, envisioning, making, exploring materials, trying something over and over, etc.
	Displaying motivation or investment through affect or behavior	• Showing emotions such as joy, pride, disappointment, frustration • remaining after they appear "finished," and starting something new
Initiative and Intentionality	Setting one's own goals	• setting goals / posing problems • planning steps for future action • developing unique strategies, tools, objects or outcomes • stating intention to continue working outside Studio
	Seeking and responding to feedback	• actively seeking out feedback or inspiration from materials/environment • anticipating further outcomes • innovating approaches in response to feedback
	Persisting to achieve goals in the problem space	• persisting toward their goal in the face of setbacks or frustration within the problem space • persisting to optimize strategies or solutions
	Taking intellectual risks or showing intellectual courage	• disagreeing with each other's strategies, solutions, or rationales • trying something while indicating lack of confidence in outcome
Social Scaffolding	Requesting or offering help in solving problems	• requesting or offering ideas and approaches • offering tool(s) or materials in service of an idea
	Inspiring new ideas or approaches	• noticing, pointing out, or talking about others' work • innovating and remixing by using or modifying others' ideas or strategies • leaving something of their work behind to share with others
	Physically connecting to others' works	• Producing work that physically interacts with others' work

(*Continued*)

Table 10.1 (Continued)

Learning Dimension	*Indicators*	*Description of Learners' Interactions*
Development of Understanding	Expressing a realization through affect or utterances	• showing excitement when expressing a realization • claiming to realize or newly make sense of something
	Offering explanation(s) for a strategy, tool, or outcome	• Offering or refining explanation(s) for a strategy, tool, or outcome, possibly by testing and retesting
	Applying knowledge	• connecting to prior knowledge, including STEM concepts • employing what has been learned during tinkering • complexifying by engaging in increasingly complicated and sophisticated work
	Striving to understand	• Indicating *not* knowing (e.g., through surprise, bewilderment, confusion) and remaining in the problem space to explore confusion and build an understanding

or "messing about," they quickly become absorbed in what they're doing or they move onto something else that interests them more. The typical dwell time in the Tinkering Studio is 25 minutes on average, and sometimes visitors spend several hours. One gauge that we tend to use in developing tinkering experiences is that if the phenomenon or activity is interesting to us and is framed as an invitation for others to join in the investigation along with us, chances are good that others will find it interesting too.

A good example is working with circuit boards, an activity that typically gets one of two reactions: people are either drawn to it because they're familiar with it and enjoy electronics or they are less interested and perhaps even intimidated by the idea of working with circuits or electronics. We like to mitigate this by mixing more familiar pieces with ones that are unfamiliar or surprising in some way. By combining traditional electronic components like light bulbs and batteries with dissected toy parts that move in whimsical ways, it makes for a more compelling activity. By watching others trying things out, hearing laughter and the delighted expressions of surprise, this often can be enough to get people interested enough to try things out. These qualities or cues may help someone get started, but intrinsic motivation and interest is what keeps them going past sticking points or challenges they encounter along the way. The more people work with the materials at their own pace, the more confident they become, developing fluency and interest in the process (for more on motivation in the making process, see chapter 6 of this volume).

Iteration and Complexification

Tinkering Studio experiences are designed to encourage learners to complexify their thinking over time. By offering a variety of more and less complex parts, learners of many different experience levels are able to find something to start with. This means beginners can start with quick success and then alter and complexify their designs as their ideas progress. All of the activities in the Tinkering Studio are designed to become more complex than the entry point.

Iteration (working on something over time, making small but important adjustments as you go) is what drives tinkering. When participants test a design to see how it moves, flies, or operates, each refinement of their design is part of the iterative process. These steps are taken in direct response to what's happening with the phenomena; the learner may notice something outside of what they were going for—something that seemed surprising in what happened. This can set off a whole series of investigations involving constructing, testing, refining, observing, reflecting, remixing or reimagining, trying the next thing—building fluency with tools, material, and phenomena and one's current ability to manipulate things in that way is what development of understanding is all about. The ability to iterate is strengthened over time and with practice and is something we try to reinforce in the way we facilitate. A constant checking of assumptions and advancing understanding reinforces our belief that learning is a cumulative process that draws on prior experiences to shape new ideas in the moment.

Persistence

One of the defining qualities of a tinkering experience is that frustration and failure are common occurrences; the path from idea to execution is never straightforward, and there are many steps that seem to go in a direction opposite of success. Part of this is intrinsic to the nature of tinkering as a mode of making: the absence of a prescriptive plan, using materials in ways they weren't intended to be used, setting highly personalized goals, encouraging quirky ideas, etc., all naturally lead to people getting "stuck" in a problem, getting themselves into trouble, if you will. This could be scary in a more traditional setting, like a classroom. Students may get frustrated, or not know how to move forward in their project, or reach a point they might identify as a failure. Not only do we not mind that these moments occur while tinkering, we actively design for them and try to help learners see frustration as natural and failure in the process of tinkering as valuable feedback. For example, we choose sets of materials that are not optimally suited for the task at hand in an activity like Marble Machines (learners construct a pathway for marbles using common hardware store parts). If the tracks are precisely machined and very stable, it takes something away from the process. Instead, we use lengths of corner molding from building supply stores that have a tendency to roll from side to side on the pegs. The tracks are imperfect, but the result is an interesting tension between what the materials afford and the vision a learner has for what to do with them in order to make them work. This is an opportunity for the learner to persist through frustration, developing a sense that it is worth not giving up on an idea just because its execution is difficult. This breakthrough in thinking, persisting in the problem space, is one of the fundamental outcomes of tinkering. It is about finding the capacity in oneself to look carefully at the problem, reframe a solution, try it out, and assess the outcome.

Shifting Goals

Tinkering activities are often constrained on several dimensions: the materials that are made available to build with have been carefully selected and often narrowed down to an intentionally limited set; the environment has been designed to encourage and favor certain types of interaction; and the prompts and facilitation are chosen to keep the activity tilted towards a fairly specific set of goals. We often call this set of constraints the problem space within which participants operate. We try to find the right balance or set of constraints that simultaneously feel open enough to invite learners in, but not so open that it's a free-for-all. Achieving the right balance so that there is more than one possible goal to solve is what we're after.

When introducing Marble Machines, we often will ask people to "make the marble travel from the top to the bottom as slowly as possible." This leaves a lot of room for interpretation as to what constitutes success. Exactly how slow is "as slowly as possible"? This constraint also encourages lateral thinking and creative solutions for circumventing the goal; it almost goads people into trying to subvert what we're asking them to do. Participants often ask "could we add height at the top to gain more travel time? Can we get a marble to go back up for a while, or get stuck in a loop? Can we use multiple marbles, an elevator, multiple pathways?" In the course of this rapid brainstorming, the original goal is often joyously forgotten and let go, as more interesting and exciting ideas leap to mind. "Maybe we could use rubber bands as trampolines and get the marble to jump across tracks! How about a teeter-totter that releases a second marble down an alternative path? These copper tubes sound nice; let's build a musical marble machine." This is what we think of as the macro-level goal flexibility: the theme and overall marker for success is highly individualized and can develop during the course of messing around with materials and gaining experience and proficiency with the activity itself. Shifting goals is often the biggest contributor to the innovative ideas that emerge through tinkering.

Personal Expression

Personal expression can be seen as frivolous and inconsequential, simply decoration on top of a STEM-based activity—and indeed, if that's all the activity offers in terms of meaningful interaction, it can be. However, when you allow learners to inject some of their personal choices, preferences, aesthetic predilections, and most importantly narratives into the physical representation of their thinking, you open the door for development of understanding that has deeper roots and relevance.

The two main driving forces behind personal expression are aesthetic choices and the development of personal narrative.

Aesthetics is sometimes dismissed in school as being inconsequential, having to do with just the "looks" of it, or merely decoration. But a sense of aesthetics emerges very early on in development (Hetland, Winner, Veenema, & Sheridan, 2007) and we see it manifesting itself in very young kids through tinkering activities. There is not much that a 4-year old gets to choose in her life, but she will have very strong opinions already about what color markers should be used as legs for her scribbling machine, or whether to send the yellow or the green marble down the track. We respect and value these choices as the legitimate expressions of a point of view and as tools of empowerment toward defining an individual's path towards understanding and creative expression. They can fundamentally guide what gets made, which questions are asked, and how satisfying the answers are.

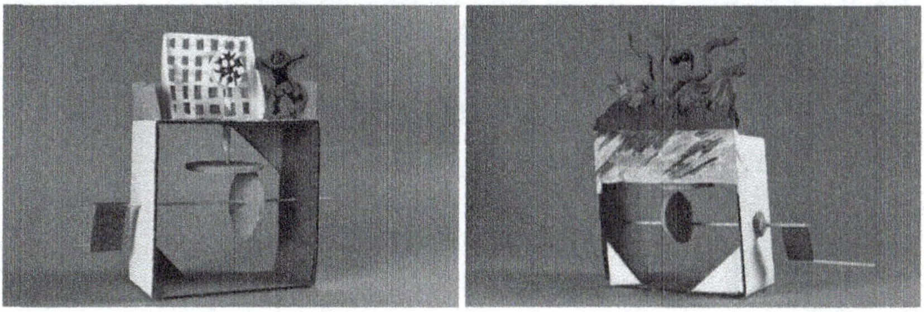

Figure 10.2 Cardboard Automata.

Exploratorium

Telling stories and adding a narrative element is a fundamentally human way of making meaning out of the world. We interpret almost everything we do through a narrative lens, and, of course, that remains true of the things we make and even the process involved in making them. We've noticed how powerful narrative storytelling can be a driving force in the tinkering process. Creating conditions that encourage narratives to emerge can have positive impacts on what gets made, the creative direction that the tinkering experiences take on, and the types of solutions people come up with.

Certain activities encourage a narrative lens right from the get-go, while others emerge out of working closely with materials and phenomena. With Cardboard Automata, for example, learners are asked to create a scene or a mini-story that is animated by a set of cams and elements of simple machines; this can lead to the creation of something like a twirling ballerina figure, but often even straightforward creations are intertwined with identity and personal history. People like to tell stories about things that are relevant in their lives: a favorite team or hobby, skateboarding, music idols, etc. Narratives can even provide for interpersonal relationships to develop or be expressed: a daughter making a Paper Circuit card for her mom, or a valentine for a sweetheart.

People often express that they *love* their projects. Many pull out their cellphones to snap a photo or video of what they've made. This is something

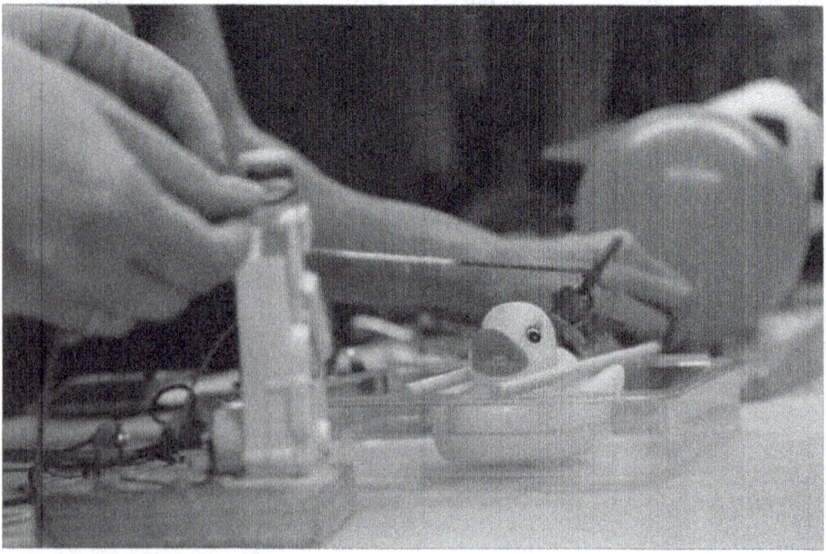

Figure 10.3 Chain reaction.

Exploratorium

that learners will carry with them in a lasting way, much more so than if they had gone through the motions of making something by following step-by-step instructions that resulted in an identical object to everyone else around them. There is still value in those types of projects, but tinkering isn't prominent and neither is personal expression.

Humor and Whimsy

One way or another, humor and whimsy are always present in Tinkering Studio offerings. We enjoy unusual juxtapositions of topics, like sewing with circuits or using familiar materials in unfamiliar ways, and use humor to lower the barriers for entry for those who might approach the activities more tentatively. Humor and whimsy is the driving force behind our Chain Reaction activity, partly inspired by playful artists and illustrators, such as Rube Goldberg and Bruno Munari, and partly by the supply of materials on hand for learners to construct with. This collaborative build activity culminates in setting off a series of cause-and-effect events that visitors have constructed. This physical act of participating in something larger than yourself, while having to explore and exploit the possibilities within a wide range of objects, leads to comical results that everyone can enjoy because they can identify with the tasks that others have gone about solving.

Oftentimes it is the unusual whimsical objects, like a severed plastic hand or a dancing Frankenstein monster, that sets the tone for people to start acting in more playful ways from the start of the exploration. Playful and whimsical aspects of activities set a tone for what we value beyond science learning and hint that these tinkering experiences might go beyond traditional didactic science learning.

Varied Outcomes

Tinkering is not a prescribed set of steps that everyone is expected to follow. Each person comes away from a tinkering experience with a slightly—and sometimes significantly—different artifact or takeaway. Sometimes the takeaway isn't a physical object at all, but more an attitude or idea. This breadth of outcomes is a mark of a successful tinkering activity and a testament to the importance we place on the role of individual learners and their pathways to understanding. There are two main ways we design for varied outcomes; one is to create constraints that allow for tinkering to occur and the other is to introduce a palette of materials that are varied enough, but not so varied that the learners move outside the territory being explored. Finding that sweet spot between constrained enough and open enough is what *we* are tinkering with all the time.

By structuring the tinkering experience around the learner's questions, tentative ideas, and initial insights, you end up with varied outcomes. This is not a trivial act—empowering people to trust their instincts and feel competent in pursuing their own pathway to understanding. To be truly rich and transformative, what gets constructed must start with the learner's existing collection of experiences and build from there. The Chain Reaction activity is the ideal example to illustrate a variety of outcomes used to solve a problem. Every time we facilitate this activity, we experience wildly different construction attempts, spectacular failures, and unusual finales.

We deeply believe that learning isn't linear and it's never "done." By modeling the fact that there isn't one single right way of doing something or a simple linear path to follow when pursuing an idea, we give the learner permission to follow their hunches and further develop a tinkerer's disposition in the process. Allowing for varied outcomes gives you more richness in terms of results, but also more interest and investment on the part of the learners, which is a hallmark of tinkering for us. It builds upon intrinsic motivation, resulting in learners that are more interested and invested in their own creation, intrigued enough by what they see happening to keep the process going.

Case Study—Alma's Top

We'd like to use a common Tinkering Studio experience as an example to show how the Dimensions of Learning and the design principles we've been discussing unfold in real time.

Figure 10.4 Tops activity.

Exploratorium

Alma (a pseudonym) was a 12-year-old girl who spent some time in the Tinkering Studio when we were hosting a top-making activity. Three weeks after Alma's initial visit, we interviewed her about her experience. We showed her photos of her process and asked her to tell us about what was happening in them.

Alma arrived with her younger brother and was greeted by a facilitator who introduced what we were doing that day. He showed them a table filled with commercially made tops, where other visitors were testing them to see how they spun. Nearby, a film by Charles and Ray Eames, called *Tops*, was playing. Both the film and the sample tops were meant to set an informal tone for exploration and serve as inspiration for the activity taking place. Once Alma had spun a few tops, the facilitator asked if she'd like to try making one, directing her to a materials table, pointing out a few of the materials—things like yogurt cups, plastic plates, cardboard pieces, lids, etc.—and encouraging her to start by trying to make things spin. This is where we started asking about her experience:

> ***K: What did you do first?***
>
> *Alma: I was kind of . . . I wasn't even using the process of elimination, I was just picking random things up off the table and seeing how they worked in the top . . . this looks kinda cool maybe I'll try it.*

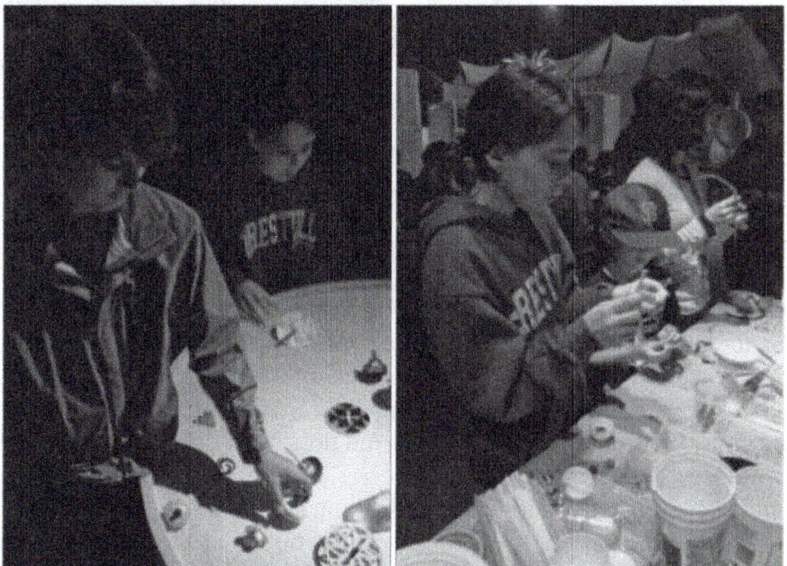

Figure 10.5 Experimenting with tops.

Exploratorium

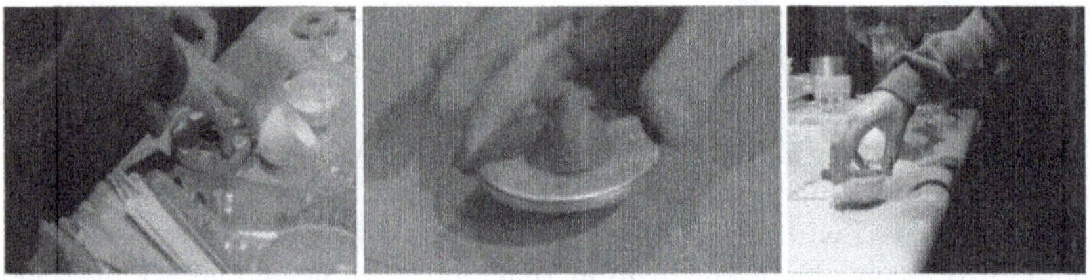

Figure 10.6 Exploring materials.

Exploratorium

Figure 10.7 Testing the height of the spindle.

Exploratorium

It took Alma a while to settle on a specific direction with her top, but once she started building she tried a variety of different materials, which is a terrific way to begin—getting to know the materials by "messing about" (Hawkins, 1974) with their properties and possibilities. As Alma went along she was developing fluency in this process by adding an element, trying to spin it, watching what happened, and taking action based on what she saw and wanted to do next. This process of iteration is at the heart of tinkering. By offering opportunities for people to iterate on their ideas through a range of possible materials, you're also creating opportunities for choice and the development of initiative and intentionality. This also, naturally, leads to a variety of outcomes.

K: How did you know what to do to make a top?

Alma: I was just testing it out . . . what would happen if I did this . . . what would happen if I did that . . . if I took that away . . . if I added more. . . . I was just testing, does it work better like this? Or like that? And would it look better with this? If I added more weight would it look better? If I took away weight would it work better?

K: I noticed you decided to use one of those large washers you had been playing with on its own earlier.

Alma: I think . . . it kind of balanced out the egg. The egg when it was lighter, it kind of just flopped. I don't really know how to put it, but it just didn't work light like that. Once it started not really working as well, as light, then I put the washer in and it got heavier. Then I spun it and it got better. I kind of came up with the idea that if I make this top heavier then it'll be able to do better. Maybe it'll become better if I make it heavier.

K: What does a top need to spin?

Alma: It really works to have more weight in the center . . . you need balance around the edges and weight in the center so it keeps its place. So I just kept adding weight along that straw part and I think that kind of helped it to get a lot better because the center was more stable, and I don't know why that might have worked but for some reason by adding more and more washers to that part, so they stacked up it made it taller and more stable in the bottom—it helped it a lot.

This type of construction was the core part of her exploration. She spent most of her time working on these elements (adjusting the distribution of mass, the height of the spindle, and perfecting her launch technique). Even though the initial prompt was very open-ended, Alma was able to find a direction for herself and move through a series of trial-and-error adjustments, receiving little more from the facilitator than encouraging

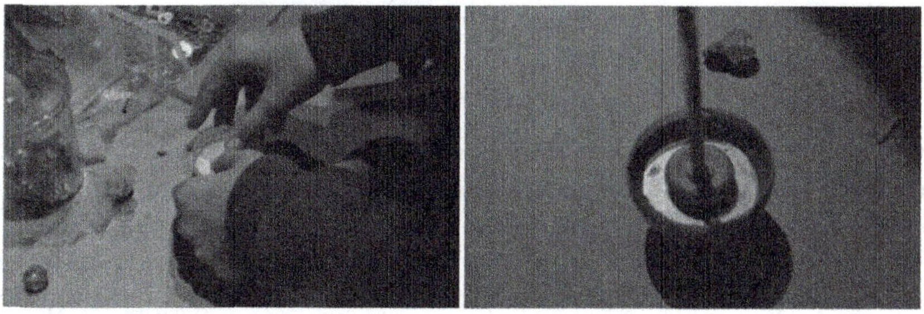

Figure 10.8 Adding a large washer.

Exploratorium

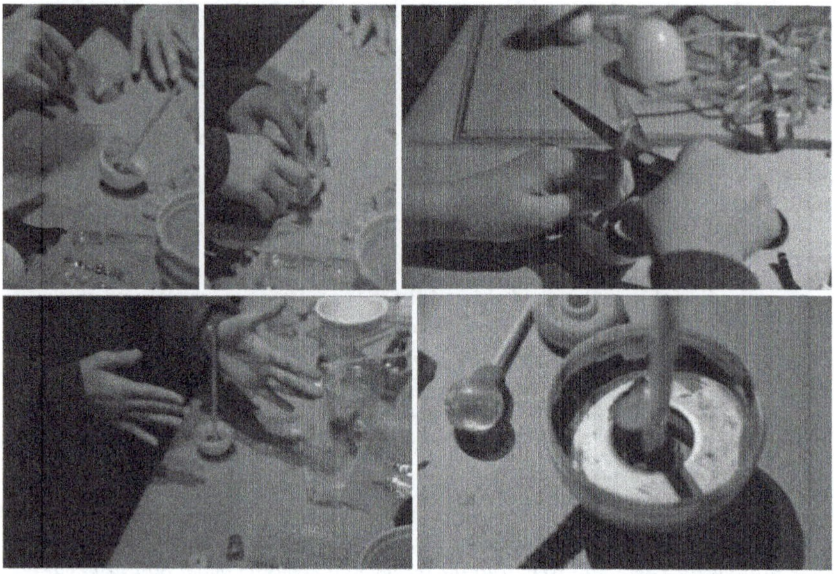

Figure 10.9 Changing the height of the spindle.

Exploratorium

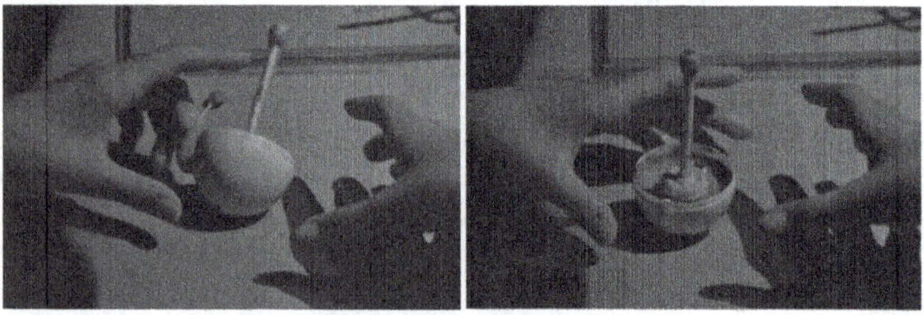

Figure 10.10 Adding weight to the top of the spindle.

Exploratorium

words about what she was doing, even when things weren't working or didn't appear to be the results she had in mind. As educational experience designers, we believe tinkering is not just about problem solving, but allowing the learner to ask questions or pose problems that are meaningful to them, then go about solving those problems rather than ones they're given to solve. Persisting in a problem space and learning to be comfortable there is a hallmark of tinkering, pushing past frustration or failures. We value this type of intentionality because the learner is able to take action, even when those actions lead to dead ends or ultimately don't work out. Alma did this again and again throughout her top-building experience, eventually creating something that did work, but not without encountering many more ideas that didn't work. This is what real learning looks like—problematic and messy.

> ***K: What did you do to get your top to work so well?***
>
> *Alma: I started off using the straw like really tall and anchoring it to the bottom. . . . I think it just made the egg less, the top . . . less balanced. I don't know what it was but when you spun it, the stick seemed to like want to go out and fall . . . so that caused it to get wobbly. I know I didn't want a wobbly top, like too wobbly . . . I ended up with a top, that it didn't wobble but it moved around a lot and I liked that. So I think my top is good at moving.*

Here she is describing a process of iteration that ended when she was pleased with the outcome. She mentioned that the resulting calmer movement here made it seem like the top was "alive." Her goals seemed to shift at this point, from wanting a top that spun in one spot to enjoying the surprising result of its wandering movement and wanting to incorporate that into her design.

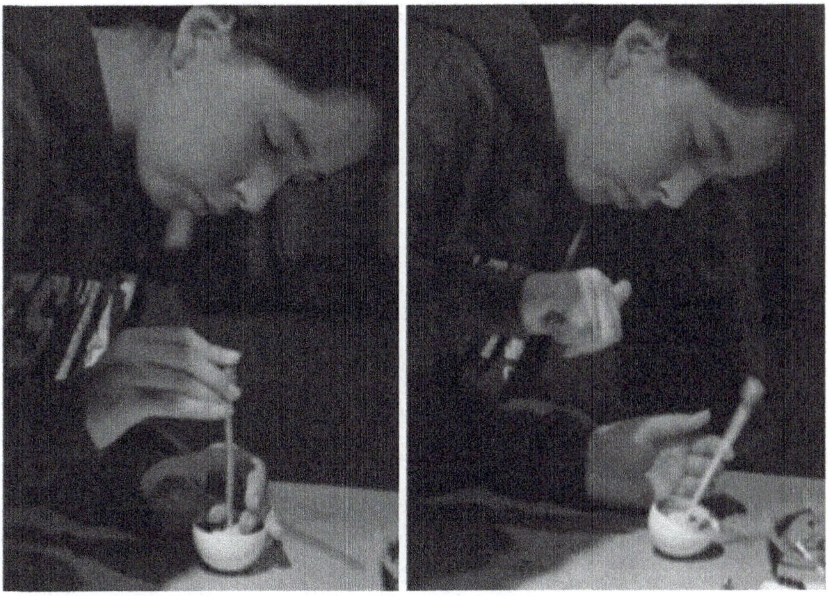

Figure 10.11 Testing the new spindle.

Exploratorium

She took it one step further and wanted to add more decorative elements to her top, to enhance its "creature-like" qualities:

> *Alma: I was like okay, my top is perfected, it just needs googly eyes. I'm obsessed with googly eyes. They are one of my favorite things . . . Cause I'm all like . . . it's kinda like a little creature, it needs googly eyes. And they were like "well we have lots of googly eyes."*
>
> (These materials were not out on the table, but the facilitator went and got them for her)

As noted earlier, we see narratives frequently in the Tinkering Studio where learners create objects that turn into creatures of some kind, because an object takes on characteristics they can relate to. We encourage this type of storytelling because it allows learners a personally meaningful way to connect to the activity and to become more invested in the process. Developing narratives is a natural way for kids to express themselves; it's delightful to see ideas originate from ordinary materials and objects that don't possess those qualities initially. Compelling for both the learner and the facilitator, this demonstrates how invested learners are in the process and how empowering it can be when others share that enthusiasm.

In terms of the activity design, it's important to note that we could have developed this experience much differently. If we had only egg parts with precut stems or spindles, this would have made it easier for us to gather

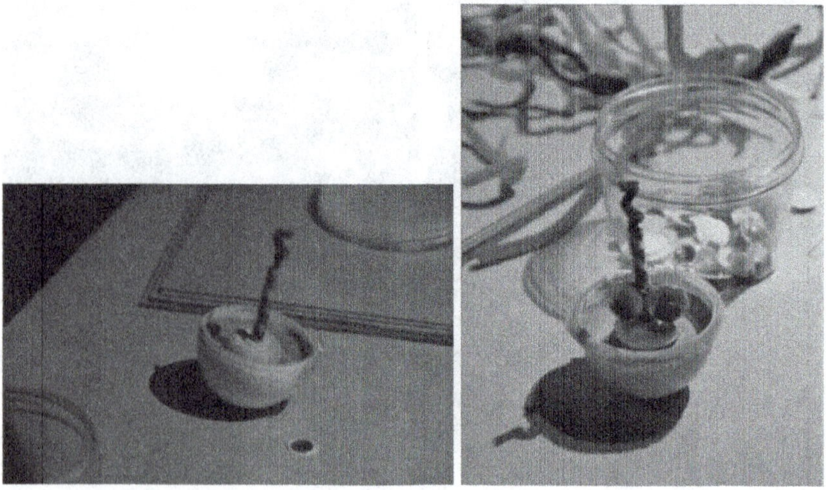

Figure 10.12 Decorating the spindle.

Exploratorium

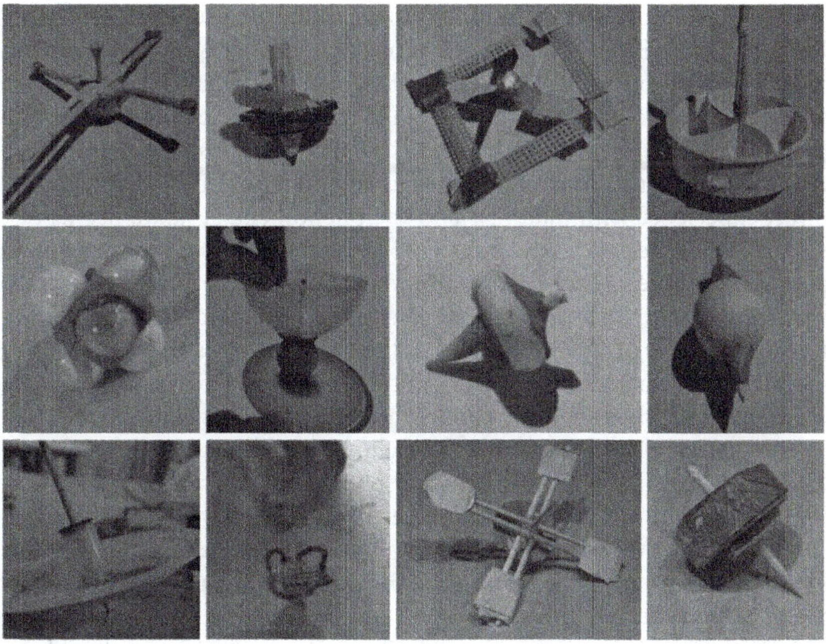

Figure 10.13 Top variations.

Exploratorium

materials and prep for the activity, but it would have made for more uniform-looking tops in the end, with less variation for the learners. As it was, Alma's top looked very different from other tops around her. Others made tops out of bottle caps or rolled up cardboard, tops with pointed ends or flat ends, square tops and tops that were shaped like an X; this only added to the territory that got covered in terms of science content. While it's true that not everyone came away with similar understandings, what developed this way is a much more durable type of understanding that relates directly to the learners' investigations and one that will stick with them for a longer time because they owned the process.

Towards the end of our interview and conversation, we asked her what advice she might give to someone else interested in building tops.

> *Alma: I think that balance is definitely something that is key to tops. Some weight, but there are light tops. Tops that are really light that work, but that I noticed that the more weight I added the better mine got, but I had a different kind of top than most people would think of as a top. Yeah, tops are confusing.*

This statement says all sorts of things to us. It's interesting that after spending such a long time working on her top, Alma ends the interview by saying, "yeah, tops are confusing." Rather than being discouraged by this statement, we think it indicates that Alma was able to truly immerse herself in the top-building experience, enough to see that it is a complicated and multifaceted endeavor. Tinkering is a playful inquiry process that develops based on direct experience with materials and the phenomena at hand; in this case spinning tops. Because Alma built a top herself, she was able to home in on an important idea—that balance is key and that weight distribution really matters when it comes to spinning. Her early experience with the sample tops was that all of them were very lightweight, and this is still something she's trying to consider. This may indicate that she's actively analyzing the experience, which is an important learning indicator for us.

Understanding how tops work develops over time as one tries things that are successful, but it's often what doesn't work or fails that is more informative and essential to the tinkering process. Instead of the single "aha" moment, we witness many tiny breakthroughs along the way that inform the learner's investigation and help reinforce experimentation and the development of a tinkerer's disposition. Because we believe learning to be cumulative, with one experience feeding into the next—you don't learn

Figure 10.14 Spinning top.

Exploratorium

something and then you're done—Alma's experience with tops will follow her into future learning experiences, allowing her understanding to deepen over time.

One can often overlook the learning that's taking place because at times it looks like play or can seem rather uneventful, lacking those "aha"-type breakthroughs traditionally expected with science education. Our constructionist philosophy guides our development process, and the Tinkering Studio experience itself is reliant on the action of the learner to create something tangible. That's where it begins, this act of constructing something—or what we refer to as thinking with your hands. The Learning Dimensions Framework has been an invaluable tool for our design team to refer to (and reflect on) when we are in the process of prototyping new tinkering experiences. Along the way, facilitators and often other visitors get drawn into an investigation, and the creation of intangibles often result, those that have to do with creating a culture of curiosity and the development of a tinkerer's disposition.

References

Hawkins, D. (1974). *The informed vision: Essays on learning and human nature.* New York: Agathon Press.

Hetland, L., Winner, E., Veenema, S., & Sheridan, K. (2007). *Studio thinking: The real benefits of visual arts education.* New York: Teachers College Press.

Papert, S. (1980). *Mindstorms: Children, computers, and powerful ideas.* New York: Basic Books, Inc.

Petrich, M., Bevan, B., & Wilkinson, K. (2016). Tinkering with MOOCs and social media. In K. Peppler, E. Halverson, & Y. Kafai (Eds.), *Makeology: Makerspaces as learning environments* (Volume 1) (pp. 175–189). New York, NY: Routledge.

Section 3
Connecting Making to the Disciplines

CHAPTER 11

Making as a Pathway to Engineering and Design

LEE MARTIN AND COLIN DIXON

Introduction

While making and the Maker Movement have developed and flourished primarily in out-of-school and informal spaces, there is substantial and growing interest in the education community for bringing making and elements of the Maker Movement into K–12 schools to reinvigorate science, technology, engineering, and mathematics (STEM) curricula. This excitement is understandable—observation of people, young, old, or in-between, hard at work on maker projects often reveals a playful atmosphere, persistence through difficulty, creative problem solving, sharing of ideas, and the creation of fun, exciting, or novel creations. For those concerned that STEM education in K–12 has become rigid, abstract, and unexciting, making looks like a welcome antidote. Yet questions remain about the extent to which it can and should be integrated into more formal educational endeavors.

In this chapter, we consider the potential of making as a set of activities that can set the stage for work within the discipline of engineering. There are obvious connections to be made here: engineers design and build things, often with the use of technological tools, and makers do the same. Yet there are also important differences in these practices that need to be explored. Making is not engineering, nor is it a unitary activity. Instead, it is a diverse set of activities that occurs under a variety of circumstances. Using the recently developed Framework for the Next Generation Science Standards (NGSS; National Research Council, 2011), we consider how making aligns with this view of engineering and present the theoretical framework of *adaptive expertise* to guide our thinking. Next, we present vignettes of two brothers participating in an out-of-school maker club, comparing and contrasting their experiences. We close with a brief consideration of how our data may inform efforts to integrate making into K–12 engineering education.

Background: Making and Engineering as Design

How well is making aligned with engineering? There is no simple answer, as what young people learn while making, and the extent to which it can be connected to engineering, depends on the particulars of what they are doing and the context in which they are doing it. One approach is to look for topical points of connection in particular activities, such as a shared focus on electronics projects in the two communities. While useful at times, a narrow focus on topics can be limited, suggesting an outmoded view of learning that seeks *identical elements* to transfer between disparate contexts (cf. Thorndike & Woodworth, 1901). Moreover, a topic-centric approach to exploring alignment between making and engineering would treat the diversity of approaches to making as a barrier to alignment. In our studies of youth, we have seen substantial variety: we see youth who write code, and those who do not; those who sketch and prototype relentlessly, and those who begin with the "final" materials; those who collaborate and engage in constant discourse with their team, and those who work quietly as individuals.

Instead, we can take a broader view of making and engineering, considering *practices* that are central to each. Given this view, there are points of connection between making and K–12 engineering that extend beyond surface-level correspondence of topics (e.g., robotics) and skills (e.g., creating a CAD model). Chief among these is the focus on and practice of *design*. The Framework for K–12 Science Education (National Research Council, 2011), which serves as the conceptual basis for the Next Generation Science Standards, defines engineering as "a systematic and often iterative approach to designing objects, processes, and systems to meet human needs and wants" (p. 202). Design is a central idea throughout the framework. In the framework, "engineering design" is one of two "Disciplinary Core Ideas for Engineering, Technology, and Applications of Science" (the other is "links among engineering, technology, science, and society"). Likewise, the first principle put forth in the comprehensive NRC report on K–12 engineering education is that "engineering education should emphasize engineering design" (National Research Council, 2009, p. 151).

The centrality of design in K–12 engineering provides a strong potential connection point for making and tinkering, as within these activities it is common for people to design and build things. In the NGSS framework, the authors specify that they "use the term engineering in a very broad sense to mean any engagement in a systematic practice of design to achieve solutions to particular human problems" (National Research Council, 2011, p. 11). Depending on how one defines "systematic," this definition opens a wide door for a variety of design activities to count as engineering. Moreover, Quinn and Bell (2013) identify substantial overlap in the engineering design practices listed in the NGSS framework and commonplace practices in the making community.

This is not to say that the relation between making and engineering is simple or unproblematic. Resnick and Rosenbaum (2013) explicitly differentiate engineering, with its planful orientation, to tinkering, where creations emerge more dynamically in interaction with materials. Moreover, the making and engineering communities are distinct, and an interest in making can develop in many directions, of which engineering is only one (e.g., see chapter 2 of this volume for the variety of disciplinary areas covered in *MAKE* magazine). Certainly many of the youth we have studied strongly identify as makers, but not as engineers in training (Martin & Dixon, 2013). In addition, there are artistic, playful, and subversive elements in making that fall outside definitions of tinkering or engineering (e.g., Kuznetsov & Paulos, 2010). Although we focus here on connections between making and engineering, we emphatically reject the notion that other aspects of making are unimportant.

With a focus on design experiences, we can consider how making may or may not be part of a trajectory toward engineering design competence for any particular young person. For youth who love to build things, and whose interests and opportunities align, maker experiences may play a significant role in a *line of practice* that eventually includes engineering (Azevedo, 2011). Because making contexts typically emphasize a creative, playful approach to projects, they are fruitful contexts to study when and how young people can become creative, thoughtful designers, rather than rigid adherents to a narrowly conceived design process. To explore these questions, we now turn to the theoretical framework of adaptive expertise as one lens with which to view the transition from novice to expert.

Key Making Concept: Adaptive Expertise

Research contrasting the capabilities of experts and novices has long been a staple of educational research. However, not all forms of expertise are equivalent. Hatano and Inagaki (1986) showed that while all experts are efficient, able to perform skills in their area of expertise quickly and accurately, some are also able to go beyond their existing knowledge to learn new things and solve novel problems. They called these experts *adaptive experts*, in contrast to routine experts. While all experts have procedural knowledge—knowledge of how to perform actions—adaptive experts also have deep conceptual knowledge. They understand how and why things work the way they do, and thus are able to deal with unexpected problems and innovate new solutions. For example, procedural knowledge in cooking will allow you to follow a recipe efficiently and produce quality results under standard conditions, but conceptual understanding is needed to invent clever substitutions (e.g., replacing butter with avocado) or develop new recipes.

Hatano and Inagaki (1992) explored the conditions under which conceptual knowledge, and thus adaptive expertise, is most likely to develop. Their theory emphasizes four primary conditions that enhance the likelihood of developing conceptual knowledge:

1. Frequent experience with events that disconfirm expectations. This condition is frequently met with natural objects (e.g., animals), but rarely with standardized objects. They note that violations of expectation motivate efforts to understand when a person cares about the target of her interest.
2. Experience engaging in "frequent dialogic interaction," including debate and discussion. Such interactions aid comprehension through several mechanisms, including the need for people to make their ideas explicit and well organized.
3. A community that values comprehension and explanation and does not focus strictly on efficient performance. Hatano and Inagaki (1992) give the example of kindergarteners who had the job of caring for animals at the start of the school day. When teachers insisted on speedy performance of these tasks, children did not take time to explore their own questions and curiosities that arose.
4. Some distance from punishment and reward structures. Rewards tend to motivate efficient and routine approaches to problem solving, and comprehension efforts are typically inefficient, at least at first.

A number of researchers have applied the adaptive expertise framework within the context of engineering education research (see McKenna, 2014, for a review). For example, Pandy, Petrosino, Austin, and Barr (2004) studied the development of adaptive expertise within an undergraduate biomechanics course. They operationalized adaptive expertise as high scores on tests of both factual and conceptual knowledge, along with the ability to transfer this knowledge to new problems. They found that the challenge-based instructional program they designed was more effective in fostering adaptive expertise than standard instructional practice.

In contrast, Walker, Cordray, King, and Brophy (2006) used design scenarios to assess adaptive expertise in freshman and senior engineering and design students. As predicted, seniors were much more innovative problem solvers than freshmen, but both groups showed improvement over the course of a semester. Interestingly, results showed that improvements were multifaceted: not only did solution quality improve, but other process-level factors, such as question quality, also improved.

Rayne et al. (2006) examined the development of adaptive expertise in biomedical engineering ethics in a study that included high school students, early undergraduates, and more advanced undergraduates. Instruction was similar for all students and consisted of a three-day problem-solving experience. Adaptive expertise was assessed by having students respond to newspaper articles that discussed complex ethical issues related to stem cells. All students had high levels of knowledge at post-test, but younger students actually showed higher levels of adaptiveness at the end of the intervention. The researchers suggest that their lower level of initial knowledge may have benefitted them in their ability to take up new ideas through instruction. They take this as evidence that instruction focused on promoting adaptiveness needs to occur early in students' educational careers. All of the aforementioned studies employed challenge-based instructional approaches, where students need to engage in problem solving around a complex topic. They all found that such an approach leads to gains in adaptive expertise, however, it was operationalized. These findings suggest that learning environments that center on problems and projects hold substantial promise for fostering the development of adaptive expertise in engineering educators.

Our research has focused on youth making in highly open-ended out-of-school learning environments. We believe that these contexts often provide challenging environments that satisfy Hatano and Inagaki's (1992) four conditions. As such, they can provide a promising context for the development of knowledge, skills, and attitudes needed to place youth on a trajectory toward adaptive expertise in design. The open-ended nature of making in informal learning environments allows youth substantial freedom in what and when they learn, making it difficult to assess learning gains on knowledge and skills defined *a priori*. Instead, we examine the ways in which making in informal settings can align with Hatano and Inagaki's (1992) four conditions.

Making and Adaptive Expertise

We present here the experiences of twin brothers Carter and Jacob, who participated in a maker club with six other boys. Though they participated in the same group, their contrasting experiences highlight ways that making may support, or at times fail to support, conditions for the development of adaptive expertise. We briefly introduce these two projects and describe the nature of work on the projects, based on field notes, videotapes of the work session, and reflections on their work that youth participants, parents, and mentors shared with us in one-on-one interviews.

To collect this data, we worked with *Maker Club*,[1] an organization that helped youth find mentors and coordinated their participation at Maker Faire, to find four case study groups that represented a range of participation structures and experience levels. We followed these groups for approximately four months leading up to the presentation of their projects at the regional exposition. We conducted pre- and post-project interviews with the youth participants, and post-project interviews with parents and mentors. We observed and made video and audio recordings of work sessions and public presentations, and we took pictures of projects, sketches, and other artifacts. The group and participant experiences we describe here were unique in the particulars of their projects and group structure, but the interactions we highlight are representative of the kind of participation we saw across all of the case study groups we followed.

The *Hillside Makers* were a group of eight boys, ranging in age from 12 to 17, most of whom were first-year participants in Maker Club and most of whom knew each other from their local public school. A parent initiated the group, hoping to channel her son's intellectual energy and connect him to a group of peers with similar interests. She did not have the technical expertise she felt would best support the group, so the group found two community mentors. The group met weekly and most meetings were held at the homes of the mentors, who brought experience with digital technologies and design work, as well as access to tools and workspaces. The parent organization, Maker Club, facilitated the formation of local clubs, like Hillside Makers, and provided presentation space at Maker Faire, but had no involvement in local club meetings. In addition, Maker Club sponsored monthly meetings to share ideas and works in progress.

The group's first mentor, Chris, a creative professional and father who had hosted a Maker Club (of different kids) the previous year, was suggested to the group by a Maker Club regional staff member. Chris saw that making infused many aspects of his professional work and, after working with his own children on projects the last two years, believed that the experience of being able to try out new tools and skills, meet young people with similar interests, and work on something to completion was very valuable to young people. While he worked hard to introduce a new idea or skill to the group at each meeting, he allowed ideas to wander and did not pressure the group members to find and finish individual projects. He also provided the group access to a 3D printer at his workplace and to a network of makers who gave periodic demonstrations to the group.

The second mentor, Kevin, joined the group a few weeks into their maker "season." Kevin worked in IT and had been looking into helping with FIRST Robotics (www.firstinspires.org). Instead, he found the Maker Club website, saw a club in his area, and got in touch with the group. With Chris as the more experienced mentor, Kevin saw himself as a resource: "I didn't have any individual goals for the kids. I just kind of viewed my role as being there to help out, and to help them achieve whatever goals they had set for themselves, help them learn something along the way, provide them whatever information they might need." Kevin spent time researching aspects of the group members' projects, helped obtain materials, shared his own expertise, and made his home available as a workspace. By the end of the work period, he seemed to have become an advisor and project partner trusted by the young group members.

Beginning in January and continuing until a local Maker Faire in May, Kevin and Chris introduced technologies and skills to the group members—soldering, carpentry, 3D design—and discussed project ideas. This discussion often alternated between serious and playful. As the group members presented ideas or talked about recent progress, considerations and difficulties were mentioned, but the group would also discuss potential uses and modifications, spinning out ideas for things to add, potential uses, and completely new projects. For example, an idea for a wand that would shock people led to fanciful talk about what kind of reactions it might provoke, as well as a technical discussion about electricity and safety.

Case 1: Robotic Hand Design

Early in the work period, Carter, age 13, settled on a project idea, the "robotic hand," a life-size hand made out of 3D printed fingers that he would be able to control with a smartphone. Culled from a longer list of potential projects that were too complicated or not interesting enough, the project offered Carter a chance to try something ambitious while using the 3D printer, a tool he did not usually have access to and was eager to learn about.

After discussing and sketching with a friend in the group, Carter began designing the hand using TinkerCad, an online CAD tool introduced by one of the mentors. He ran into trouble because, in his own words, he "had considered the 3D printer, at that time, perfectly accurate." He had designed small, precise fingers that printed out "too fat"—intricate features turned into "little bumps." Carter had to redesign the fingers multiple times, each week sending a new file to Chris to print out before the weekend meeting, testing the newly printed components, and adjusting the design for a subsequent print and test cycle.

With these difficulties, the robotic hand project offered early and frequent experience with *events that disconfirm expectations.* The printed parts and the design did not work as expected, requiring many cycles of testing and redesign. Later, with a week left until Maker Faire, he modified his goals, planning to mount just two fingers that would go up and down, one controlled with a string and one with a smartphone button. Carter talked with his dad about how this would allow the Maker Faire audience to try out the robotic hand and demonstrate the mechanism and its potential. He told us,

> A lot of things weren't working great. We had one last [work] day . . . we probably got half the work on the entire project just *done* in that couple of hours, 'cause we just figured out, hey, let's just do the rubber band thing, and let's see if we can get *one* finger to work.

Over the course of a couple hours in the group's last work session, Carter worked with Kevin, his dad, and another parent to develop, refine, and troubleshoot placement and attachment of a small servo motor, opting for creative use of rubber bands instead of a more permanent solution. He discovered problems with the servo motor and worked to design a modification to the motor's arm. He also coordinated the work of another peer who agreed to help with the computer code that would allow him to control the servo motor. By the day of Maker Faire, Carter had a workable, if rough, prototype of his robotic hand. He was able to commit to physical form his hypotheses about how something might work, and then confront results that supported or disconfirmed his mental models.

While solving these problems, Carter engaged in *dialogic interactions* with parents, mentors, and peers. He shared plans, received feedback, answered questions, and integrated new approaches and ideas. Such discourse continued at the regional exposition as well as in informal presentations to family members and friends. Carter had opportunities not only to consolidate knowledge about the technologies, mechanisms, and computer programs that his project relied upon, but also to describe and reflect upon how he created the robotic hand—his process of design and construction.

In a presentation guide given to youth participants, Maker Club organizers told students to "collect photos, sketches, prototypes . . . anything that tells the story of how and why your projects came to be." They asked youth presenters to be ready to answer questions about how their projects worked, what past experiences they had, and what parts were most difficult, fun, or surprising. These guidelines, with their emphasis on explanation and storytelling, show the organization was a *community that valued comprehension*, explanation, and experimentation.

The adult mentors who worked with Carter also seemed to value youth understanding and autonomy in their interactions. For example, when Carter would bring a new idea to his mentor Kevin, Kevin would provide feedback and ask questions, but often take a hands-off stance, saying, "yeah, that could work," and leaving Carter to return to discussions with peers or to constructing the new iterations. Carter's father told us he viewed the project not as a "father–son project," but as "the son's project," and avoided inserting his ideas too often into the project, letting Carter retain decision-making control.

This focus on youth autonomy and metacognitive knowledge of design and building processes is important. Building knowledge of processes relevant to engineering and of one's own learning and working strategies are important steps on a trajectory toward engineering design expertise. Reflecting on the project, Carter felt he learned a great deal about the need to simplify and prototype, identify priorities early on, and set benchmarks for progress. His father saw in him new abilities to understand and appreciate how things were designed and fabricated and new knowledge of what it takes to get from an idea to a product.

Finally, Carter's work took place in a context that was largely *free of punishments and rewards* and that supported playful experimentation. At the community level, Maker Club organizers emphasized noncompetiveness, requesting and celebrating descriptions of project "failures." At the group level, mentors and parents seemed to share this embrace of failure and worked to keep stakes low, but excitement high. Carter's father described his perspective, echoing similar statements from Kevin and Chris: "I could possibly have [helped with more details], but for whatever reasons I didn't. I was seeing value at other levels . . . I don't think the sign of success was a kid actually implementing or not. I saw growth and positive experiences for both [brothers], at whatever level they happened to be at."

The presentation deadline was certainly a major motivator for Carter, but the lack of rewards or competition made it easier to scale back plans and show an early prototype. The time pressure did sometimes push Carter toward a nonideal solution. He told us that, near the end, "we were pretty much out of time . . . and we were trying to come up with all these things, we were drawing, and it was like, 'what's the simplest, basic thing I can do to fix it, even if it's not very good.'" Nonetheless, the youth and parents we interviewed frequently described creativity, curiosity, and openness as important characteristics of making and being a maker, as well as of design, engineering, and other technical work. These shared community values made less likely that a deadline would motivate a move toward efficiency over creativity.

Case 2: Automatic Tripod / Tesla Coil Design

We now briefly turn to projects that Jacob, age 13, worked on. Jacob began work in Hillside Makers at the same time as his twin brother Carter, interacted with the same mentors and parents, and spoke about some of the same values and interests, but his experience differed in important ways.

At the beginning of the work period, Jacob was interesting in building an "automatic tripod" that would level itself automatically. He sketched ideas and did a little research, but lost momentum when he, like some of the other boys in the club, failed to find an idea he really cared about. Jacob described his process of not making progress, then procrastinating, and "then you're not making progress, and you don't want to do it even *more*. . . . I was trying to get people to help me, and it wasn't really working, 'cause no one was really interested in it, and *I* wasn't super interested in it myself . . . and [then] the Tesla coil project sort of came along."

With five weeks left until the Maker Faire, Kevin, a mentor, realized that many of the young makers' projects had sputtered. He initiated a large group project that he hoped would catch their interest and provide opportunities to both learn about electricity and participate in Maker Faire. Building from the young makers' jokes and conversations about voltage and amperage, Kevin asked the group if they would like to make a Tesla coil, a device that uses large capacitors to create a dramatic arc of electricity.

Because it involved many parts and needed to be finished in a relatively short period of time, the Tesla coil provided opportunities for almost all of the group members to contribute. Mentors explicitly taught principles of electricity, parts of an electrical system, and how to safely use these in construction. They taught and discussed use of fabrication tools as they brought in new materials. The boys developed a jig to help the tedious process of coiling thin copper wire. Parents and visitors frequently asked the boys how it all worked.

Despite its complexity, the Tesla coil offered few surprises and few sticking points for the youth (Jacob included) to troubleshoot, and the well-planned design did not require revision. The work demanded using tools and materials that the boys were not familiar with, and they learned a number of new skills, but the high stakes of the project—the Tesla coil could be unsafe if not constructed properly—meant that there was little room for risk taking and variation. Therefore, Kevin researched the plans online and gathered most of the supplies. In Jacob's words, "I don't really remember ever getting stuck on anything, because it was pretty well planned out—what pieces were going to be made and how they were going to be put together."

At the Maker Faire, the Tesla coil generated few opportunities for Jacob to engage in meaningful dialog, to share what he had learned, or to receive feedback, critique, and questions. Two of the other boys in the group did see these opportunities, as they would usually speak for the group in informal situations and at the regional exposition. In Jacob's words, "I don't think I ended up showing [the Tesla coil] that much. Other people did. But it drew a lot of attention—a gigantic coil."

The particular division of labor seen in this group project left Jacob with few opportunities to develop adaptive design expertise. While the community value of conceptual knowledge remained in place, the other conditions for the development of adaptive expertise were weaker. There were few violations of expectation, as the project was built from an existing design and largely preformed as expected. There was little opportunity for experimentation due to the dangers of a high voltage project. Finally, while there were opportunities for dialogic interaction, they were not evenly distributed, and Jacob missed out.

However, we do not suggest that Jacob gained little from his experience in the Maker Club. Like Carter, Jacob talked in interviews about realizing the importance of planning, drawing from the dissolution of his originally planned project, the automatic tripod, as well as from participating in an expert-led building process with the Tesla coil. As Jacob's dad confirmed in our interviews, working on the Tesla also gave Jacob an opportunity to gain new insight into electricity concepts, new appreciation for the design and manufacturing processes behind everyday objects, and allowed him to carry forward and broaden an existing interest in technology.

In addition to a playful, reflective, and collaborative atmosphere in which to engage with technology and design, working on the Tesla coil may provide a technical and socioemotional foundation from which Jacob can build in the future. Vossoughi and Bevan (2014) caution against dismissal of the potential of *assembling* to be "intellectually generative." This potential is illustrated by Chris's comments after the Maker Faire.

> It was also for me a strong desire of like, this is the first time the kids are going through [Maker Club]; it's easy to fail, because they're all nervous and learning. If you can do something like [the Tesla coil], they'll be engaged next time around. They'll be a little more independent, a little more confident.

Discussion

Making and engineering can certainly align in the topics and skills they employ, as seen in the extensive exploration of electricity in both Carter's and Jacob's experiences. We believe that a deeper, more important connection can be made in the shared focus on *design* in making and in engineering. Furthermore, we believe that engaging in making can do more than simply build skill in and procedural knowledge of design (e.g., learning and practicing steps in the design process), but under the right circumstances can help youth develop *adaptive expertise in design*—the ability to learn new things and work through unexpected circumstances. Good designers, after all, do more than simply follow a design process faithfully. They must, among other things, collaboratively engage in inquiry and decision making in contexts characterized by ambiguity and uncertainty (Dym, Agogino, Eris, Frey, & Leifer, 2005), conditions which require flexibility and creativity.

Our analysis of Carter's and Jacob's experiences in Maker Club highlights some important opportunities that engaging in making and its community can bring, as well as some of the dimensions along which conditions may differ. Carter's case shows that making can satisfy conditions for the development of adaptive expertise in design. More evidence is needed to understand how and when such expertise can be translated into a more formal engineering design context, but we believe our data give strong reasons to be hopeful that such translation is possible.

Jacob's case shows that youth experience in making can differ in significant ways, even within a similar context. Jacob had a positive experience. He helped with a dynamic and exciting project, learned new skills, and had fun. One can credit mentor Kevin for creating a project that engaged the group collectively after a number of individual projects fizzled out. Nonetheless, this case shows that conditions for the development of adaptive expertise are not automatically met. We believe that more careful attention to the nature of these conditions, and the pedagogical moves needed to sustain them, may help educators to create more fruitful learning environments (e.g., Blikstein & Worsley, 2016, in volume 1 of this series; see chapter 3 of this volume for a specifically design-centered approach).

Although our data are drawn from an out-of-school context, we see in them lessons relevant to those working to bring making into the school context. Classrooms experience forces pushing them toward valuing procedural efficiency, toward external reward and punishment structures, and away from open-ended discourse and experimentation. Yet within making, with its distinctive blend of playful yet technical student-driven projects, there is a distinctive opportunity to upend the traditional and well-worn curricular pathways of schooling to embrace learning activities in line with conditions for the development of adaptive expertise. In our work, we have seen these conditions arise in places where young people experience ample support, substantial autonomy, freedom to explore, and a rich context to talk about their work, yet there are certainly many other ways to foster these conditions, which can and should be explored.

Note

1 All names of organizations and people are pseudonyms.

References

Azevedo, F. S. (2011). Lines of practice: A practice-centered theory of interest relationships. *Cognition and Instruction*, *29*(2), 147–184.

Blikstein, P., & Worsley, M. (2016). Children are not hackers: Building a culture of powerful ideas, deep learning, and equity in the maker movement. In K. Peppler, E. Halverson, &

Y. Kafai (Eds.), *Makeology: Makerspaces as learning environments* (Volume 1) (pp. 64–79). New York, NY: Routledge.

Dym, C. L., Agogino, A. M., Eris, O., Frey, D. D., & Leifer, L. J. (2005). Engineering design thinking, teaching, and learning. *Journal of Engineering Education, 94*(1), 103–120.

Hatano, G. & Inagaki, K. (1986). Two courses of expertise. In H. Stevenson, H. Assume, & K. Hakuta (Eds.), *Child development and education in Japan* (pp. 262–272). New York: Freeman.

Hatano, G. & Inagaki, K. (1992). Desituating cognition through the construction of conceptual knowledge. In P. Light & G. Butterworth (Eds.), *Context and cognition: Ways of learning and knowing* (pp. 115–133). Hillsdale, NJ: Lawrence Erlbaum and Associates.

Kuznetsov, S. & Paulos, E. (2010). Rise of the expert amateur: DIY projects, communities, and cultures. In *Proceedings of the 6th Nordic Conference on Human–Computer Interaction (NordiCHI): Extending Boundaries* (pp. 295–304). Reykjavik, Iceland.

Martin, L. & Dixon, C. (2013). Youth conceptions of making and the Maker Movement. *Presented at the Interaction, Design, and Children (IDC) Conference, 2013*. New York.

McKenna, A. F. (2014). Adaptive expertise and knowledge fluency in design and innovation. In A. Johri & B. Olds (Eds.), *Cambridge handbook of engineering education research* (pp. 227–242). New York: Cambridge University Press.

National Research Council. (2009). *Engineering in K–12 education*. Committee on K–12 Engineering Education, National Academy of Engineering and National Research Council of the National Academies.

National Research Council. (2011). *A framework for K–12 science education: Practices, crosscutting concepts, and core ideas.* Committee on Conceptual Framework for the New K–12 Science Education Standards, Board on Science Education, National Research Council. Washington, DC: National Academies Press.

Pandy, M. G., Petrosino, A. J., Austin, B. A., & Barr, R. E. (2004). Assessing adaptive expertise in undergraduate biomechanics. *Journal of Engineering Education, 93*(3), 211–222.

Quinn, H. & Bell, P. (2013). How designing, making, and playing relate to the learning goals of K–12 science education. In M. Honey & D. Kanter (Eds.), *Design, make, play: Growing the next generation of STEM innovators* (pp. 17–33). New York: Routledge.

Rayne, K., Martin, T., Brophy, S., Kemp, N. J., Hart, J. D., & Diller, K. R. (2006). The development of adaptive expertise in biomedical engineering ethics. *Journal of Engineering Education, 95*(2), 165–173.

Resnick, M. & Rosenbaum, E. (2013). Designing for tinkerability. In M. Honey & D. Kanter (Eds.), *Design, make, play: Growing the next generation of STEM innovators* (pp. 163–181). New York: Routledge.

Thorndike, E. L. & Woodworth, R. S. (1901). The influence of improvement in one mental function upon the efficiency of other functions. *Psychological Review, 8*, 247–261.

Vossoughi, S., & Bevan, B. (2014, October). Making and tinkering: A review of the literature. *National Research Council Committee on Out of School Time STEM*, 1–55.

Walker, J. M. T., Cordray, D. S., King, P. H., & Brophy, S. P. (2006). Design scenarios as an assessment of adaptive expertise. *International Journal of Engineering Education, 22*(3), 645–651.

CHAPTER 12

Making, Tinkering, and Computational Literacy

MATTHEW BERLAND

Introduction

One powerful way to become computationally literate is to learn how to express yourself through the making of computational artifacts. That said, developing computational literacy is difficult and developing working artifacts involves a lot of failure: wires can short; LEDs might not light up; your batteries could be the wrong voltage; you have picked out the wrong materials; or your code might not compile. Those failures can be frustrating, but they serve a valuable purpose—they sit at the core of how you learn to build, engineer, and solve complex problems, both creative and technical. In this chapter, I discuss how making—in particular, tinkering and fiddling around with creative projects—can help people in becoming more computationally literate.

The Maker Movement (Dougherty, 2012) has significant potential in helping people learn computational literacy. In particular, the practice of tinkering in making—the playful fiddling that characterizes a lot of the fun in hobby engineering—can be a principled and theoretically sound way to gain expertise with complex technical content. In this chapter, I investigate what makes tinkering useful, what aspects of making specifically involve tinkering, why computational literacy can be valuable, and what aspects of computational literacy may most help budding makers.

So what is computational literacy? Broadly, it describes how one can use computation as a tool, as a *lens*, to understand and communicate with the world. A print-literate person is someone who not only reads books well or writes sentences well, but can create well and communicate effectively. A computationally literate person can create, communicate, and problem-solve with computation. This is useful for any number of reasons: creative expression, effective communication, and access to jobs and resources.

Background: Computational Literacy

This chapter follows diSessa (2001) in defining computational literacy as consisting of three component aspects: material, social, and cognitive. *Material computational literacy* can be defined as making things with computation—primarily programming and electronics. This kind of material literacy can come in many forms: through facility in making a complex spreadsheet in Excel; from the ability to pack your luggage using the most efficient procedure; or through evaluating various data structures in program code. Most of what is considered to be material computational literacy is simply the ability to write and craft program code to express oneself and build usable artifacts. *Social computational literacy* describes the ability to articulate, discuss, communicate, and understand what you and other people need from those computational artifacts. This is fundamentally distinct from material computational fluency—more *to whom* and *for whom* computation is valuable then *how* to make a computational artifact work or run. Articulating meaningfully about programming is difficult: it requires overlapping teaching skills, speaking skills, and technical skills. Having some of those skills does not imply that you have all of them: many people who have significant programming ability often lack the ability to articulate the meaning and process of creating computational artifacts. Linking the social and the material is, in part, *cognitive computational literacy*—often called computational thinking. I discuss computational thinking later in the chapter, but, in short, it can be defined in terms of the ability to think about problems, contexts, and the world in terms of what computation can and cannot do, where and why it is useful, and how it exists as a tool. If material literacy is *how* and social literacy is *where* and *for whom*, cognitive literacy primarily describes *why*.

There are multiple reasons why someone might decompose literacy in this way, but a primary benefit is that it provides a "handle" with which to build curriculum, makerspaces, and communities. Many communities—even complex and well-established ones—focus only on one aspect of computational literacy, while ignoring the others. For example, some learning environments (and makerspaces) provide great tools but no explicit structures for encouraging experts to teach new participants how to use them; some provide an engaging social environment and vivid discussions but focus heavily on making only one "kind" of thing (e.g., "battle-bots"); some provide a diverse set of experiences but do not engage new participants in making something social or vital (thus missing out on valuable experience and context). As diSessa (2001) compellingly argues, those approaches will likely struggle to create more engaged learners who can transfer their understanding to new environments because they cannot engage students in building computational literacy holistically.

The communitarian ethos underlying the Maker Movement (as described by Dougherty, 2012) gives the movement the potential to succeed in supporting learners' computational literacy by creating social spaces (such as makerspaces) in which people learn together by building together. The articulation, argumentation, and social orientation found in these spaces are deeply connected to what we know about how people learn (e.g., Vygotsky, 1980) and specific learning practices, such as reflection. Indeed, teaching each other to make things (whether formally or informally) has been found to be one of the best practices for learning complex content (Chi, Siler, Jeong, Yamauchi, & Hausmann, 2001).

In addition, determining what to build and then building projects that you or the community actually wants or needs is a classic engineering problem. Atman, Cardella, Turns, and Adams (2005) found that identifying the wants and needs of the community is, perhaps, the skill most vital but hardest to teach in introductory engineering classes; it was the identification, specification, and refinement of the problem space in which novices and experts most differed—not skills, math, or theory, as others had predicted. This corresponds to findings in other fields in which understanding the problem and the connections underlying the problem space is far more salient a predictor of expertise than any specific skill. That describes, in a nutshell, the development of a *lens*—an understanding of how to read, evaluate, and engage with new situations using an understanding of complex content.

Constructionism (Papert & Harel, 1991) is a *framework for action* (diSessa & Cobb, 2004) that frequently uses diSessa's computational literacy construct to teach people to express themselves with computation. The notion of constructionism also underlies many of the more successful efforts in the Maker Movement. Research in and with constructionism suggests that people learn best when they are making *authentic* artifacts (as per Shaffer & Resnick, 1999). Constructionism, as a framework for teaching and learning, meshes well with the Maker Movement, as many makers engage in active construction of authentic artifacts for the benefit of (or, at least, potential use by) other people. Kafai and Burke (2014) use the term *computational participation* to identify this constructionist engagement with the social, authentic community-focused perspective of computation. Computational participation helps both the maker and the people for whom the maker is making. Work on service learning in engineering (e.g., Bielefeldt, Paterson, & Swan, 2009) intuitively suggests that makers (and engineers more broadly) will invest more time and energy into a project when they believe that it will be used. Authentic construction has the added benefit that it generates real feedback—if people cannot use a tool that they need, they will tell you why and how.

Rapid feedback is a hallmark of good learning environment design (Koedinger & Corbett, 2006), good game design (Gee, 2004), and best practices in learning theory (Bransford, Brown, & Cocking, 2000). Learners that get "just in time" (JIT) feedback both can build their learning around that feedback (or "expectation violation," as per Schank, 1983) and construct more effectively around that feedback. Making can work as a best practice for learning by *triangulating rapid feedback* across the aforementioned three aspects of literacy.

Triangulating rapid feedback can be defined as "using rapid feedback from different sources about different aspects of making to inform" (in this case) how and why someone builds an artifact. When I have built digital-physical artifacts in a makerspace, I have received feedback from a diverse set of sources. I get voluminous social feedback in terms of what the other people in the makerspace found valuable (or not) about what I was building; sociomaterial feedback about tools I was using (correctly or incorrectly); sociocognitive feedback about how they would build something differently; material feedback from the actual building of the artifact (which did not work correctly for quite a while); and cognitive-material feedback from watching other peoples' problems wrestling with helping me build my artifact. Much of the feedback was implicit (simply watching people do things differently than I had expected), but feedback from the compiler (say) was quite explicit (syntax or runtime errors). Understanding comes, in part, by connecting what is shared across all of the different forms of feedback. Making is, in part, about bringing those feedback practices out in public.

Computational Literacy in Tinkering and Making

Focusing in on how best to motivate and construct in practice, tinkering emerges as a best practice for generating meaningful rapid feedback both for cognitive literacy and material literacy. In particular, tinkering has several specific features that make it a *cognitive-material practice* (i.e., a potential best practice for developing computational literacy). To do so, it is important to establish both how tinkering works and why tinkering may be specifically valuable.

In Berland, Martin, Benton, Petrick Smith, and Davis (2013), we enumerate eight relevant definitions of tinkering which overlap into an *orientation* and a *set of activities*, as such:

> The tinkering orientation is essentially atheoretic—tinkering, bricolage, and playful experimentation describe the act of either having or needing no plan in the process of creating or modifying a computer program. The set of activities described as tinkering include trial and error, messing around or fussing, finding and using feedback mechanisms (such as testing), or combinations of those activities.
>
> (p. 568)

Interestingly, tinkering is both a novice practice and an expert practice; this sets it apart from many of the classroom practices with which novices learn engineering and computer science. For a long time, people avoided teaching novices to tinker because it was considered a naïve set of habits that prevented people from properly planning out projects (as identified by Turkle & Papert, 1990). However, experts use it frequently for many of the same reasons that novices do (Danielak, 2014), likely because it provides frequent just-in-time feedback. As an expert programmer myself, I can (anecdotally) confirm that my colleagues and I frequently tinker with programs until they work. That said, experts also tend to use high-level plans, structure their work more effectively, understand the problem space better, and can bring many other practices to bear on a problem. Simply because both experts and novices tinker does not make it better or worse, but it does make the practice *professionally authentic*. This is important for the maker community, as making tends to focus on authentic behaviors in professionally authentic settings (e.g., makerspaces, hackerspaces, and FabLabs) used by diverse audiences of makers, ranging from beginners to experts. Common practices can engender easier modes of interaction simply because people are using the same tools in the same ways.

In Berland et al. (2013), we found that tinkering can be characterized by attempting short fixes to problems, a directed exploration of the space, trial and error behavior, and the acquisition of new expertise through feedback on failures on the errors in tinkering. To figure out exactly how and why tinkering may be valuable, it is helpful to consider both expectation violation and productive failure as learning practices. Schank (1983) suggested that much of learning for understanding could be considered a function of *expectation violation*—that to learn something new, it both must be based on current knowledge and understanding and must somehow violate the predictions of that current understanding. Schank argued that humans build up linked, recursive models (called *scripts* and *schema*) and learn when those models prove insufficient. Importantly, this can be true at the largest sense of a conscious thought that "this should probably work" and—far more commonly—at the unconscious level in which someone typically acts.

In some sense, tinkering can be a name for a bridge between the conscious and the unconscious practices of making. You may tinker until something goes wrong without knowing why it will go wrong, learning only when things inevitably fall apart. Rarely do I know exactly what will go wrong when I am tinkering. In the last month, I have experienced compiler errors, runtime errors, physical explosions that splattered paint all over me, simple nonfunctioning behavior, and everything in between. In the cases in which I do have solid predictions of what will happen, the practice is less similar to our local definitions of tinkering and more similar to something significantly closer to systematic exploration or experimentation. There is nothing at all wrong with experimentation—it is often quicker than tinkering—but, crucially, it requires *prior understanding* of the problem space. Before you can guess exactly what will happen, you have to learn what might happen. That is a value of tinkering: *learning what might happen through making semidirectedly and failing*. This is consistent with research into *productive failure* (Kapur, 2008), which shows that more open-ended, ill-structured problems can focus learners' attentions on problem analysis, critique, and evaluation, which, as described above, are aspects of engineering and computer science education with which students have specific difficulty.

That move to "learning what might happen"—perhaps better rephrased as "understanding the problem space"—is a key move towards literacy rather than raw skill or knowledge. This understanding is called either *computational thinking* or the cognitive computational literacy (as per diSessa, 2001, described previously).

Tinkering in the Practice of Making a Robot

One example from my work (Berland et al., 2013) is a study using an iOS game ("IPRO") that our team designed and developed, in which 60 novices in a high school girls' summer camp each constructed a virtual soccer-playing robot (see Figures 12.1 and 12.2). We found that novices followed a relatively small set of pathways in learning to program their robots. That is, people started to program in similar ways; we characterized the general pattern of how they started to program as *EXTIRE* for *ex*ploring, *ti*nkering, and *re*fining. Learners mostly began the session by exploring the space of possible programs and possible program elements—they tried out many tools to explore how and why they could be used to make something, without much direction overall. This corresponds to my personal experience of new and unknown complex learning spaces; it is difficult for me to know what is possible or what is meaningful without figuring out what exists.

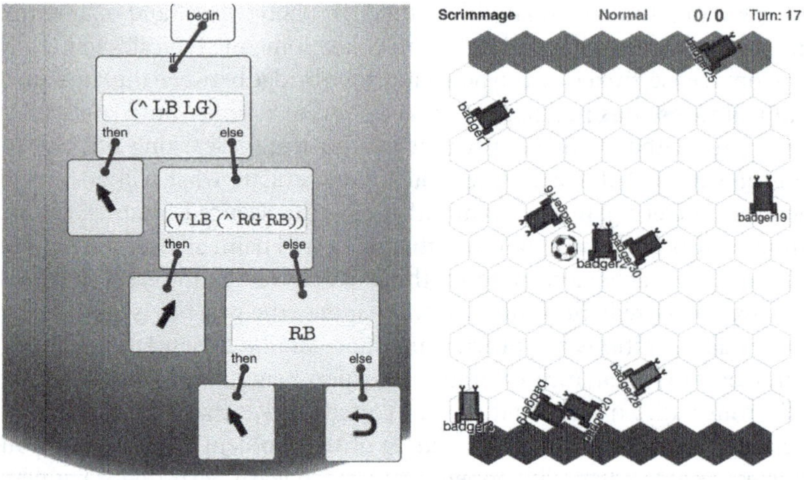

Figure 12.1 The IPRO interface, including programming screen (left) and soccer pitch (right).

Figure 12.2 Students playing IPRO.

As learners began to understand the game, they focused on achieving smaller "local" objectives; rather than trying to win the game outright, they, for instance, tried to make their robot move in a circle or block one other robot. To get there, the players' tinkering practices became very focused—they would fiddle with the tools and materials that they had identified in their exploration phase and, through trial and error, work their way to a solution (showing material computational literacy). However, the targets that you first identify are rarely the targets on which you will end—learning often involves coming to understand what is most valuable in context (building cognitive computational literacy). It is rare to enter a new problem space knowing which actions, practices, or facts are most valuable or relevant, even as an expert.

After tinkering to achieve local objectives, the players began refining their programs. They started isolating and improving elements that they deemed most valuable in order to debug, focus on more globally valuable targets, and generally work toward solving broader problems in the game (such as "being an effective goalie" or "scoring many goals"). It is important that they identified these goals (local and global) by engaging with their teammates. In itself, this is obvious—a forward and a midfielder need to work together to win—but, crucially, their tinkering is structured around the social goals that they identify (exhibiting their social computational literacy).

It is interesting, and perhaps obvious in retrospect, that the quality of their programs (as measured by number of goals scored minus number of times scored upon) went up most quickly during the tinkering phase. Students naturally fell into the rhythm of using rapid feedback to try out an idea, see if it works, and iterate until the idea has reached fruition. They did this by engaging their robots in soccer matches with everybody else's robots and against simulated "dummy" robots. They began to mimic each other's strategies (even more than their code) and, in the process of doing so, came up with novel ways of articulating both code and roles in the game to each other, using tinkering to reinforce each other's sociocognitive literacy skills (Petrick, Berland, & Martin, 2011).

Discussion: Tinkering, Making, and Computational Literacy Practices

The Maker Movement offers hope for computational education, because it offers possibilities to learn computational literacy in a holistic, meaningful way in an environment that encourages play and tinkering. It is valuable to fail in public—you can learn a lot by making things that do not work for other people and then tinkering them into a semblance of functionality. The encountering of many small failures in the process of building something useful—in which many of the failures might be ones only you encounter because of your specific background and your specific prior knowledge (or lack thereof)—will provide feedback for you as you build a lens that you can use.

In Martin, Berland, Benton, and Smith (2013), we found that the learners improved on a variety of computational literacy transfer tasks after engaging in a constructionist tinkering-building game; constructionist theory (diSessa, 2001; Harel & Papert, 1990) suggests that this may be due to the fact that the technical is embedded in an authentic social space, and, through discussion and reflection, learners notice connections together. The specific value of *tinkering together* remains underappreciated. Other work by authors in this series have highlighted specific cases in which students have learned together. In particular, Fields and Lee (2016, in volume 1 of this series), Vasudevan and Kafai (chapter 9 of this volume), and Peppler (chapter 13 of this volume) describe how craft construction can bring people together around tinkering and computation.

Developing computational literacy is a complex prospect—computational literacy requires using diverse skills in multiple contexts across cognitive, social, and material dimensions. But all practice and repetition is not equal. It takes deliberative practice that features rapid material feedback (tinkering—so you don't keep doing the wrong things), rapid social feedback (community—so you can start doing the right things), and rapid cognitive feedback (authentic problem spaces—so you can develop transferrable skills). Makerspaces and the Maker Movement hold promise to create areas in which learners can engage in this kind of optimal deliberative practice.

References

Atman, C. J., Cardella, M. E., Turns, J., & Adams, R. (2005). Comparing freshman and senior engineering design processes: An in-depth follow-up study. *Design Studies, 26*(4), 325–357.

Berland, M., Martin, T., Benton, T., Petrick Smith, C., & Davis, D. (2013). Using learning analytics to understand the learning pathways of novice programmers. *Journal of the Learning Sciences, 22*(4), 564–599. doi:10.1080/10508406.2013.836655

Bielefeldt, A., Paterson, K., & Swan, C. (2009). Measuring the impacts of project-based service learning. In *American Society for Engineering Education (ASEE) Annual Conference Proceedings* (pp. 1–15). Chicago, IL.

Bransford, J. D., Brown, A. L., & Cocking, R. R. (2000). *How people learn*. Washington, DC: National Academy Press.

Chi, M. T., Siler, S. A., Jeong, H., Yamauchi, T., & Hausmann, R. G. (2001). Learning from human tutoring. *Cognitive Science, 25*(4), 471–533.

Danielak, B. A. (2014). *How electrical engineering students design computer programs*. Dissertation, University of Maryland, College Park.

diSessa, A. A. (2001). *Changing minds: Computers, learning, and literacy*. Cambridge, MA: MIT Press.

diSessa, A. A. & Cobb, P. (2004). Ontological innovation and the role of theory in design experiments. *Journal of the Learning Sciences, 13*(1), 77–103.

Dougherty, D. (2012). The Maker Movement. *Innovations, 7*(3), 11–14.

Fields, D. A., & Lee, V. R. (2016). Craft technologies 101: Bringing making to higher education. In K. Peppler, E. Halverson, & Y. Kafai (Eds.), *Makeology: Makerspaces as learning environments* (Volume 1) (pp. 121–137). New York, NY: Routledge.

Gee, J. P. (2004). *What video games have to teach us about learning and literacy*. New York, NY: Palgrave MacMillan.

Harel, I. & Papert, S. (1990). Software design as a learning environment. *Interactive Learning Environments, 1*(1), 1–32.

Kafai, Y. B. & Burke, W. (2014). *Connected code*. Cambridge, MA: MIT Press.

Kapur, M. (2008). Productive failure. *Cognition and Instruction, 26*(3), 379–424.

Koedinger, K. R. & Corbett, A. (2006). Cognitive tutors: Technology bringing learning sciences to the classroom. In K. Sawyer (Ed.), *The Cambridge handbook of the learning sciences* (pp. 61–78). New York: Cambridge University Press.

Martin, T., Berland, M., Benton, T., & Smith, C. P. (2013). Learning programming with IPRO: The effects of a mobile, social programming environment. *Journal of Interactive Learning Research, 24*(3), 301–328.

Papert, S. & Harel, I. (1991). Situating constructionism. In I. Harel & S. Papert (Eds.), *Constructionism* (pp. 1–12). New York, NY: Ablex Publishing.

Petrick, C., Berland, M., & Martin, T. (2011). Allocentrism and computational thinking. In G. Stahl, H. Spada, & N. Miyake (Eds.), *Proceedings of the Ninth International Conference on Computer-Supported Collaborative Learning (CSCL)* (pp. 666–670). Hong Kong.

Schank, R. C. (1983). *Dynamic memory: A theory of reminding and learning in computers and people*. New York, NY: Cambridge University Press.

Shaffer, D. W. & Resnick, M. (1999). "Thick" authenticity: New media and authentic learning. *Journal of Interactive Learning Research, 10*(2), 195–215.

Turkle, S. & Papert, S. (1990). Epistemological pluralism: Styles and voices within the computer culture. *Signs, 16*(1). Retrieved on October 1, 2014 from www.jstor.org/stable/3174610

Vygotsky, L. S. (1980). *Mind in society: The development of higher psychological processes*. Cambridge, MA: Harvard University Press.

CHAPTER 13

ReMaking Arts Education Through Physical Computing

KYLIE PEPPLER

Introduction

The Maker Movement is an amalgam of low-tech and high-tech traditions, though it is the invention and incorporation of new technology that propels its current attention and reach. Similarly, there has been increasing attention paid to the role of new technologies in visual and performing arts education, reflected in the creation of new "media arts" national standards (www.mediaartseducation.org). Though both spheres evaluate technology for its functional and expressive purposes, media art places a greater emphasis on visual culture and linear media, whereas computational media factors more prominently into the broader Maker Movement. Given that computation is taking a more central place in the palette of many of today's professional artists, it is worth investigating whether a greater conversation between arts education and Maker Culture could better prepare youth for entrance into the professional discourse of today's contemporary art.

Over the last two decades, professional artists have mastered computation alongside the visual and aesthetic thinking necessary to the arts (Maeda, 2004; Reas, 2006). Artists approach code as though it were a type of material, like clay or paint, with distinct characteristics, affordances, and limitations. Through an intimate familiarity with the material and a variety of cultivated techniques, artists shape computer code to envision new forms, interfaces, and applications. Because code is so central to expression in new media, a number of scholars, educators, and artists have argued for the inclusion of computation as one of the "new fundamentals" of media art, necessitating the adoption of new computational tools that enable users to engage the computer as a new medium (Maeda, 2004; Peppler, 2010a, 2010b; Reas, 2006) and further arguing that new tools make it possible for even the youngest of artists to engage in computational creativity (Peppler, 2010a; Peppler & Warschauer, 2012).

This chapter takes a closer look at what a maker approach to arts education might look like, one that enhances traditional arts instruction with approaches for producing art that interacts with its environment, facilitates expressive modalities of wearable technology, and takes advantage of the latest breakthroughs in art, technology, and science. Creative production like this can be seen in array of art venues from the colloquial to the curated, including Do-It-Yourself (DIY) creative practices (Kafai & Peppler, 2011), showcased in venues like Maker Faires, as well as the work of professional artists like Cory Arcangel or in the tech-enhanced fashion designs of Hussein Chalayan exhibited in the world's premier art museums. Because of the centrality of "physical computing"—new forms of computational creativity to control and respond to our physical environment—to artistic expression, this chapter argues that we must expand our vision for the arts in education by adding physical computing, a quintessential maker method of production, to the K–16 arts curriculum.

Seeking to address the feasibility of narrowing the gap between arts education and maker practice, this chapter explores the extent to which youth are able to engage in authentic and creative forms of physical computing. Data is pulled from a two-week e-textiles summer workshop with non-dominant Chicago Public School students (Buechley, Peppler, Eisenberg, & Kafai, 2013). E-textiles blend computation, craft, and electronics and involve the sewing of wearable computers, sensors, LEDs, and small motors into cloth using conductive thread. The e-textile can then be programmed using novice-friendly software like Modkit (Baafi & Millner, 2011) and uploaded to the wearable computer. Examples of middle school youth engaging in the creative production of e-textiles are presented in this chapter to illustrate how youth can easily be introduced to the basics of physical computing, which encompass a range of techniques and processes, including (1) learning about electronic construction and theory, (2) learning to code creatively, and (3) learning traditional and high-tech craftsmanship. This chapter concludes with a discussion surrounding the implications that physical computing represents for 21st-century K–16 arts education.

Background

Maker Practice, Physical Computing, and Media Arts

The arts reflect the current historical moment. As such, it should come as no surprise that new technologies are being used ubiquitously as creative tools in the arts. This emergent domain of art involving new technologies is an expansive and somewhat amorphous area, commonly referred to as "media arts," "new media," "digital art," or "interactive art" (Nalven & Jarvis, 2005; Paul, 2003). Although the terms have a good deal of overlap, the term "media arts" is used here to "encompass all forms of creative practice involving or referring to art that makes use of electronic equipment, computation, and new communication technologies" (Peppler, 2010a, p. 2119). Media arts encourage designing, creating, and interacting with technology in new ways, which are being widely explored in contemporary art practice.

This mix of tools, materials, techniques, and concepts brings contemporary artists in touch with a number of traditional design and technology domains, including fashion design, product design, arts, crafts, textile design, game design, media design, interaction design, architecture, and interior design, as well as a number of traditional technology domains, including digital technology, wearable technology, material science, electrical engineering, wireless technology, and nanotechnology, among others. In fact, many contemporary media art is created by artists that have either cross-disciplinary training or by teams of collaborators that each specializes in different areas.

Undergirding the work of these artists and many others in contemporary art is the leveraging of software and hardware to sense and control the physical world. Physical computing, in the broadest sense, means building physical systems, sculptures, or environments that are interactive through the use of hardware and software that can communicate with people by using sensors and output devices controlled by small computers, called "microcontrollers." Generally, physical computing can be viewed as a way of describing the relationship we have with the digital world.

Existing Toolkits and Educational Approaches to Support Physical Computing

Currently, there is a larger national push to include technology in the schooling curriculum and new momentum to include new technologies in the arts education curriculum (Arts Education Partnership, 2004), as evidenced by the adoption of media arts curriculum in large schooling districts like Los Angeles Unified (e.g., LAUSD Arts Branch, 2005). However, new media arts programs are often limited by their exclusive adoption of software that emphasize image manipulation (e.g., Adobe Photoshop) as opposed to tools that allow youth to explore the medium of the computer through learning to creatively code (Peppler, 2010b). Those few academic programs that have provided entryways into these areas have taken place almost exclusively in elite higher education institutions steeped in Fine Arts traditions. However, designers over the past several years have created and marketed novice-friendly toolkits with varying degrees of creative potential that would be suitable for adoption in arts education.

First, there is a body of artistic work that has emerged around robotics kits for artists that employs simple gears, pulleys, levers, and microcomputers to sense and control lights, sounds, motors, and other output devices. For example, the commercially available LEGO Mindstorms NXT construction kit allows designers to create robots using unique combinations of microcomputer LEGO bricks, programmed using a visual building block language to take inputs from touch, color, and/or ultrasonic sensors. Other, more advanced robotics toolkits include the Arduino Platform—the toolkit of choice for most artists, designers, and DIY hobbyists—which includes a small microcontroller and accompanying software that can be used to control any number of input and output devices (Banzi, 2008). Although robotics toolkits like these are typically associated with science and technology courses, courses on robotics have also been taught in Fine Arts programs at the undergraduate level (Turbak & Berg, 2002).

A second approach to physical computing toolkits involves a body of work that has emerged around soft circuits or e-textiles. E-textiles are fabric artifacts that include embedded computers and other electronics (Berzowska, 2005; Buechley et al., 2013; Marculescu et al., 2003; chapter 8 of this volume). Instead of focusing on practices like soldering and desoldering, this genre of physical computing involves learning about sewing, quilting, crocheting, knitting, or other techniques that have historically been the domain of seamstresses and crafters. In this tradition, new materials like conductive thread, conductive fabrics woven from copper, silver, or other highly conductive fibers, conductive yarn, and conductive paints are engendering new genres of work that look and feel different from traditional circuits soldered together with insulated wire. There is a range of internationally available toolkits to support e-textile production, including the LilyPad Arduino, i*CATch, fabrickit, and Aniomagic. These toolkits have been deployed to cultivate various aspects of physical computing in a range of educational applications, including in-school, out-of-school, and higher education environments (Buechley et al., 2013; Fields & Lee, 2016, in volume 1 of this series; Kafai, Fields, & Searle, 2014; chapter 5 of this volume).

This chapter takes a qualitative approach to examining youth in the process of art making involving physical computing with e-textiles in order to address the extent to which e-textile production facilitates opportunities for youth to engage in authentic and creative forms of physical computing. More specifically, we were interested in the extent to which e-textile production facilitates opportunities for youth to engage in (a) electronic construction and theory, (b) creative computing, as well as (c) traditional and high-tech craftsmanship. The development of these skills puts youth in a place where they can combine new technologies and traditional materials in artistically expressive ways.

The E-Textiles Summer Workshop

While many educational approaches have been developed to support physical computing and a wide range of hands-on activities, our two-week summer workshop centered on youth designing with e-textiles for their natural connections to interests in fashion, design, arts, crafts, and new technologies, as well as their ability to engage traditionally marginalized youth (Peppler, Salen, Gresalfi, & Santo, 2014), especially young women (Buechley, Eisenberg, Catchen, & Crockett, 2008; Kuznetsov & Paulos, 2010).

The summer workshop was taught by four professional K–12 teachers at a university facility in Chicago over a period of two weeks, meeting an average of four hours per day, Monday through Friday. The teachers, all newcomers to the world of e-textiles, taught in teams of two in two separate classrooms equipped with interactive whiteboards, large project tables, and one laptop per child. A concerted effort was made to keep didactic modes of instruction to a minimum; the majority of youths' learning would come from playful exploration with the materials and observations of each other's projects and processes. This workshop concentrated on the development of the youths' individual sensibilities within the structure of specific thematic assignments (Rusk, Resnick, Berg, & Pezalla-Granlund, 2008). Emphasis was placed on independent investigations and creative problem solving.

The workshop was offered freely to middle-school-aged youth in the public schools and attracted 53 participants—57% of whom were African American, 15% Caucasian, 9% Latina/o, 9% Biracial, and 19% declined to state. The group included nearly equal numbers of female ($N = 27$) and male youth ($N = 26$). The youth were rising 6th- and 7th-grade students and more than 80% were from low-income communities.

Over the course of the workshop, we collected extensive videotaped observations of classroom interactions, youths' sketchbooks, and informal interviews with youth. Two cameras with wireless microphones were used to capture the workshop events and dialogue. These cameras were consistently focused on eight of the workshop participants who wore the wireless microphones over the course of the workshop. Randomly selected but representative of the diversity of the youth participating, youth recorded their notes and ideas for their projects in a personal sketchbook throughout the workshop. The sketchbooks contained all of the participants' notes, as well as their circuit diagrams, initial designs, and finished project sketches. At the end of the workshop, these notebooks were collected to aid in our data interpretation process, since they provided insights into the youths' design process and contained information that was difficult, if not impossible, to capture through video alone.

The 200+ hours of videotaped observations were first logged according to the focus and the current workshop activity and were subject to further analyses. The observations were then tagged for recurrent practices involving physical computing, e-textile production, and art making. We then chose a selection of these vignettes that were both representative of the dataset yet were illustrative of what physical computing can look like with middle-school-aged youth.

Youths' Media Art and Physical Computing

These data sources offer us a closer look how youth create media art via physical computing, informing us about the new materials, processes, and tools required for meaning-making and creative expression with new media. Each aspect of physical computing is presented in greater depth below with attention paid to the extent that youth are able to engage aesthetically and creatively in these introductions beyond merely meeting technical requirements.

Electronic Construction and Theory

The following vignette is of two youth working to construct their first e-textile circuit, after having participated in introductory activities using electronics (see Table 13.1). Amber, a White 7th grader in a well-worn purple T-shirt printed with peace signs, is partnered with Antoine, an African-American 6th grader in basketball shorts and whose height makes him look a little older than his age. The two are working on a project that involves two sock puppets that will complete a circuit when they make contact.

One of the hand puppets was intended to be "reddit robot," who is the "mascot" of reddit.com. In a storyboard that Amber and Antoine created around their puppets, reddit robot sets out to "make people lazyer" [sic] by adding the music to the Nyan Cat Internet meme that rose to prominence at the time of the workshop.

In the sock puppet version of reddit robot, the youth employed their electronics domain knowledge to advance this narrative; the LED on the robot's antenna illuminated when it touched that of the second puppet (equipped with the battery and the other half of the circuit), which represented the content that reddit robot was uploading to the Internet. Having successfully sketched the circuit design earlier, the following vignette depicts the two in the process of making their circuit operational before stitching into the puppets. The youth designed and created their own custom battery holder that sandwiched a 3V battery between two pieces of insulating felt with a small hole cut in the top and bottom sides to create an access point for conductive fabric to touch the battery. The youth ensured a tight connection on either side of the case by affixing a rubber band around it, crossing

Table 13.1 Video transcript of Amber and Antoine troubleshooting the circuitry on their e-textiles project

Video transcript	*Gesture*	*Interpretation*
1. **Amber:** Hold that there. Nah, that ain't going to work—there's not enough pressure . . . It's the rubber band [holding the battery case together] that might not work.	Amber *and* Antoine *place both strips of conductive fabric to the top of the battery holder. The LED fails to illuminate.*	After a first attempt to connect the conductive fabric between the battery and the LED, Amber offers a troubleshooting hypothesis: maybe the connection isn't secure between the battery and its case.
2. **Antoine:** Excuse me, Ms. B—it's not working.		
3. **Amber:** We're testing it with the LED 'cause they [need] more volts, but it's not working.	Ms. B *approaches and places her hands on the project.*	Amber uses domain-appropriate terminology, like LED and volts, to describe the problem.
4. **Ms. B:** Do you think maybe you might have those on the wrong side?	Ms. B *flips the battery holder over, moving both strips of conductive fabric to the underside of the case.*	Ms. B checks to see if the youths applied their knowledge of electrical polarity to their circuit to make sure that the battery is positioned in the right direction respective to the LED.
5. **Antoine:** We tried switching 'em around.		Antoine indicates that they have already tried turning the battery over in a prior attempt—a second hypothesis for why the project might not be working.
6. **Amber:** And they're not touching on the inside [which would cause a short].	*Points to conductive pads on the opposite sides of the battery holder.*	Amber realizes that the next appropriate step to debug the project would be to see if they made the battery holder correctly. She verifies that they have not inadvertently created a battery holder that would cause a short circuit, referencing another domain-appropriate concept—a third hypothesis for why the project isn't working.
7. **Ms. B:** OK, they're not touching . . .	Ms. B *opens the battery case to check.*	

8. **Amber:** Our battery might be dead?		Amber considers a fourth hypothesis: their battery is dead.
9. **Ms. B:** We need to problem shoot again.	Ms. B *applies pressure to the ends of the conductive fabric on the LED prongs. Nothing changes. Then she slides one of the legs of the LED to the backside to connect with the negative side of the battery holder and leaves one of the legs on the positive side of the battery holder. The LED lights up for the first time!*	
10. **Amber:** Huh! She fixed it!	Amber's *face lights up and her speech gets excited.* Antoine *punches his fist in the air.*	
11. **Ms. B:** Nah, I didn't fix it—y'all just weren't holding 'em right. So you *do* have a good connection.		Ms. B verifies that their circuit design was good; the problem lay in the way they were holding the various pieces of their circuit together.
12. Amber: Yeah! Perfect! . . . OK, so we figured out how we're going to do it.	Antoine *and* Amber *head back to their table excitedly.*	

over the middle of the conductive fabric on either side of the battery holder. Moments before the start of this vignette, Amber and Antoine confirmed that the battery holder worked with a multimeter. The pair is holding the electronic components of their puppets together to check whether their homemade battery holder on one puppet is capable of lighting a traditional two-leg LED that will be positioned on the other.

While the youth took initial pains to align what they saw as the negative side of the battery with the negative prong of the LED and vice versa, they didn't realize that both of the connecting fabric strands were resting on the top (positive side) of the battery only. They ultimately, with the help of the instructor, realized that one of the conductive fabric strands would have to reach beneath the battery case to make a complete circuit. By identifying the error and making the corresponding changes to their puppets, the youth were afforded a more robust understanding of how electronic theory works than had they limited their activities to pen and paper explorations.

This mirrors the material exploration of traditional arts instruction, which encourages students to explore a wide range of media, particularly drawing attention to the movement between two- and three-dimensional expressions of ideas. This is used to develop artists' conceptualization of space and its representation, an aspect often proven to be difficult for students.

Once the pair returned to their table, a nearby researcher engaged them in an informal interview about their project. Immediately, the youths' language around the puppet shifted from specific technical qualities as exemplified above, toward incorporating the electronics into their creative vision for the project.

Amber: Our puppets are going to be antennae firing.

Antoine: Yeah, like both have an antenna, and when their antennae touch, her antenna is gonna light up.

Amber: 'Cause mine's a robot. (Points to the peace signs printed on the sock. The pattern is similar to the one on her T-shirt.) A very *peaceful* robot.

Antoine: The battery . . . it's like a switch. If *that* isn't touching *that*, then the circuit is open and energy can't flow through.

Amber and Antoine incorporated the functionality of the circuit into how they described their project—it was no longer just about a functional circuit, it became more about creating an action through electronics that enhanced how viewers saw their puppets' character (see Figure 13.1). Yet, even though the circuitry is in service of a narrative they created for their puppets, their description of how the puppets interconnect were rich with a remarkable amount of domain-specific language, naming not only the physical components of their electronic constructions (e.g., LED, battery) but also the unseen ones (e.g., volts), as well as the ways they work together (e.g., switch, energy, open circuit). A grasp of electronic theory transmitted through the act of working with e-textiles is not only evidenced by the way they incorporated a functional circuit formation into their puppets, but also in their ability to think flexibly in the act of troubleshooting; the youth, after all, came up with three alternative hypotheses to test when their LEDs initially failed to light.

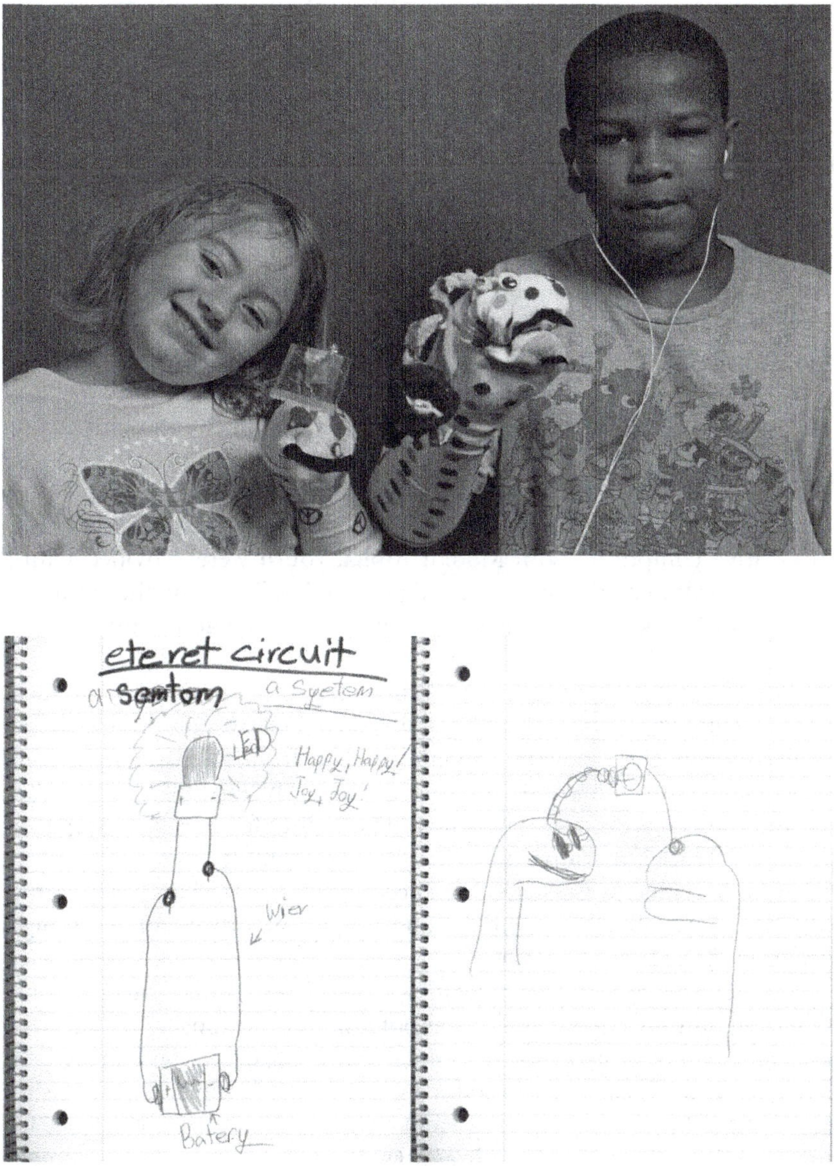

Figure 13.1 Top: Portrait of Amber and Antoine displaying their sock puppets. Bottom left: Planning diagram for the electric circuit in their sock puppet. Bottom right: Planning diagram for the puppet interaction to light the LED.

Creative Computing

As a backbone to arts projects sitting at the intersection of physical and digital media, learning to expressively and creatively approach computing is an essential skill. While overlapping with goals of computer science, the goals of creative computing is less about the efficiency (as few lines of codes as possible) of the code and more about the functionality and aesthetic possibilities of the code. Typically, in courses on digital arts and physical computing in higher education, students explore text-based languages like Arduino in combination with physical computing, as well as experiences with Pure Data (PD), Adobe Flash, C, and Python (Peppler, Sharpe, & Glosson, 2013). Our workshop utilized a new user-friendly alternative to text-based languages like Arduino, called Modkit Alpha.

After the first foray to basic electronic theory and circuit construction with e-textile materials, youth were introduced to microcontrollers and how they could be programmed to control lights, sound, and several other types of output. To assist youth with independently learning the basics of creative computing with Modkit Alpha, youth were provided with a series of cards depicting how to configure the LilyPad using the Hardware settings in Modkit, as well as sample blocks of code and additional tips (Figure 13.2).

"My First Blink" kinds of programming activities can act as initial starting points for youth to envision possibilities for creative computing. By way of illustration, the following vignette is taken from a 7th-grade African-American youth, Omarion, working on his "My First Blink" and then extending his discoveries to imagined possibilities for physical computing (see Table 13.2). Omarion sits at a long table surrounded by six of his peers. Prior to this vignette, Omarion had successfully uploaded his first program to the LilyPad—the "slow blink"—and was in the process of executing a program for a faster blink rate.

Despite the aspects of recreating code from initial "instructions," Omarion and his peers saw the real potential in transposing digital commands into physical behaviors. Omarion, in particular, anticipated the "meta-medium" features of producing media art (Peppler, 2010a) in the connections he made to many different types of artistic practices, all departing from the variations of an indicator light's blink rate. Across these unique connections, Omarion imagined how digital signals could be translated to audio, visual, and movement. Each of these visions incorporates a multimodal "story" of some kind, involving sound and motion. As a foundation for what it means to creatively code, much of the practice of computer programming in the context of the arts begins with an intention (be it visual, audio, gestural, or interactional) which leads to seeking out commands or

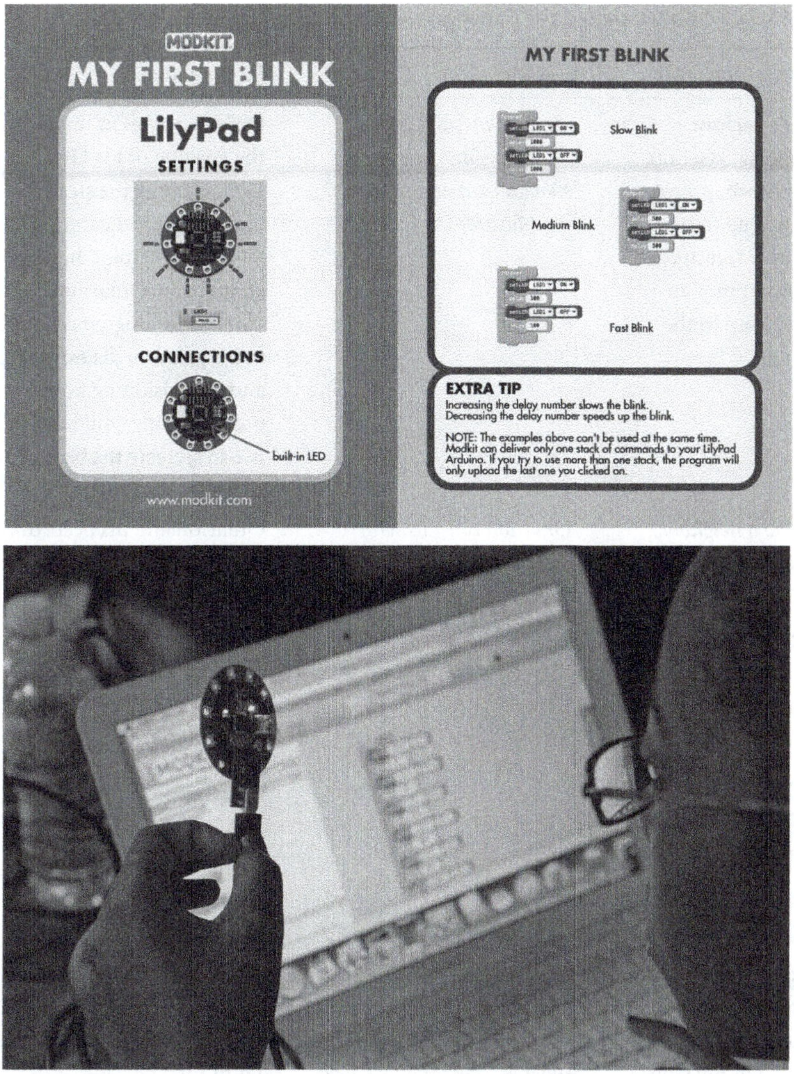

Figure 13.2 Top: Modkit card to assist with "My First Blink" programming activities. Bottom: Youth engaging in physical computing via manipulating code and physical materials.

groups of commands that help to realize this idea, often letting the two coevolve. In his final act in which he uses the Modkit cards to create a program in order to make his abstract "saw" go faster, Omarion enacts the central definition of how artists creatively code: the utilization of programming in order to realize a higher aesthetic aim.

Table 13.2 Video transcript of Omarion experimenting with ModKit code

Video transcript	*Gesture*	*Interpretation*
1. **Omarion:** *(singing)* "Get up, get down, put your hands up to the sound. Get up, get down, put your hands up to the sound . . ."	*His singing trails off as he consults with the Modkit card and makes modifications to his code.*	Omarion sings in time with the flashing of his LilyPad LED, likening the steady blink of the indicator light to a musical pulse. In this connection, Omarion connects a programmed light to his prior media experiences and is envisioning how programming could be put to use to recreate the beat of one of his favorite songs.
2. *(to a neighbor)* Hey, what about 1 [as a delay signal value]?	*Omarion consults with peers on the opposite side of the table with delight as they show off the varying rates their LilyPads blink.*	Omarion and his peers draw inspiration from each other's programs, specifically in the interaction between their programs and the effect on the physical object. The exploration is social and motivates the youth to try out new combinations of code.
3. **Jake:** *(to peers at table)* I'm doing 5.	Jake *holds up his LilyPad to show off the blink.*	Jake shows others how a 5-millisecond delay produces a very quick blink.
4. **Omarion:** Wait-wait! Give it to me, give it to me . . . Let me see 1, let me see 1 . . . Oh my God, dude!	*Omarion walks around the table to closer inspect Jake's program. He and peers go back to showing off what different programs look like on their LilyPads. Omarion returns to his chair and resumes programming his LilyPad. He uploads a new program to the LilyPad and observes the "uploading program" blink default.*	Jake's project appears to inspire Omarion, who replicates Jake's code in his own program as a departure point for a new idea.

5. *[in a high voice, like a sonar. Starts slow and increases in speed and pitch, climaxing in an explosion sound]* Boop . . . boop . . . boop . . . Boop. Boop. Boop. Boop . . . Boopboop boopboopboop . . . **Buggsssssschhhh!**	*The rapid "upload blink" ceases and the LilyPad light starts blinking at steady and moderate pace, as per Omarion's uploaded program. Omarion gazes at the blinking light, then holds up the LilyPad and rotates it slowly in a spiral.*	Like before, Omarion connects the blinking light to an external reference—a sonar or a time bomb. This time, he is inspired by the changing rate of the blinking light that confirms that a program has been uploaded to the LilyPad; first moderate (from the previous uploaded program), then more rapid (the faster, "uploading blink.")
6. *(to anyone who'll listen)* This is a saw. *Zzzzzzsch!* The faster this goes, the faster the revolution of the saw is. So it goes like this: *Zzzsch-Zzsch! Zzzzzzsch Zzzzzzsch Zzzzzzsch!*	*Omarion circles the circumference of the LilyPad with his pointer finger—fast and clockwise at first, then more slowly and counterclockwise. He maintains this moderate speed, still humming melodically, for about 20 seconds.*	The new rate of the blinking light gives Omarion a new vision: a saw. He envisions how the code could be translated into motors and gears. This connection also seems to incorporate the physical design of the LilyPad: its circular shape and reflective metal.
7. I'm about to make it go faster!	*Omarion puts down the LilyPad and stops humming. He looks down at the support materials and begins to make small modifications to the code, toggling between typing and looking at the support materials.*	Omarion switches gears; while his prior visions took flight from something that the LilyPad reminded him of, he now leverages support materials to realize an idea that begins in his mind, moves through the programming environment, and is fully realized on the physical object.

Traditional and High-Tech Craftsmanship

Craftsmanship skills required in physical computing vary depending on the form of materials being used. In the summer workshop, youth learned to thread a needle, tie knots, and sew a basic running stitch—all basic staples of traditional sewing practices that, though foreign to today's younger generations, are cultivated through creating e-textiles. And yet, e-textile craftsmanship differs from its more traditional counterpart in that it necessitates exploring fabrics and decorative materials beyond their look and durability. E-textile creation requires that attention be paid to the physical properties of the materials (e.g., whether something is elastic, conductive, or insulating), as well as to the alignment between the materials used and the goals of the circuit (e.g., a zipper can become a switch in an e-textiles project). Furthermore, the conductive thread must make specific and well-stitched connections between the microcontroller and the components in order to accurately bring the programmed elements of the project to life, bringing new meaning to the quality of youth's sewing techniques. What results is a hybrid approach to traditional craft that infuses electronic theory into the choices youth make when sewing their circuits into their projects.

The following vignette illustrates how youth move flexibly between traditional and high-tech crafting traditions in the production of e-textiles, merging what they know about electronic construction and theory to realize their designs with both traditional and novel crafting materials (see Table 13.3). This vignette features Darryl, a 6th-grade African-American male, as he meticulously stitches a programmed LilyPad and LEDs into a T-shirt. Darryl previously decorated the T-shirt using fabric paint to look "spray painted," creating a large, eight-pointed star-like shape in its center. At this stage in the project, Darryl is sewing his LilyPad to the center of the star, in addition to four LEDs to the radiating points of the star, each of which were programmed with a unique behavior so as to augment the exploding gesture painted on the shirt (see Figure 13.3). To get started, Darryl works with an embroidery hoop to create a flat surface for stitching, and begins stitching with conductive thread through the sew holes of one of the LilyPad's petals. Throughout the process, Darryl issues himself verbal reminders of best practices for sewing as well as circuitry requirements (recalled from his previous work stitching LEDs in parallel into an electronic bracelet) while in the process of stitching his electronic components into the T-shirt design.

From here, Darryl moves through the remaining holes on the LilyPad with equal precision, gaining accuracy and speed. Throughout, Darryl leverages an arsenal of crafting techniques to independently fix emerging problems, including quickly threading and rethreading his needle; consistently toggling between the front and the back of the T-shirt design to check whether his thread has any loose or hanging loops that could be later tangled or knotted; performing a series of methodical checks to the sewing; and sewing an even running stitch (particularly for a novice) to his LEDs. He is also notably slow to rip everything out and start over—something most novices are prone to do. Instead, he works with the mistake and creatively problem-solves.

Table 13.3 Video transcript of Darryl stitching a LilyPad and LEDs into his "ElectriciTee"

Video transcript	*Gesture*	*Interpretation*
1. **Darryl** (talking quietly to himself): And then, so . . . and go back through because I have to make the negative tight, so I'm gonna have to keep going through . . .	Darryl *pulls the needle through a sew hole on the LilyPad from beneath the fabric, turns the needle over, and pushes the needle back through the shirt. This starts to secure the LilyPad to the fabric and ensure the conductive thread will transmit a signal to another component along the circuit.*	Darryl begins his stitching with aesthetic and functional goals simultaneously in mind: starting with the knot on the underside of the shirt ensures that the tail of the knot won't short the circuit. Aesthetically, hiding the knot beneath the fabric also ensures a cleaner look, even though it is harder to execute.
2. I move the LEDs out of my way . . .	*Still holding the needle partially protruding through the fabric,* Darryl *picks two LEDs off the top of the hoop and places them on the table.*	Darryl pays meticulous attention to organization—a key crafting practice. Having placed the LEDs on the T-shirt as part of his planning process, he moves them to the side so as not to lose them.
3. Then, I'm gonna pull this through, like that . . .	Darryl *pulls the thread taut from beneath the embroidery hoop.*	Darryl is mindful of moving slowly and methodically.
4. And gonna . . . straight . . . gonna have to go back through here . . .	*He lifts up the shirt, reaches in through the neck, turns the needle around, and pushes it back up through the same sew hole on the LilyPad. He struggles to get the needle all the way back through the fabric. He pulls the needle harder and the thread pulls out of the needle.*	Darryl starts to sew back through a second time for the secure connection. But, because the needle is single-threaded (Darryl prefers to use a single-threaded needle, leaving a 3" tail on the one side, instead of a double-threaded one taught in the workshop), the needle becomes unthreaded.
5. *Tsk.* Oh, man.	*He grabs the short amount of thread that made it through on the last push and tries to pull it all the way taut.*	Darryl works within the constraints of the problem. Instead of starting over, he starts to investigate what went wrong and continue from the successful parts of the previous gesture.

(*Continued*)

Table 13.3 (Continued)

Video transcript	*Gesture*	*Interpretation*
6. So, I just made a *big mistake.* I'm gonna put the needle in here . . .	*He cleans up the thread and pins the needle into a nearby pincushion. He turns the hoop over to inspect the problem. He discovers that the shirt and the thread have become entangled.*	He is still investigating what went wrong, treating it like a 3D problem. He toggles between front and back, he traces the whole thread line—these are critical to discovering the root of the problem.
7. Oh, *that's* what it was. Okay.	*He uses his fingers to methodically undo the knot and separate the threads.*	Darryl talks himself through the problem, feeling confident that he can deal with the setback.
8. That was okay. Yeah, that's okay.		
9. Now I'm gonna have to somehow pull this out 'cuz I just made a mistake.	Darryl *pulls the thread back into a straight line and reaches it over to the pin in the pincushion.*	This is a traditional crafting technique: reorganizing and resuming. Darryl remains confident in his ability to problem-solve. He does this without skipping a beat, all motions are fluid and intentional.
10. I'm gonna have to connect this back on . . .	*He snaps the thread back into the self-threading needle.*	
11. Okay. Now. I'm gonna go back through here. And then I'm gonna sew . . . through . . .	*He picks up where he left off, trying to make a firm connection with the sew hole of the LilyPad. This will be the second loop through the same sew hole.*	Darryl ensures a strong connection between the microcontroller and the conductive thread that will connect the LilyPad to the LED.

The vignettes featured here illustrate how youths' work in e-textiles seems to lend itself to both authentic and creative forms of physical computing, well aligned to professional practice. At the heart of youths' creative production with physical computing is the ability for youth to forge connections between multiple domains in compelling new ways beyond the screen. This form of expression ties together multiple strands of domain knowledge—many, if not all, of which are being introduced to this age group for the

Figure 13.3 Detail of Darryl's ElectriciTee. The LilyPad is placed in the center of the design and the four LEDs are placed on the four larger points of the star. Meticulous running stitches complete a path for electricity to flow throughout the design.

first time (e.g., electronic construction and theory, computational creativity, and traditional and high-tech craftsmanship), yet these findings suggest that e-textile production presented advantageous opportunities for youth to not only engage in authentic technical practices of each specific domain, but also provided a flexibility for youth to build upon each domain toward a specific, accumulating vision. This is a noteworthy accomplishment given the high level of technical expertise that physical computing presents, which can bring to mind didactic, step-by-step forms of instruction. Examples like the ones presented here not only represent model ways in which these tools present novel opportunities to tinker, explore, and create, but also how classrooms can be set up to accommodate playful forms of self- and peer-directed learning with ideas that resonate with youth interests.

In sum, the central tenets of physical computing present us with a new vision of what a maker frame to arts education can look like in today's classrooms—not an abandonment of time-honored tools, but an opportunity to think and express across physical and digital forms. Such an effort situates new technologies within the landscape of historical traditions and practice. In a time where pervasive digital technology is changing our relationship to images and artworks, hard-and-fast distinctions between genre, place, and form are becoming increasingly blurred, thus expanding the possibilities for experimentation and innovation in contemporary art. Capitalizing on these multimodal trends, a 21st-century arts classroom should be just as open to new technologies and responsive to new media as an increasing amount of subject areas in K–16 education. This vision—arts education "ReMade"—situates art making with new technologies alongside traditional materials, embracing new media as a material in which to be sculpted for artistic expression.

References

Arts Education Partnership. (2004). *The arts and education: New opportunities for research.* Washington, DC: Arts Education Partnership (AEP).

Baafi, E. & Millner, A. (2011). A toolkit for tinkering with tangibles & connecting communities. In *Proceedings of Tangible, Embedded, and Embodied Interaction (TEI)* (pp. 349–352). Funchal, Portugal.

Banzi, M. (2008). *Getting started with Arduino* (1st ed.). San Francisco, CA: O'Reilly Publishing.

Berzowska, J. (2005). Electronic textiles: Wearable computers, reactive fashion, and soft computation. *Textile, 3*(1), 2–19.

Buechley, L., Eisenberg, M., Catchen, J. & Crockett, A. (2008). The LilyPad Arduino: Using computational textiles to investigate engagement, aesthetics, and diversity in computer science education. In *Proceedings of the Special Interest Group on Computer–Human Interaction (SIGCHI) Conference on Human Factors in Computing Systems (CHI)* (pp. 423–432).

Buechley, L., Peppler, K., Eisenberg, M., & Kafai, Y. (Eds.). (2013). *Textile messages: Dispatches from the world for e-textiles and education.* New York, NY: Peter Lang Publishing.

Fields, D. A., & Lee, V. R. (2016). Craft technologies 101: Bringing making to higher education. In K. Peppler, E. Halverson, & Y. Kafai (Eds.), *Makeology: Makerspaces as learning environments* (Volume 1) (pp. 121–137). New York, NY: Routledge.

Kafai, Y. B., Fields, D. A., & Searle, K. A. (2014). Electronic textiles as disruptive designs: Supporting and challenging maker activities in schools. *Harvard Educational Review, 84*(4, Winter), 532–556.

Kafai, Y. B. & Peppler, K. (2011). Youth, technology, and DIY: Developing participatory competencies in creative media production. In V. L. Gadsden, S. Wortham, & R. Lukose (Eds.), *Youth Cultures, Language and Literacy: Review of Research in Education, 35*(1), 89–119.

Kuznetsov, S. & Paulos, E. (2010). Rise of the expert amateur: DIY projects, communities, and cultures. In *Proceedings of the 6th Nordic Conference on Human-Computer Interaction (NordiCHI): Extending Boundaries* (pp. 295–304). Reykjavik, Iceland.

LAUSD Arts Branch. (2005). *Media arts study group report.* Los Angeles, CA: Los Angeles Unified School District (LAUSD) Arts Branch. Retrieved August 31, 2007 from artseducation.lausd.net/portal.php?id=MEDI

Maeda, J. (2004). *Creative code.* New York: Thames & Hudson Inc.

Marculescu, D., Marculescu, R., Zamora, N., Stanley-Marbell, P., Khosla, P., Park, S., . . . Nakad, Z. (2003). Electronic textiles: A platform for pervasive computing. *Proceedings of the IEEE, 91*(12), 1995–2018.

Nalven, J. & Jarvis, J. (2005). *Going digital: The practice and vision of digital artists.* Boston, MA: Thomson Course Technology.

Paul, C. (2003). *Digital art.* New York, NY: Thames & Hudson.

Peppler, K. (2010a). Media arts: Arts education for a digital age. *Teachers College Record, 112*(8), 2118–2153.

Peppler, K. (2010b). The new fundamentals: Introducing computation into arts education. In E. P. Clapp & M. J. Bellino (Eds.), *20Under40: Reinventing the arts and arts education for the 21st century* (Ch. 19, pp. 294–309). Bloomington, IN: AuthorHouse.

Peppler, K., Salen, K., Gresalfi, M., & Santo, R. (2014). *Short circuits: Crafting with DIY technologies.* Cambridge, MA: MIT Press.

Peppler, K., Sharpe, L., & Glosson, D. (2013). E-textiles and the new fundamentals of fine arts. In L. Buechley, K. Peppler, M. Eisenberg, & Y. Kafai (Eds.), *Textile messages: Dispatches from the world of e-textiles and education* (Ch 8, pp. 107–117). New York, NY: Peter Lang Publishing.

Peppler, K. A. & Warschauer, M. (2012). Uncovering literacies, disrupting stereotypes: Examining the (dis)abilities of a child learning to computer program and read. *International Journal of Learning and Media, 3*(3), 15–41.

Reas, C. (2006). Media literacy: Twenty-first century arts education. *AI & Society, 20*(4), 444–445.

Rusk, N., Resnick, M., Berg, R., & Pezalla-Granlund, M. (2008). New pathways into robotics: Strategies for broadening participation. *Journal of Science Education and Technology, 17*(1), 59–69.

Turbak, F. & Berg, R. (2002). Robotic design studio: Exploring the big ideas of engineering in a liberal arts environment. *Journal of Science Education and Technology, 11*(3), 237–253.

Closing

CHAPTER 14

Making—Writing—Coding

MITCHEL RESNICK, ELYSE EIDMAN-AADAHL, AND DALE DOUGHERTY

This final chapter is a shortened and edited version of a keynote address given by three innovators and leaders in the Maker Movement at the 2014 MIT Scratch Conference.[1] Dale Dougherty is the founder and executive chairman of Maker Media, Inc., which launched *MAKE* magazine (analyzed in chapter 2 of this volume) in 2005, and hosted the first Maker Faire event in 2006. Elyse Eidman-Aadahl is the executive director of the National Writing Project, which was founded in 1974 with the mission to improve writing and learning in schools and communities (for more on the NWP's efforts to connect writing and making, see Cantrill & Oh, 2016, in volume 1 of this series). Mitchel Resnick is the director of the Lifelong Kindergarten group at the MIT Media Lab, which developed the programming software Scratch. Resnick is also the cofounder of the Computer Clubhouse network.

Introduction

Mitchel Resnick: It's a great pleasure and an honor to be joined by Dale Dougherty and Elyse Eidman-Aadahl to be talking about the topic "Making, Writing, and Coding." Yesterday we talked about the fact that *coding* is not just a technical skill or some particular new skills for getting a job, but rather it's a pathway towards new ways of thinking, new forms of expression, and new ways of communicating in the world. As we try to think about how we can support coding as a new form of expression and a new way of communicating in the world, it's great to look to other people who have been exploring those same types of questions, but across different media.

I see lots of links to the work that's being done with one of the oldest forms of communication, *writing*, which has been around for 5,000 years or longer. Elyse is the Executive Director of the National Writing Project and thinks a lot about engaging people in expression through writing. *Making* has been around even longer than writing. People have been making things since humans started to walk around and use their hands. Recently, of course, there's been a new surge of interest in making—and the learning opportunities that can come through making. Through his position as CEO of Maker Media, which publishes *MAKE* magazine and produces the Maker Faires, Dale has really been at the forefront of supporting this new Maker Movement, examining how people can engage with the world in new ways through making.

Another thing that connects making, writing, and coding together is that even though writing and making have been around for a long time, new technologies always get us to rethink what it means to write, what it means to make, and the ways that we engage through writing and making.

Dale Dougherty: *MAKE* magazine is 10 years old, and Maker Faires are about 9 years old. We started out inspired by old *Popular Mechanics* and *Popular Science* magazines of the '50s and how they encouraged you to do lots of different things. And I felt it resonated with the hackers who were trying to make things, whether it's programs and software or physical objects, to do something they wanted it to do. And that sense of direction and control and playfulness I thought, well, it would be fun to create a magazine full of projects, things to do, and show what other people are doing. Then Maker Faire came to be because I was meeting such interesting people that I thought many other people would enjoy meeting them. It's the old-fashioned show-and-tell to talk about something you make. It's actually easy even for shy, geeky people to talk about things that they've made.

I think what happened over the years was we began to see a flood of kids at Maker Faire; we started with adults and moved to high school and teenagers. You see now makers in kindergarten, which makes sense since it was the original makerspace. That has drawn me into thinking about education and how to get making, which has been on the margins of our culture, back into education, into our cities, and into our lives. We set up a nonprofit Maker Education Initiative, which has a program called Maker Corps, where college-aged students work as mentors in science and community centers around the country with the purpose of engaging kids in making and doing and creating.

Elyse Eidman-Aadahl: The National Writing Project is about 40 years old now. It started out at the University of California Berkeley with one group of teachers, K through university and across the curriculum. This group of people came together one summer in a peer learning model to try and work together as practitioners to think about what writing really was and how they could support young people becoming better writers. Through their initiative, and the initiative of other practitioners, the Writing Project spread to other locations. Now we're a network of about 200 local Writing Project sites. They're all hosted at universities across the country, with a couple abroad. These are all practitioner collaboratives where people work together in continuous inquiry and action research to learn how to better their teaching or their mentoring. Most people are in formal education settings, but some are in museums and libraries—increasingly, we see folks in out-of-school settings.

There are several core ideas that unite all of those local writing project sites. One is this vision that engaging powerfully in practice is, in its way, a generation of knowledge. So practitioners, through inquiry around practice, generate and create knowledge about teaching and learning that needs to be surfaced, needs to be shared, and needs to be brought into the conversation. Another idea that unites them is that they work together across the borders and boundaries like secondary, elementary, middle, or formal/informal, or K–12 and higher ed. The final big idea is our broad concept of writing. Most of us have probably had schooling that has narrowed a concept of what writing is instead of broadening it. We believe that writing happens in text, it happens in media, it happens in image, audio. It happens for example when you code a digital story in Scratch.[2]

Creating Meaning Through Making

Mitchel Resnick: One thing that unites the three of us is our interest in the idea that *people create meaning through the things that they create*. We're all inspired by the importance of creating things, making things, producing things. For a long time, that has taken a back seat. For example, in the world of literacy, the Writing Project focuses on writing, but if you go into schools there's a lot more attention paid to reading. We're all in favor of reading. On the other hand, as valuable as reading is, there should be more attention on writing, not just reading. There are parallels in the coding world and the making world. Learning how to interact with a computer or an app is somewhat like reading—while learning to code is more like writing. And, as with writing, not enough attention goes to coding. Elyse, maybe you can say more about that relationship between reading and writing in the literacy world, why there is more attention on reading, and what you're doing to try to get more attention to the production of meaning side of things.

Elyse Eidman-Aadahl: You certainly see it in assessment; you see it in many, many formal structures, that literacy equals reading. They'll say,

"Literacy, oh yes, literacy *and* writing." I'll say: "Actually, literacy is really both. It's reading *and* writing." People write stuff so that other people can read it, and they read what other people have written. They really go together. We've spent thousands of years creating learning institutions that create and hold content, and then in order to have people able to access that prior knowledge, they need to learn how to read. That makes complete sense. So if you think of the start of formal schooling, much of that was about learning to read. Read your Bible. Learn to read and access the stuff in the library. Learn to read and access the stuff that's delivered to you via the Internet on the computer.

But actually nobody really wants people to only consume. We want people to produce and participate, and so that's the active side, the production side, not the consumption side. So what if we thought about what people will produce, how they'll be knowledge makers, creators, and writers? How would we teach reading if our end goal were that people became strong, powerful, authoritative, engaged, participatory writers? In both coding and making, there's this notion that your real emphasis is not on the consumption side but on what somebody will produce themselves or with their peers. How would it be different in teaching and learning if our emphasis were on what you're going to do now as a maker, a doer, a creator, a writer? That shifts everything.

Mitchel Resnick: Certainly by its name, the Maker Movement and *MAKE* magazine highlights that it's about the production side of things, so there's not much confusion there. But for me one of the things that's been so important about the Maker Movement is that it's not just about making. Because as much as we all believe there's so much to be gained by engaging people in designing, creating, making, and expressing, we also know that if all you do is follow the instructions to make something, that's not going to live up to what we're hoping for.

Dale Dougherty: Similar to reading and writing, there's using technology and there's making technology. One driving force in the world of technology is to make everything easy to use from the consumer side, so that people can buy it. From the making side, it's always going to be harder. Some of the meaning that comes from it is because you have to learn how to do this and that means something to you. If it was just simple, it really wouldn't have the value that it does. The challenge that's in making is part of the value.

Mitchel Resnick: Similar issues come up in coding. As we develop Scratch, some people in our group are always emphasizing that we shouldn't focus on making things easy to use. Of course we don't want things to be needlessly hard, but we want things to be engaging, meaningful, and motivating, not easy.

Connecting With People

Dale Dougherty: One of the things I've realized about Maker Faire is how many people create things to *interact with people*. It's like they're using technology and they're using other things, which could be knitting, sewing, electronics, or robots, but they're actually putting it out to create that interaction with someone else, which could be a game or just a conversation. Many of the things we build have those qualities. We write to communicate. We don't write just to put it away in a diary. We want to communicate and connect to other people, so it's a very human thing.

Elyse Eidman-Aadahl: It's less of a singular vision that either writing or making or coding in and of itself is the thing. In our writing process work, or in the current Maker Movement, or what you all are creating in Scratch, what's important is what surrounds the thing that's being created. That is the thing that enables people to create a different model of joyful and engaged learning, where people can bring a kind of *passion* and *play* with *peers* to a *project*—your four Ps. That's really the key.

I'm thinking of a conversation I had with a professor in a school of engineering who was looking at a makerspace for kids. He was happy to see the beginnings of an excitement around engineering, but then wondered why most engineering schools killed it. One of the things that he said was, "Here people are actually making things. Engineering schools are not about making things. They're about preparing later to make really serious things." This notion of a deferred engagement, a deferred participation, and "let's fill you up with everything you need know to do something really serious later"—that can affect all of these tools and all of these movements.

Dale Dougherty: Some of the spaces I see at universities, specifically in the design profession, say they need to create a space where students could choose to fail. They wouldn't do that in formal programs because students are getting graded. We see that a lot. The competitive nature of a lot of school-based activities takes it away from being play. We have an expression around Maker Faire that I think is pretty nice: exhibition, not competition. We show work rather than saying, well, this is against this, or this is better than this. The same is true for a library of Scratch programs you can look at. You can have challenges and give people motivation to do something, and that's cool. But really what we're looking for is to increase the body of work and visibility into the body of work, not just find a few good things.

Mitchel Resnick: In the Scratch community, we have the Scratch Design Studio. It's more of a place where you exhibit some work, as opposed to having a weekly contest to show the best project—it's not about that. There is some value to rallying people together around some themes; we certainly see this in the Maker Movement. You want to have ways that people can come together and have some structure that they're participating in, but where everyone is able to develop their own voice. In robotics competitions, there's making involved there, but I sometimes worry when it gets focused just on who's going to do the best, and who's going to plan it out, execute it, and deliver, as opposed to focusing on the creative process and the diversity of things that might come out of that process.

Schools, Assessment, and Identity

Mitchel Resnick: Over the last decade with the Maker Movement, people are becoming increasingly interested in introducing making into formal education. There has been a lot of interest around introducing coding into schools as well. But there's a risk of making and coding getting narrowed down in ways that we've seen with writing. Writing has been in schools for a long time, but not always in the way you would want. There are some parallels, with too much focus on the syntax and vocabulary, as opposed to the expression.

Dale Dougherty: I was once at the Department of Education in DC. Someone recognized me, and without even a conversation said, "Tell me, is there some maker project that every 7th grader in America could do?" It was that checkbox mentality: do this activity and then we've got the making. There's a similar mentality with getting students coding. It's really a much more deliberate long-term process that we're talking about here, and I think it involves a community of people that influence learners' participation and shape it. One of the things that interests me about making is that it's become a cultural thing and it's about a cultural change, not just, "here's a technology" or "here's a practice." It's really how we think about making and its influence on us and where do we see it going.

Elyse Eidman-Aadahl: Writing has a special problem in that it's a primary mode of transaction for assessment. For people who write, this is very counterintuitive. If you think of people who write in the wild, people who are writing for their own purposes, not as part of a school assignment, typically you write something for someone who needs to read it from you because you know something about it and they don't. They are seeking to learn from you. And that's a more natural writer/reader transaction. Writing in assessment, writing in testing, the essay test or the short answer test, is exactly the opposite of that. You're generally writing to an assessor who knows more about the topic than you do. So the construction of that reader/writer relationship is backwards. So, if almost all of your writing experiences are writing-as-testing, your sense of yourself is that you are always being tested by a judgmental reader. What kind of model does that set about what writing is—and how hard is it to grow beyond that and out of that? It's why people will say often, when they have a very powerful writing experience, that they've discovered they really are writers. Of course, they've been writing in some form for years and years and years, but they experience that *being* a writer is a very significant mental shift.

I think being a maker is similar. You've made and created things your whole life, but at some point you say "now I see myself as a maker." So there's some identity shift that's really powerful in all of these. For us in the writing project, and I think it's true at Maker Faire and it's true in the Scratch community, there's something important about going through that identity shift yourself, experiencing it yourself. In the National Writing Project, people come together to do a lot of things: to demonstrate practices to each other, to read together, to do research together. But we always write. We experience what it's like to be a writer. Whatever it is you're working on, you have to do the thing too, so that you can experience that inside. When you do experience that, a lot changes. You realize how you used peers, or mentors, or models. You realize how the design of space enabled or constrained you. You understand differently how you can apprentice yourself to someone who knew something that you wanted to learn.

So going through that identity shift is really, really critical. In many cases, we create learning situations where people aren't able to make that identity shift. We might emphasize just a lot of initial engagement activities: gateway activities. Now, you may need the gateway activities. You may need to play with stuff a while in order to go through the identity shift. But one of the things in all of our communities is that we often emphasize the gateway activities, but we don't have a sustained overall engagement with an environment and with peers that we can really learn from and apprentice ourselves to over time. No one goes through that identity shift with a one-hour activity or a single engagement with making a digital story in Scratch. You do that over time by being around other people who think and express differently because they have gone through that shift, and then you sort of say, "Wow, that's the way to be. I'd like to be one of them."

Dale Dougherty: That captures a lot of things here. You started with assessment and you're almost saying the real validation comes from the community, and we don't get that through our school assessments. Too often, schools teach STEM not as a way of thinking, but as a body of knowledge, and not as a way of experiencing the world and interacting with the world. I was looking through a test for students in California. One page looked like it came from a textbook because it was explaining what a microscope was. It had all the callouts of the pieces and components of a microscope. It described in hifalutin language what it was, but it never really conveyed the idea that it was a new way of seeing things that you can't see. It asked a question about if you adjusted the microscope knob the wrong way would it break the glass. Why would you ask that question? Instead of "What do you see with a microscope and what kind of worlds are you exploring with the microscope?" *That's* science, not this we-can-catch-you-on-something-and-get-a-good-question.

What Are They Learning?

Mitchel Resnick: This opens up the question: What do we hope people are going to learn through the activities of making and writing and coding? Too often, people are focused on learning specific concepts, and there's nothing wrong with learning specific concepts, but I don't think that's what drives us. With making, it's not about learning specific concepts. It's about different practices, strategies of designing, creating, thinking. Similarly with coding, it's less about just learning about variables or conditionals. It's more about strategies for designing, creating, debugging. And it's similar in writing.

Dale Dougherty: One of the things that is very powerful about making is that it's personal, and I feel like it wants to start inside of you. The do-it-yourself, DIY, idea isn't necessarily that you do everything yourself, but you have to initiate that expression of an interest, making a choice of what to do. I really think what you're trying to do is create self-directed learning and self-directed learners. That's the quality that I see in innovators and creators that ties them together, and yet we don't necessarily encourage that properly in school.

When I talk about making, you might think that I'm talking about hands-on activity, but it's more about the learning that I'm interested in, and seeing yourself as a competent, capable learner. One of the fundamental pieces of making is it gives you lots of feedback. It's not a test that you take and you get back three weeks later. It's something that gives you constant feedback as a process, and I think it makes you a better learner, and it engages you so that you are learning.

This is more about setting up experiences that accumulate in meaning and value to you than it is whether you know this concept. I believe makers will encounter those concepts, and there's a place to introduce and talk about them. I think the perfect activity in making is something that you build, that you get to play with. And the thing you're playing with, like a racecar or a robot, you look at the performance of that thing and you begin to say how it changes to be better or different or faster or slower. That starts to introduce you into some of the conceptual frameworks, but it grounds you in engaging in relevant experiences. I think that the dominant mode in education sadly is efficiency. It's easier to show you a picture of a microscope than to set up microscopes and have you experience them, and there's a huge difference.

Or the middle ground today is we'll simulate that so it looks like you're using a microscope, but it's an app. Let's give them the damn microscope.

Elyse Eidman-Aadahl: A lot of that resonates with our experiences with writing. In our vision of writing, whether you're making a video, a film, writing a dissertation, writing a poem, whatever it might be, one key is iteration. We called it "draft" in the old days: this is a first draft, this is a new draft, this is my last draft, this is a "doggy" draft, because it is a "rough-rough" draft. When you start to see that everybody works at the craft, draft by draft, that they iterate, it's like watching someone that you thought was amazing at building something, but actually it took them whatever period of time to do it, and they worked through all kinds of failed prototypes on the way to it. A draft is a more or less successful prototype.

Another key is sharing with others. You share your draft with others because you need to get people who are not living inside your head and already know what you need to say reading your draft and giving you feedback. Another key is working in an environment where you collaborate, use peers, in a kind of virtuous circle of, "I will help you with yours, you will help me with mine." So the way that a peer group or network of people share and push each other towards improved performance, that's another key.

How you can learn about writing from the writing that's all around you is another key idea. We teach reading in many cases, schools and out-of-school and elsewhere, as if the only reason you would read would be to get the main idea. "What's the theme? Can you identify the main idea?" Okay, that is a good thing to do. But when we write, we may read dozens of things just to understand how someone else approached the same problem. All those texts that are around me in the newspapers, on the wall, everywhere else, they can be mentors to me. There's even this phrase "the mentor text." I think in fact we do that when we study how other people solve a problem in coding, when we look at other people's prototypes or making activities. We learn from what is around us.

So how does this translate into ideas about teaching and learning? Well if you think about how we are all about people doing work, and if you think of "workshop" as the environment that privileges the idea of people working and producing, then the design of the workshop is one instructive model. Whether it's a makerspace, a writing center, or a hacker weekend, there are principles for designing educational environments in those places. But the model that goes back centuries, of the lecture, of the priest at the front reading to the congregation, that model has come to define formal education. The workshop is always on the side.

It would be interesting if we could flip that, so we were mostly in a workshop and just occasionally heard from mentors or others, if the lecture format were the addition to an environment that was really about the work. That could be a simple flip that would be a very powerful thing.

Dale Dougherty: It's really important that you document the work you're doing, that you describe either the procedure you use to make something or what the experience of making meant to you. There are so many ways that this communications side should be integrated. Just as there might be a speech class, there might be a demo class in how to give a good demo or explain something. The folks at TED-Ed have a program to teach kids how to do TED Talks. I'd love to have a similar program where, apart from what you make, it just focuses on how do you give a good demonstration and how do you anticipate questions, how do you deal with things that go wrong. There's a great relationship here between this kind of procedural writing and code. Making an Instructable (see Peppler & Hall, chapter 10 of volume 1) is really a series of steps. You have to think about what you do first and what the next step is and connecting those steps. It's very much how you think about code.

Tinkering

Mitchel Resnick: All of the activities that we're talking about do support organizing your thinking, but sometimes people misinterpret to think it's a straight line to organize your thinking. It can be a meandering path to organize. The iterative process is important in all of these activities, whether it's making or writing or coding. We sometimes use the word *tinkering* to describe this process. Some people are dismissive of tinkering, thinking that you need to make a plan ahead and then execute it. But for all of us, tinkering captures the idea of iteration—trying it out, experimenting, being willing to fail, but then adapting and moving forward.

Dale Dougherty: There's a lot of informal things that happen here that if we're honest are kind of mysterious. We don't completely understand them, and then we sort of formalize them. One of my critiques of design thinking is we teach it as a formal process. I'd rather have kids get the experience of design. Then you could talk about that formalization, rather than have them recite the four steps in a process. A point of origin for me with *Make* was the sense of playfulness, and that comes out of that state of mind that you're in where you're experimenting and trying, and you don't care if you fail. It's a really, really great environment to try things out and learn from that, and I feel like that's so much richer than a lot of our models.

To support this type of learning, there's an opportunity to rethink spaces. We need spaces to support group activity where kids are learning from each other. But how much more interesting it is if they're actually doing different things in that space rather than the same thing, and they can talk about it and they can look at it. I think it's one of the big differences in what tinkering used to be 50 years ago and today—I call it "the social tinkerer" rather than the lone tinkerer. You can do this, and should do this, with other people. It makes it better.

Elyse Eidman-Aadahl: One of the things we do in the National Writing Project is host the YOUmedia Learning Lab Network, which is a network of libraries and museum people who are trying to create production spaces in their institutions (Larson et al., 2013). Many libraries and museums, particularly fine arts museums, were created as places for you to consume and perhaps not even touch—admiring the work of others, as so much better than anything that you could create, or aspire to create. It's remarkable for these institutions to create places for people to make and create, inside of institutions whose centuries of history are the opposite.

We have this opportunity now, this moment, brought to us by the Internet. We've created the most powerful tool for knowledge distribution and access ever created. So everything that the library or the museum was created to do, to be able to gather and distribute content, is bested by the Internet, freeing these institutions a little bit from that historic mission, allowing them to be more playful about themselves. We collectively hold the moment to say, "Will those new tools be used primarily by institutions as a new means of distribution, or will we actually turn over the tools, put in the hands of everyone to create new value for themselves?" Is that what we will teach everyone to do with the Internet and with digital tools?

Mitchel Resnick: That's a good note to end on. One thing that the three of us have in common is our commitment to putting more power in the hands of people from all backgrounds, enabling everyone to develop their voice and express themselves, whether it's through making, writing, or coding. There's a special opportunity right now. There's a greater openness to the ideas of learning through projects, peers, passion, and play. But that moment could also slip away, so it is all the more important to make connections and join forces with other communities with shared values, to make sure that all children have the opportunity to grow up as full and active participants in tomorrow's society.

Notes

1 The video of this keynote is available at www.media.mit.edu/video/view/scratch-2014-08-08.

2 Scratch is an online programming platform used by people of all ages to create interactive stories, games, and animations (Resnick et al., 2009; see also chapters 6 and 9 of this volume).

References

Cantrill, C., & Oh, P. (2016). The composition of making. In K. Peppler, E. Halverson, & Y. Kafai (Eds.), *Makeology: Makerspaces as learning environments* (Volume 1) (pp. 107–120). New York, NY: Routledge.

Larson, K., Ito, M., Brown, E., Hawkins, M., Pinkard, N., & Sebring, P. (2013). *Safe space and shared interests: YOUmedia Chicago as a laboratory for connected learning.* Irvine: Digital Media and Learning Research Hub.

Peppler, K., & Hall, T. (2016). The Make-to-Learn Youth Contest: Gaining youth perspectives on learning through making. In K. Peppler, E. Halverson, & Y. Kafai (Eds.), *Makeology: Makerspaces as learning environments* (Volume 1) (pp. 141–157). New York, NY: Routledge.

Resnick, M., Maloney, J., Monroy-Hernandez, A., Rusk, N., Eastmond, E., Brennan, K., . . . Kafai, Y. (2009). Scratch: Programming for all. *Communications of the ACM, 52*(11), 60–67.

About the Contributors

Luigi Anzivino is a Scientific Content Developer at San Francisco's Exploratorium. He wants to live in a world where people can learn by doing in messy, unusual, and inventive ways, without fear of failure. Hoping to pull that off, he works as a Tinkering Content Developer at the Exploratorium, where he helps design, prototype, and facilitate hands-on making activities in the Tinkering Studio. After 24 consecutive years of formal education culminating in a PhD in Behavioral Neuroscience, Luigi discovered informal education, constructionism, and tinkering; he never looked back to academia. In his work at the Exploratorium, Luigi focuses on developing, documenting, and sharing rich learning experiences, with the goal of creating a physical, cultural, and social space that is safe for trying out tentative ideas, not knowing the right answer, and developing the skill of posing—even more than solving—interesting problems.

Brigid Barron is an Associate Professor at the Graduate School of Education at Stanford, a faculty co-lead of the LIFE center, and directs the YouthLAB (Youth Learning Across Boundaries) research group (youthlab.stanford.edu). She takes an ecological approach to understanding social processes of learning in and out of school with a focus on how digital technologies can serve as a catalyst to learning across settings and time. She develops biographical and ethnographic methods to document the evolution of interest-based learning, mapping children's activities to reveal the networks of partners and resources that have supported expertise development.

Sophia Bender is a Graduate Research Assistant in the Creativity Labs at Indiana University. She is interested in studying creative expression in learning contexts, whether that's through art, design, e-textiles, writing, other forms of making, personally meaningful learning choices, or interest-driven exploration. She also hopes her work will help to break down barriers in education, specifically the barriers between disciplines and the barriers leading to educational inequity—especially in STEM fields. Her ultimate goal is to make school more fun and fulfilling for all students. As part of this work, she has helped to bring e-textiles to Girl Scout troops, public libraries, Maker Faire Education Day, and even to an entire public school district. She is a leader in a campus organization promoting more female involvement in technology. Her favorite form of making is writing stories.

Matthew Berland is an Assistant Professor of Digital Media in the Department of Curriculum and Instruction at University of Wisconsin–Madison, a member of the Games+Learning+Society group, and the director of the Learning Games Play Data Consortium—a national consortium of learning scientists, educational researchers, and game designers dedicated to helping people better use data to understand how people learn with games. He uses design-based research methods, learning analytics, and data mining to create and analyze constructionist learning environments supporting students' creativity in learning computer science and engineering.

Lisa Brahms is the Director of Learning and Research at the Children's Museum of Pittsburgh and a Research Scientist with the University of Pittsburgh Center for Learning in Out of School Environments (UPCLOSE). Lisa has been an educator and designer of formal and informal learning experiences and environments for over a decade, working in schools and at numerous children's, art, and history museums. Lisa earned her PhD in Learning Sciences and Policy at the University of Pittsburgh, and holds a master's degree in Museum Education and Childhood Education from Bank Street School of Education. Lisa's research considers the design of informal learning environments for meaningful participation in creative processes with digital and physical media.

Edward P. Clapp is a Senior Research Manager and a member of the core research team working on the Agency *by* Design (A*b*D) initiative—an investigation of the promises, practices, and pedagogies of maker-centered learning—at Project Zero, an educational research center at the Harvard Graduate School of Education (HGSE). Edward's current research interests include creativity and innovation, maker-centered education, design thinking, and contemporary approaches to arts teaching and learning.

In addition to his work as an educational researcher, Edward is an HGSE Lecturer on Education and co-instructor of the HGSE course "Thinking and Learning Today and Tomorrow: Project Zero Perspectives."

Kevin Crowley is a Professor of the Learning Sciences and Policy at the University of Pittsburgh, where he also directs the University of Pittsburgh Center for Learning in Out-of-School Environments (UPCLOSE). He works in partnership with museums, community organizations, and other informal educators to develop innovative out-of-school learning environments. Crowley's group conducts basic learning sciences research in informal settings and develops new theories of how people learn about science, technology, engineering, and art. Crowley has a PhD in psychology from Carnegie Mellon University and a BA in psychology and education from Swarthmore College.

Colin Dixon is an Educator and Doctoral Candidate in the Learning & Mind Sciences at the UC Davis School of Education. He spends time in makerspaces, citizen science groups, bike shops, and other places where people make stuff to use. He looks at when and how young people adapt, and adapt to, new situations in ways that make it possible for them to use and further develop interests and areas of expertise. He is especially interested in the pathways that people create as they encounter obstacles and opportunities, big or small.

Dale Dougherty is the founder and CEO of Maker Media, Inc., in Sebastopol, CA. Maker Media produces *MAKE* magazine, which launched in 2005, and Maker Faire, which was held first in the San Francisco Bay Area in 2006. *MAKE* has been the catalyst for a worldwide Maker Movement that is transforming innovation in industry, hands-on learning in education, and the personal lives of makers of all ages. *MAKE* invites everyone to become a maker and integrate creative goals with technical skills. Dougherty was a cofounder of O'Reilly Media, where he was the first editor of their computing trade books, and developed GNN in 1993, the first commercial website. He coined Web 2.0 in 1993. *MAKE* started at O'Reilly Media and spun out as its own company in January 2013. Dougherty grew up in Louisville, KY.

Elyse Eidman-Aadahl is Executive Director of the National Writing Project (NWP), a network of nearly 200 professional learning and research communities located at universities across all 50 states, the District of Columbia, Puerto Rico, and the US Virgin Islands. Based at the University of California-Berkeley, the NWP leads nationally networked learning and research initiatives with a focus on writing and connected learning for educators working in K–12, university, and out-of-school settings. Eidman-Aadahl's work focuses on the design, experience, and impact of communities of practice for educators in the formal and informal learning spheres. She is coauthor of *Because Digital Writing Matters* and *Writing for a Change.*

Deborah A. Fields seeks to understand the power of connected learning by studying how students' learning is enriched when school, home, friends, and playful online spaces are combined. She is a Temporary Assistant Professor of Instructional Technologies and Learning Sciences at Utah State University and an independent Research Scientist. Her work focuses on the creative objects that students make and how their interests, physical and virtual communities, and identities come into play in design decisions. At Utah State University, she pioneered the Craft Technologies course where students from every college combine use handcrafts and digital technologies to create light-up reactive clothing, sewn electronic sensors, and interactive quilted game controllers. Professor Fields is also the coauthor of *Connected Play: Tween Life in a Virtual World* published by MIT Press, the culmination of a decade of research documenting kids' play, learning, and development in virtual worlds.

Erica Rosenfeld Halverson is an Associate Professor of Digital Media and Literacy in the Department of Curriculum & Instruction at the University of Wisconsin–Madison. Her work focuses on what it means to learn in and through the arts across a range of contexts including out-of-school arts organizations, museums, libraries, and arts-based classrooms. In 2010, Dr. Halverson received the Jan Hawkins Award for Early Career Contributions to Humanistic Research & Scholarship in Learning Technologies for her research on how filmmaking serves as a vehicle for positive identity development and sophisticated literacy learning for young people who are disaffiliated from school. Dr. Halverson codirects the "Learning in the Making" research lab with Dr. Kimberly Sheridan, where they are currently focused on what and how young people learn through making and how new technologies can be leveraged for more inspired and engaged making processes. She is the cofounder of Barrel of Monkeys, a Chicago-based nonprofit arts education organization that works with Chicago's most underserved elementary school students on creative writing and performance. While working on Barrel of Monkeys, Erica received her PhD in Learning Sciences from Northwestern University.

Sherry Hsi is a Learning Engineer and Researcher at the Concord Consortium, a nonprofit educational technology laboratory for science, math, and engineering. For more than 20 years, she has created and studied how different learning environments, materials, and technologies can be designed to help improve learning in science, engineering, technology, and math. She created a makerspace, the TechHive teen design internship program at the Lawrence Hall of Science, and cofounded Howtosmile.org, a STEM digital library. With support from National Science Foundation and the National Institutes of Health, Dr. Hsi has codesigned an augmented reality sandbox exhibit and DIY apps for children, families, and visitors. She is currently leading Paper Mechatronics, an exploratory project to develop low-cost kits for engineering education. Hsi has a BS and an MS from UC Berkeley's engineering program and received her PhD in Science Education from UC Berkeley.

Yasmin B. Kafai is a Researcher and Developer of online tools and communities (scratch.mit.edu, stitchtfest.org, and ecrafting.org) to promote equity and diversity in coding, crafting, and creativity across K–16. Her books include *Connected Code: Why Children Need to Learn Programming*, *Connected Play: Tween in a Virtual World*, and *Minds in Play: Computer Game Design as a Context for Children's Learning*, as well as edited volumes *Textile Messages: Dispatches from the World of Electronic Textiles and Education*, *Beyond Barbie and Mortal Kombat: New Perspectives on Gender and Gaming*, *The Computer Clubhouse: Constructionism and Creativity in Youth Communities*, and *Constructionism*. After studying in France and Germany, Kafai earned a doctorate from Harvard University while working with Seymour Papert at the MIT Media Lab. She is Professor of Learning Sciences at the University of Pennsylvania, an elected Fellow of the American Educational Research Association, and a past President of the International Society for the Learning Sciences.

Caitlin K. Martin is a Senior Researcher at the YouthLAB (Youth Learning Across Boundaries) research group at Stanford University (youthlab.stanford.edu) and at the Digital Youth Network in Chicago (digitalyouthnetwork.org). Her work focuses on the design and research of environments that offer youth from diverse communities opportunities to deeply learn, understand, and use digital media and technology across formal, informal, and online settings.

Lee Martin is an Assistant Professor in the School of Education at UC Davis. His research focuses on ways in which people create and use social and cognitive tools and resources to propel their own thinking and learning in the face of new and challenging problems. He studies making as a set of activities that may help people to become more flexible and adaptive in their thinking and problem solving. His research looks across in-school and out-of-school settings to investigate the varied ways that people assemble social, material, and intellectual resources to help them to meet their goals.

Mike McGalliard has launched a series of companies in the education sector over the last 24 years, including LA's Promise, which was awarded more than $15 million in grants to help turnaround schools in Los Angeles Unified School District (LAUSD), and Metro Charter, the first public elementary school in the burgeoning core of downtown LA. In 2011, Mike worked with chef Jamie Oliver to improve child nutrition in LAUSD. Their work together was featured in the Emmy-nominated Season 2 of "Jamie Oliver's Food Revolution." In 2014, as founding President of the Imagination Foundation (a nonprofit launched from the success of the film, *Caine's Arcade*, to foster child creativity), Mike and his colleagues designed a play-based educational model that was named Champion in a global competition sponsored by LEGO and Ashoka to "Re-imagine Learning." Mike studied literature at Reed College and lives in Los Angeles.

Kylie Peppler is an Associate Professor of Learning Sciences at Indiana University. An artist by training, she engages in research that focuses on the intersection of arts, media, new technologies, and informal learning. Peppler's book publications include *The Computer Clubhouse: Constructionism and Creativity in Youth Communities* (Teachers College Press), *Textile Messages: Dispatches from the World of E-Textiles and Education* (Peter Lang), and *New Creativity Paradigms: Arts Learning in the Digital Age* (Peter Lang), as well as a four-book series titled *Interconnections: Understanding Systems Thinking Through Digital Design* (MIT Press, 2014). Peppler also leads the Make-to-Learn initiative of the MacArthur Foundation, which leverages DIY culture, digital practices, and educational research to advocate for placing making, creating, and designing at the core of educational practice. Her current work on maker culture is supported by the National Science Foundation, the US Department of Education, the Moore Foundation, and the John D. and Catherine T. MacArthur Foundation. Find out more at kpeppler.com.

Mike Petrich is Director of the Making Collaborative at the Exploratorium. He designs and facilitates personally meaningful making and tinkering contexts for people to develop first-hand experiences and understanding of the world. This work has developed over the past 25 years, with audiences as diverse as museum visitors, primary school students, Tibetan monks, prison inmates, and graduate school researchers.

Mitchel Resnick is Professor of Learning Research at the MIT Media Lab. His Lifelong Kindergarten research group develops new technologies that, in the spirit of the blocks and fingerpaint of kindergarten, engage people in creative learning experiences. The group collaborated with the LEGO Company on the Mindstorms and WeDo robotics kits, and it develops the Scratch programming software and online community, used by millions of young people around the world. Resnick cofounded the Computer Clubhouse project, an international network of after-school learning centers for youth from low-income communities. He was awarded the McGraw Prize in Education in 2011.

Jessica Ross is a Senior Practitioner Specialist working on the Agency *by* Design research initiative at Harvard Project Zero (PZ). Prior to this role, Jessica taught grades 5–8 humanities for 10 years. In her classroom practice, Jessica incorporated several PZ frameworks and collaborated with researchers Shari Tishman and Patricia Palmer to create an Artful Thinking classroom practice. Working with teachers, schools, and districts, Jessica has facilitated professional learning opportunities, both internationally and throughout the United States, sharing PZ frameworks in addition to interdisciplinary-focused content courses in the Humanities. She is currently an Education Coordinator of the Project Zero Classroom Institute and a teaching fellow at the Harvard Graduate School of Education.

Natalie Rusk is a Research Scientist in the Lifelong Kindergarten group at the MIT Media Lab and is a lead developer of Scratch, a graphical programming language that enables young people to design and code interactive animations, games, and other creative projects. Natalie is one of the creators of the MIT Media Lab online course, Learning Creative Learning. In 1993, she started a model afterschool program called the Computer Clubhouse, which now has 100 sites in 20 countries.

Jennifer Oxman Ryan is a Project Manager and researcher for Agency *by* Design, an initiative exploring the promises and practices of maker-centered learning and its intersect with Project Zero frameworks. Past research projects and current research interests include maker-centered learning, arts education, school/community partnerships, and young people's engagement with digital media. Jennifer has a background in museum education and nonprofit management and is current Commission member and former Education Committee Chair for the Maine Arts Commission.

Kristin A. Searle is an Assistant Professor in Instructional Technology and Learning Sciences at Utah State University. Her work focuses on how participating in making activities (like e-textiles) can broaden students' sense of what computing is and who can do it, with a particular focus on the development of culturally responsive computing pedagogies. She is especially interested in how students' gendered and cultural identities impact their engagement with computing. Her work has appeared in a number of journals including *Harvard Educational Review*, *Games and Culture*, and the *International Journal of Learning and Media*.

Shari Tishman is a Lecturer at Harvard Graduate School of Education and a Senior Research Associate at Harvard Project Zero, where she recently served as Director. Her research focuses on the development of thinking and understanding from a dispositional perspective, learning in museums, and learning in and through the arts. She currently leads Agency *by* Design, a project that explores the intersect of design thinking, the Maker Movement, and Project Zero frameworks and codirects Out of Eden, an online learning community to accompany journalist Paul Salopek's 7-year walk around the world.

Veena Vasudevan is a Doctoral Candidate in the Teaching, Learning, and Teacher Education program at University of Pennsylvania's Graduate School of Education. She studies the relationships between youth's technology and media use, schooling, and identity. In addition, she has done research on game design for learning using educational technologies like Scratch and MaKey MaKey. Her research builds on extensive experience working in urban school districts. Veena holds a master of public administration from Columbia University.

Karen Wilkinson directs the Tinkering Studio at San Francisco's Exploratorium. A maker and tinkerer to her core, she believes deeply in studio pedagogy and is continually inspired by the beauty and complexity found in seemingly mundane materials and phenomena. She and her partner, Mike Petrich, wrote *The Art of Tinkering*, highlighting the playful intersection of art, science, and technology. In the museum field for more than 20 years, her recent roles as author and MOOC (massively open online course) producer have been some of the most rewarding of her career. Passionate about constructionism as a powerful way of learning, Karen sees herself as an advocate for this approach. She views tinkering and making as a way of reconnecting people to their own learning and inherent capabilities—a vital 21st-century skill.

INDEX

Note: Italicized page numbers indicate a figure on the corresponding page. Page numbers in bold indicate a table on the corresponding page.

Also available from Routledge

Makeology: Makerspaces as Learning Environments (Volume 1)
Edited by Kylie Peppler, Erica Rosenfeld Halverson, & Yasmin Kafai

www.routledge.com/education